ROAST
CHICKEN

AND OTHER STORIES

ROAST
CHICKEN

AND OTHER STORIES

A Recipe Book by
Simon Hopkinson

With Lindsey Bareham

Illustrations by Flo Bayley

HYPERION

New York

To my parents, and to the memory of Yves Champeau

Text copyright © Simon Hopkinson 1994, 2006
Illustrations copyright © Flo Bayley 1994

Originally published in 1994 by Ebury Press, a division of Random House

Library of Congress Cataloging-in-Publication Data

ISBN: 1-4013-0862-7
ISBN 13: 978-1-4013-0862-9

Hyperion books are available for special promotions and
premiums. For details contact Michael Rentas, Assistant Director,
Inventory Operations, Hyperion, 77 West 66th Street, 11th floor,
New York, New York 10023, or call 212-456-0133.

FIRST U.S. EDITION

10 9 8 7 6 5 4 3

Contents

Introduction   1

ANCHOVY   4
Jeremiah Tower's Montpellier butter   6
Old-fashioned egg sauce   6
Salade niçoise   7
Anchovy and onion tarts   8

ASPARAGUS   11
Asparagus soup   13
Délices d'Argenteuil   13
Grilled asparagus with Parmesan   14

BRAINS   16
Gratin of brains with sorrel   18
Cervelles au beurre noir   18
Salad of calves' brains with sauce ravigote   19
Deep-fried calves' brains with sauce gribiche   20
Sauté of calves' brains with cilantro, chillies, ginger, and garlic 21

CÈPES   22
Cèpe tarts   24
Cèpe and potato broth   25

CHICKEN   26
Roast chicken   28
Grilled breast of chicken with Provençal vegetables and aïoli   29
Poulet poché à la crème with crêpes Parmentier   30
Poulet sauté au vinaigre   32

CHOCOLATE   34
Chocolate tart   36
Saint-Émilion au chocolat   36
Milk chocolate malt ice cream   37

Chocolate pithiviers   38
Chocolate bavarois   39
Petit pot au chocolat   39

CILANTRO   **41**
Green paste   43
Salsa   43
Oriental salad   44
Dipping sauce   45
Cilantro and coconut soup   45

COD   **47**
Le grand aïoli   48
Poached cod with lentils and salsa verde   49
Deep-fried cod   50
Poached cod with pickled vegetable relish   51
Brandade de morue   52

CRAB   **54**
Crab vinaigrette with herbs   56
Crab tart   57

CREAM   **58**
Crème Chantilly   60
Fruit fool   60
Francis Coulson's strawberry pots de crème   61
Crème brûlée   62
Rice pudding   63
Caramel ice cream   64
Vanilla ice cream   65

CUSTARD   **66**
Lemon surprise pudding   68
Bread and butter pudding   68
Crème renversée à l'orange   69
Custard sauce   70
Crema Catalana   71
Passion fruit bavarois   71
Orange mousse   72

EGGPLANT   **73**
Grilled eggplant with a dressing of olive oil, garlic, and basil   75

Spiced eggplant salad   76
Creamed eggplant   77
Eggplant baked with herbs and cream   77
Grilled eggplant with pesto   78
Vinegared eggplant with chilli and spring onion   79
Grilled eggplant with sesame   79

EGGS   **81**
Piperade   82
Oeufs en meurette   82
Salade frisée aux lardons   83
Eggs Florentine   84
Lacy's oeufs en cocotte   85

ENDIVE   **87**
Braised endives   89
Endives an gratin   89
Creamed endives   90
Pickled endives   91

GARLIC   **92**
Baked new garlic with creamed goat's cheese   94
Deep-fried garlic   94
Garlic purée and garlic sauce   95
Snail butter   96
Garlic and sorrel soup with Parmesan croûtons   96

GROUSE   **98**
Roast grouse with bread sauce and game crumbs   99
Grouse soup   101

HAKE   **102**
Warm hake with thinned mayonnaise and capers   104
Fillet of hake with herb crust   105
Basque Chiorro   105

KIDNEYS   **107**
Roasted lambs' kidneys with cabbage and mustard dressing   109
Grilled veal kidneys with rosemary and anchovy butter   109
Sauté of veal kidneys with shallots, sage, and beurre noisette   110

LAMB 112
Breast of lamb Ste-Ménéhould 114
Roast leg of lamb with anchovy, garlic, and rosemary 115
Marinated and grilled lamb cutlets with hummus, olive oil, and cilantro 115
Roast best end of lamb with eggplant and basil cream sauce 117

LEEKS 119
Leeks vinaigrette 121
Leek tart 121
Leeks with cream and mint 122
Vichyssoise 122

LIVER 124
Calves' liver Venetian style 125
Richard Olney's terrine of poultry livers 125
Duck livers, crêpes Parmentier, and onion marmalade 127

OLIVE OIL 129
Olive oil mashed potatoes 131
Sauce vièrge 131
Vinaigrette 132

ONIONS 133
Roast onions 135
Grilled red onion relish 135
Onion tart 136
Creamed onions with rosemary 137
Onion soup 137

PARMESAN 139
Parmesan fritters 141
Crisp Parmesan crackers 142

PARSLEY 143
Potato purée with parsley 145
Gay Bilson's parsley salad 145
Parsley soup 146

PEPPERS 148
Piedmontese peppers 149
Pimiento salsa 149

Roulade of peppers and eggplant   150
Rowley's vinaigrette of red peppers and anchovy   151
Red pepper tart   151
Gazpacho   152
Chilled pimiento soup with basil   153

PORK PIECES AND BACON BITS   **154**
A sauce to serve with boiled ham   156
Prosciutto with warm wilted greens   156
Old-fashioned pork terrine   157
Slow-braised belly pork with soy, ginger, and garlic   158
Petit salé aux lentilles   159

POTATOES   **161**
Roast potatoes with olive oil, rosemary, and garlic   163
Potato cakes   163
French fries   164
Potato salad   165
Potato, tomato, and basil soup   165

RABBIT   **167**
Braised rabbit with white wine, shallots, rosemary, and cream   169
Stewed rabbit with balsamic vinegar and parsnip purée   170
Rabbit terrine   170
Roasted leg of rabbit with bacon and a mustard sauce   171

SAFFRON   **173**
Saffron mashed potatoes   175
Rouille   175
Saffron cream dressing   176
Saffron soup with mussels   176

SALMON   **178**
Salmon in pastry with currants and ginger   180
Poached salmon with beurre blanc   180
Grilled salmon, sauce verte, and fennel salad   182
Poached salmon, hollandaise sauce, and pickled cucumber   183
Ceviche of salmon   184

SCALLOPS   **185**
Scallops sauté Provençal   187

Scallops Bercy 187
Scallop and artichoke soup 188

SMOKED HADDOCK **190**
Smoked haddock baked with potatoes and cream 191
Omelette Arnold Bennett 191
Curried smoked haddock soup 192

SPINACH **194**
Spinach mousse with anchovy hollandaise 196
Spinach dumplings 196
Cold spinach with crème fraîche, garlic, and black pepper 197

SQUAB **198**
Roast squab with braised lettuce, peas, and bacon 199
Grilled squab with shallots, sherry vinegar, and walnut oil 199

STEAK **201**
Steak au poivre 203
Meat glaze 204

SWEETBREADS **206**
Ris de veau aux morilles 208
Breadcrumbed veal sweetbreads with tartar sauce 209
Blanquette of lamb's sweetbreads 210

TOMATOES **212**
Creamed tomatoes on toast 213
Tomato and pesto tarts 213
Pappa al Pomodoro 214

TRIPE **215**
Tripes à la lyonnaise 217
Callos a la Madrilena (Tripe Madrid-style) 217
Deep-fried tripe with green paste 218

VEAL **220**
Roast shin of veal 222
Saltimbocca alla Romana 222
Salted calves' tongue with Madeira sauce 223

Index 226

INTRODUCTION

GOOD cooking, in the final analysis, depends on two things: common sense and good taste. It is also something that you naturally have to want to do well in the first place, as with any craft. It *is* a craft, after all, like anything that is produced with the hands and senses to put together an attractive and complete picture. By "picture," I do not mean "picturesque"; good food is to be eaten because it tastes good and smells enticing.

We are all drawn to the smell of fish and chips, fried onions, roast beef, Christmas lunch, pizza, fresh coffee, toast and bacon, and other sensory delights. Conversely, to my mind, there is nothing that heralds the bland "vegetable terrine," the "cold lobster mousse with star anise and vanilla," or the "little stew of seven different fish" that has been "scented" with Jura wine and "spiked" with tarragon. I feel uncomfortable with this sort of food and don't believe it to be, how shall we say, genuine.

I do not mean to berate the cook who wishes to make food complicated or multifaceted; I just think that some ideas are misguided. For instance, one perfect piece of turbot or halibut, grilled on the bone with hollandaise sauce must surely (ask yourself) be a perfect plate of food. What is the point of marrying a little piece of Mediterranean red mullet with a similar-sized piece of Scottish farmed salmon? They just don't belong together.

Food that tastes good lingers in the memory for all time: such things as good, homemade soups, my mother's meat and potato pie, Bury black puddings, a well-made bloody Mary, prosciutto and melon, native English oysters with Tabasco, hot salted ox tongue with coleslaw, a dozen snails at Chez L'Ami Louis in Paris, the

1

apéritif maison at L'Oustau de Baumanière at Les Baux in Provence, and the home-made bresaola of Franco Taruschio at The Walnut Tree in Wales.

I have written this book, not because I am a chef, but because I like to cook and I enjoy eating good food. A novelist I know once said to me, on hearing that I had decided to embark on a cookbook, that cooks should cook and writers should write. Well, fair enough. (He is, actually, a very good cook.) I am not a professional writer, nor am I good at writing recipes on a regular basis. This is particularly so when I have to think about listing the ingredients in the right order for each recipe, or giving metric and imperial measurements, or stating exact oven temperatures and precise timings. I have had to learn to do that, and it has been interesting and beneficial to be so restricted.

Deep down in the mind of a good cook are endless recipes. It is a matter of knowing what goes with what; knowing when to stop and where to start, and with what ingredients. Thinking how a dish is going to taste, before you start to cook it, may seem an obvious instruction, but it is not necessarily common practice. It is important to cook in the right frame of mind (we are not talking everyday chores here) and to do things in the right order. Ergo: feel hungry; go out shopping (with pen and paper and money). See good things, buy them. Write down further items that will accompany previous purchases. Buy wine to go with food. Come home. Have a glass of wine. Cook the food and eat with more of the wine. More importantly, do make sure that the food you have bought is the sort that you like to eat and know how to cook. It is also a question of sympathy between the cook and the cooked-for; is there a worryingly large proportion of people, I wonder, who cook to impress rather than to please?

It's really a question of confidence. It is far better to cook food for your friends that you enjoy eating yourself. Familiar dishes are comforting; carefully prepared and simple dishes are an asset to a good lunch or dinner party. The food should not dominate the proceedings. Rather, it should enhance and enliven the occasion. There is nothing more tedious than an evening spent discussing every dish eaten in minute detail. "Oh Daphne, how *did* you manage to insert those carrots in your hollowed-out zucchini?" What's wrong with egg salad or leeks vinaigrette? Or a simple rabbit stew, or some grilled lamb cutlets. And, of course, roast chicken.

The title of this book, *Roast Chicken and Other Stories*, was chosen simply because it had a friendly ring to it, and I hope that it sounds inviting and uncomplicated. I also happen to enjoy roasting a chicken almost more than anything. It is very satisfying to look upon a fine chicken turning crisp and golden as it cooks. Even the sound of it causes salivation, and the smell of it jolts the tummy into gear.

I would like to think that this collection of recipes will appeal to all who like to cook; those who gain immense pleasure from being in their kitchens with good produce around them purchased from favorite sources—markets, butchers and fishmongers, grocers and greengrocers, delicatessens and wine shops. I would also like to imagine that *everybody* could become a good cook and have a healthy interest in the bountiful ingredients that are available in such quantity on our doorsteps.

Good food relies on good ingredients, but it has always been my belief that a good cook can turn the proverbial sow's ear into a silk purse. It takes a little knowledge and expertise, but whereas an ignorant and uncaring chef can ruin the finest free-range chicken, a sympathetic and enthusiastic cook can work wonders, even with an old boiling fowl.

Finally, I would like to thank Jill Norman for asking me to do a book in the first place: Lindsey Bareham, without whose help the book could never have been written; and Flo Bayley for her exquisite illustrations.

Simon Hopkinson

AUTHOR'S NOTE

All recipes serve four

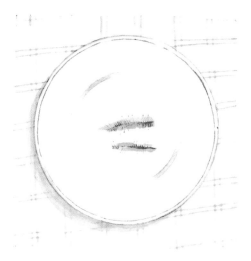

ANCHOVY

The salted anchovy, in one form or another, has been with us for some time. The Romans used to salt all sorts of fish, and from them made their all-purpose sauce, liquamen. This fermented brew seems to have been used as a seasoning and added to almost everything. Today, the Thai people use anchovies to make a fermented fish sauce—nam pla—that similarly finds its way into pretty well all their dishes.

I have liked the anchovy (it's one of the herring family) ever since discovering a bit of one stuffed inside a green olive many years ago. I am particularly keen on very salty things and I can actually eat anchovies on their own. The best I have come across so far are filleted Spanish anchovies. These are fat and juicy, a lovely pinky-red color, and their flavor is remarkably fine. They are preserved in olive oil and come beautifully packaged in large, round, colorful cans.

In disagreement with most of my food friends, I find whole salted anchovies a little disappointing. They are excessively salty, even for me. Perhaps I have never had a good one. So, it is the fillets of this little fish that I am talking about.

The strangest thing about cooking with anchovies is that they are best by far when accompanying meaty things. With fish, they seem to cancel out the inherent flavors and on occasion can even cause you to think that you are eating a piece of stale fish (the only exception to this is Old-Fashioned Egg Sauce, see page 6, which makes a good accompaniment to white fish). Not so with meat, especially when used to flavor and season a roast—lamb in particular. Little pieces of anchovy inserted deep into the muscles of a leg of lamb, together with some garlic slivers, impart the most agreeable contrast of flavors. And, curiously enough for such an intensely fishy fish, it ceases to taste fishy when used in this way.

The anchovy's uses and appearances are truly legion. You will find it on pizzas, in Caesar salad and salade Niçoise (I happen to think that the one and only fish therein should be a generous helping of anchovies), and on a good egg salad, as well as stuffed into those lovely green olives. Some continental classics would not be the same without the anchovy. Take anchoiade. This Provençal staple combines garlic, olive oil, a little vinegar, and some pounded anchovies. It is then spread onto thick slices of toast, according to Elizabeth David. She goes on to say: "This is not so much an hors d'œuvre as the sort of thing to get ready quickly anytime you are hungry and want something to go with a glass of wine. . . ." What splendid advice.

Closely related to anchoiade, and from the same region, comes tapenade. Another paste, made this time from pounded black olives, olive oil, capers, garlic, a splash of Cognac, and anchovies. Also good on toast and intensely savory. The Italian salsa verde (green sauce) is one of the very nicest lotions and consists of large amounts of finely chopped parsley, mustard, capers, garlic, olive oil, and anchovies. This is most often served with poached or boiled dishes. In all these sauces, the anchovy usually provides all the salt that is necessary.

Compound butters, for anointing pieces of grilled meat and offal, are especially good when some chopped anchovy has been introduced. A mixture of rosemary, a little garlic, cayenne pepper, anchovy, and unsalted butter is extremely good over grilled veal kidneys. But the king of savory butters, in my book, is the one called Montpellier. It combines all the flavors and smells of a Provençal marketplace. So, rather than telling you about it, here is the recipe. This version comes from Jeremiah Tower's book *New American Classics*. It is a particularly good one.

JEREMIAH TOWER'S MONTPELLIER BUTTER

6 spinach leaves
½ bunch of watercress, stalks removed
2 tbsp flat-leaf parsley leaves
2 tbsp chervil leaves
2 tbsp chopped chives
1 tbsp tarragon leaves
2 shallots, peeled and chopped
2 gherkins, chopped
4 anchovy fillets, drained and chopped
2 tbsp capers, drained and chopped
1 garlic clove, peeled and chopped
½ tsp salt
¼ tsp pepper
¼ tsp cayenne
3 hard-boiled egg yolks
2 raw egg yolks
½ cup unsalted butter, at room temperature
½ cup olive oil
1 tsp white wine vinegar

Blanch the spinach, watercress, herbs, and shallots in boiling water for 1 minute. Drain, refresh under cold water, and squeeze dry. Put them in a food processor and add the gherkins, anchovies, capers, garlic, salt, pepper, and cayenne. Purée to a smooth paste, then add the egg yolks and the butter, and process again until thoroughly mixed. With the machine running, pour in the olive oil in a thin stream. The mixture should be glossy and as smooth as velvet. Add the vinegar and check the seasoning.

OLD-FASHIONED EGG SAUCE

This is one of those forgotten British sauces that might sound unappealing and has perhaps been put in the same category as Brown Windsor Soup. Well, Brown Windsor Soup might not be very nice—I've never made it—but egg sauce *is* good and you shouldn't turn your nose up at it. It is based on a really good béchamel—and there's nothing wrong with that. A well-made béchamel sauce is truly delicious and shouldn't be thrown out in favor of the modish, overreduced, flour-free sauces one is told one should prefer.

When making a béchamel, one of the most important things to remember is to make the milk as flavorsome as possible. I heat the milk with the onion, herbs, and spices long before I need to make the sauce, so that the flavors have plenty of time to infuse.

This egg sauce is particularly good with white fish from local waters: cod, hake, and haddock (fresh or smoked). The fish is best steamed or poached.

1½ cups milk
1 small onion, peeled and chopped
4 cloves
1 sprig of thyme
1 bay leaf, torn
a few scrapings of nutmeg
salt and pepper
3 tbsp butter
3 tbsp all-purpose flour
½ cup heavy cream
1 tbsp anchovy paste
2 hard-boiled eggs, peeled and chopped
2 tbsp chopped flat-leaf parsley

Heat together the first seven ingredients until they come to the boil. (Not much salt, taking into consideration the saltiness of the anchovy paste that will be added later.) Turn off the heat. Stir well, cover, and leave to infuse for at least 1 hour, preferably longer.

Melt the butter in another pan and stir in the flour to make a roux. Strain the flavored milk into this, stirring all the time. Bring slowly to the boil, still stirring and allow to simmer very gently for up to 30 minutes—this is best done over a heat-diffuser pad, as the sauce easily stiffens. Add the cream, anchovy paste, chopped eggs, and, finally, stir in the parsley.

SALADE NIÇOISE

Of late, I have come to the conclusion that tuna is redundant in a salade Niçoise. This is purely personal and I know that some *aficionados* would heartily disagree with me. It's just that I don't think cooked tuna is anything to write home about—and I've even tried cooking my own in olive oil. So, as long as the anchovies used are of superior quality, I say just up the quantity and ditch the tuna.

The other ingredients are also a matter for debate. Rather than say what I think are key ingredients I would only ask that strips of raw green bell pepper are not included. I also like green beans to be cooked through—*not* so that they squeak when you bite them.

4 eggs

1 head Boston lettuce

8 small cooked artichoke hearts (such as those sold in jars from Italy)

a handful of haricots vert or slender green beans, trimmed, boiled briefly, refreshed,
and drained

12 small new potatoes, peeled, boiled, and drained

4 very ripe tomatoes, peeled and quartered

16 black olives

1 heaped tbsp capers, drained

1 small red onion, peeled and thinly sliced

1 small bunch of flat-leaf parsley, leaves coarsely chopped

anchovies (allow 5 per person, or more if desired)

sea salt and black pepper

For the dressing

2 tbsp red wine vinegar

a generous pinch of sea salt

black pepper

2 garlic cloves, peeled and finely chopped

¾ cup extra-virgin olive oil

First, make the dressing by mixing together the vinegar, salt, pepper, and garlic. Whisk well, then pour in the oil in a thin stream. Set aside.

Put the eggs in a saucepan of cold water, bring to the boil, and cook for 5 minutes. Refresh under cold running water for 5 minutes, then peel and quarter lengthways.

Find either a round, shallow terracotta or white porcelain dish and arrange attractively all the salad ingredients, starting with a bed of lettuce. The arrangement is entirely a matter for you, though I think the two final ingredients should be a scattering of parsley and the anchovies in a crisscross pattern over the surface. Season discriminately with salt and generously with pepper.

Give the dressing a final whisk, and spoon over the surface. Eat immediately with some crusty bread.

ANCHOVY AND ONION TARTS

The shape of these tarts came about in a lazy moment when I was rolling out a sheet of puff pastry to cut into circles for individual tarts, but didn't have time. I now prefer this free-form, squiffy-square shape with its irregular puffed-up edges.

The recipe is based on the classic southern French pissaladière, which uses bread dough and is thought to be the precursor of the ubiquitous pizza.

6 tbsp olive oil
4 large Spanish onions, peeled and thinly sliced
a pinch of salt
20 small black olives (preferably Niçoise olives), pitted
8 large anchovy fillets, split lengthways
1 heaped tsp dried herbes de Provence
black pepper
1 tbsp freshly grated Parmesan

For the pastry

¾ cup all-purpose flour
a pinch of salt
1 cup cold unsalted butter, cut into small pieces
juice of ½ lemon
½ cup iced water

Begin by making the pastry, preferably the day before; certainly several hours in advance. Sift the flour and salt together into a bowl and add the butter. Loosely mix, but don't blend the two together in the normal way of pastry-making. Mix the lemon juice with the iced water and pour into the butter/flour mixture. With a metal spoon, gently mix together until you have formed a cohesive mass. Turn onto a cool surface and shape into a thick rectangle. Flour the work surface and gently roll the pastry into a rectangle measuring about 7 × 4 inches. Fold one-third of the rectangle over toward the center and fold the remaining third over that. Lightly, press together and rest the pastry in the fridge for 10 minutes.

Return the pastry to the same position on the work surface and turn it 90 degrees. Roll it out to the same dimensions as before, and fold and rest again in the same way. Repeat this turning, rolling, folding, and resting process three more times. (Phew! This is the moment when you wish you'd bought ready-made pastry.) Place the pastry in a plastic bag and leave in the fridge for several hours or overnight.

To cook the onions, gently heat the olive oil and sweat the onions with a little salt over a moderate heat until thoroughly collapsed, pale golden, and with as little moisture left as possible. This will take about 30 minutes; you are aiming for a thick mush.

Preheat the oven to 425°F. Cut the pastry into four rough squares. Roll each one out to make four larger squares measuring about 7 inches. They should be about ⅛ inch thick. (It matters not a jot if the shape isn't exactly true; moreover, it is nicer if they are slightly irregular.) Prick the squares lightly with a fork and place on a buttered baking sheet—you may have to use two. Rest in the fridge for 10 minutes or so.

Divide the onions between the four pastry squares, leaving a border of about ¾ inch around the edges. Dot with the olives, crisscross the anchovies over the onion, and sprinkle with the herbs and a good grinding of pepper. Brush a little olive oil over the exposed pastry edges, and dust lightly with the Parmesan cheese. Bake in the oven for 10–15 minutes or until puffed up and golden brown.

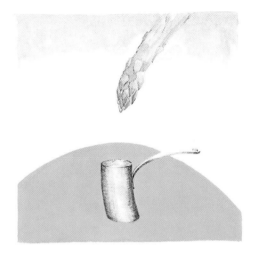

ASPARAGUS

Every year around the middle of May, I catch "asparagus fever." Our British crop is about to shoot up from underground in all its glory. And it *is* glorious, with the finest flavor in the world. In my opinion, nothing can touch the taste of that purply-green English asparagus. In France and Germany, and particularly Alsace, they grow white asparagus that has been cultivated completely underground. The green color never gets a chance to develop due to the lack of sunlight. People rave about it, but I just can't agree.

Out of season, we are bombarded with imported asparagus from (mainly) California, Mexico, and New Zealand. The spears are invariably huge and have lost most of their flavor due to their long journey. This, of course, happens to any green vegetable, however fast it is transported to your local greengrocer. Asparagus, however, seems to suffer more than most. If you have ever had the great pleasure of cutting asparagus fresh from the ground, you will see quite clearly how quickly its sap runs out. Somebody I know, who was obsessed with fresh vegetables, carried out an experiment on his own garden crop of asparagus. He erected a small Primus stove at the end of his asparagus bed and had a pan of boiling water at the ready. Next, he hurriedly collected spear after spear of asparagus and hurled them into the boiling water. This idea puts "freshly cooked garden vegetables" into a different category, but it must have been fun, and the asparagus surely the best ever.

There is a tall, very silly pan called an "asparagus pot." It has a basket inside that is slightly smaller than the pot itself. The idea is that you put your bunch of asparagus into the basket, fill the pan with water to halfway up the asparagus spears, and put the lid on. When the water comes to the boil, it is supposed to boil the parts of the asparagus in the water and steam the tips. I think this is a lot of nonsense and a waste of money, as these pots are very expensive. All green vegetables require plenty of viciously boiling, well-salted water. The more boiling water you can have around a green vegetable, the greener the vegetable will stay. And its flavor will have been, as it were, sealed in.

ASPARAGUS SOUP

This is an extravagant indulgence. Although I have tried (and succeeded) to make asparagus soup with all the trimmings, peelings, and off-cuts, it always ends up tasting a little bit like canned soup. (I can only presume that this is because that is exactly what the manufacturers do.) This recipe, however, uses a nice, trimmed-up bunch of fresh asparagus, and not much else. If you can come by the asparagus called "sprue"— which is thin and straggly and consequently much cheaper—then this can be used.

It sort of goes against the grain to turn the most beautiful of vegetables into a soup, but this simple and very pure recipe transforms it into an elixir.

½ cup butter
4 small leeks (white parts only), trimmed and chopped
3 cups water
1 potato, peeled and chopped
salt and pepper
1 lb fresh asparagus, trimmed and peeled
1 cup heavy cream

Melt the butter and stew the leeks until soft. Add the water and potato, season with salt and pepper, and cook for 15 minutes. Quickly chop the asparagus, add to the soup. Boil rapidly for 5 minutes. Blend thoroughly, then pass through a fine sieve. Add the cream and check the seasoning. This soup is equally good hot or cold.

DÉLICES D'ARGENTEUIL

The Argenteuil region outside Paris is famous for its asparagus. This pancake dish is one that I remember from my days at the Normandie (see Endive chapter). I remember what a luscious dish I thought it was, and the combination of flavors— ham, asparagus, eggs—is a perfect one. If ever there were any pancakes left over at the end of service, I would secrete them in the pocket of my coat, whip them home, and make my own hollandaise to go with them. Three délices makes the perfect midnight snack.

4 thin slices of prosciutto, halved
16 cooked asparagus spears

For the pancakes

2 eggs
1 egg yolk

1 cup milk
2 tbsp melted butter
salt and pepper
¾ cup plus 1 tbsp all-purpose flour
a little extra melted butter for cooking

For the hollandaise sauce

3 egg yolks
1 cup butter, incited
juice of ½ lemon
salt and white pepper

First, make the pancake batter. Put the eggs and egg yolk, milk, melted butter, and seasoning in a blender. Switch on and blend, then turn the motor to slow (if possible) and add the flour in a thin stream. Pass through a sieve into a pitcher and leave to rest for at least 1 hour. (This recipe will make more pancakes than you need. Why not make a few more pancakes for breakfast the next day?)

To make the sauce, whisk the egg yolks with a splash of water until thick. Use either a small stainless steel pan over a thread of heat, or a bowl over barely simmering water. Add the melted butter in a thin stream, whisking all the time until the sauce has the consistency of mayonnaise. Add the lemon juice and season with salt and white pepper. Keep warm.

Preheat the oven to 375°F, and also the grill. Heat a small frying pan, brush with melted butter, and pour in enough pancake batter, just to cover the bottom of the pan. Cook until the underside is golden, then toss or turn the pancake and cook until the second side is golden. Repeat to make eight pancakes in all.

Lay out the pancakes and place a piece of prosciutto on each one. Put two asparagus spears on each pancake and roll them up. Lightly butter a baking dish and put the pancake rolls in it, leaving a little space between each one. Heat through in the oven for 10 minutes, then take out and divide the eight pancakes among four cold plates. Spoon the hollandaise carefully along the length of each pancake. Flash each plate very briefly under a hot grill for a few seconds or until the hollandaise is lightly glazed.

GRILLED ASPARAGUS WITH PARMESAN

Apart from Délices d'Argenteuil, asparagus lends itself to the simplest of preparations. Most obvious is to serve it with melted butter, or just hollandaise on its own. I have come to the conclusion that, in fact, eggs are its favorite companion: buttery scrambled eggs, soft-boiled or poached eggs using asparagus spears as "soldiers," or eggs baked

14

en cocotte with cream and tarragon. Here, asparagus is served with hard-boiled and chopped eggs, together with Parmesan and olive oil.

24 large cooked asparagus spears
extra-virgin olive oil
sea salt and black pepper
2 hard-boiled eggs, peeled and chopped
3–4 oz Parmesan cheese, in a piece
lemon wedges, to serve

Heat a ribbed cast-iron grill or skillet. Brush the asparagus spears with some of the oil, and cook until nicely charred on all sides. Transfer to a large white dish, season lightly with salt and plenty of pepper, and sprinkle with the chopped egg. Using a potato peeler, shave slivers of Parmesan over the surface, drizzle with more olive oil, and serve with the lemon wedges.

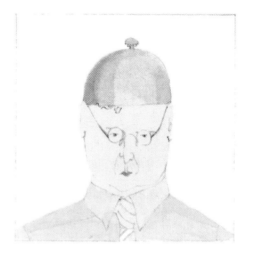

BRAINS

If only one could persuade the eating public to rid themselves of all unnecessary squeamishness about brains and to look upon them as just another delicious morsel. I suppose it's the way they look, where they come from in the body, and, of course, their name, that puts so many people off. However, I think that if one were to hand around dishes of deep-fried pieces of brain (as they are prepared in one of the following recipes) as snacks at a cocktail party, many people would proclaim, "These are absolutely yummy, what are they?" This would be a very unkind thing to do, of course, but it would be interesting to see how many people one could convert . . . Our European friends—particularly in France, Italy, and Spain— have been enjoying brains for centuries. They are highly nutritious and have a wonderful creamy texture and melting consistency. All I can say is, if you've never tasted them, you don't know what you're missing.

Some of the best brains I have eaten have been cooked by Joyce Molyneux. A particularly good dish was a gratin of brains with sorrel—but first let me tell you a little about Joyce.

FANFARE

Joyce Molyneux

Joyce Molyneux is one of those rare people. As well as being a remarkable and talented cook, she is also a sensitive and exceptionally nice person. This combination is unusual in the restaurant trade.

Joyce, with her partner, Meriel Boyden, owns The Carved Angel restaurant in Dartmouth, England. Eating there is a special experience; it has a timeless quality that is reassuring in a restaurant. If I were to try to express the feeling of elation when arriving there, it would be to suggest that each visit is like visiting a friend who always makes you feel happy.

Joyce learned to cook fine things in the kitchens of The Hole in the Wall in Bath with George Perry-Smith (see page 179), who is, incidentally, Meriel Boyden's uncle. He was a great influence on Joyce and, if I may presume, she would say that she owes everything to George.

The style of Joyce's cooking is deeply embedded in tradition, yet flirts with new ideas from around the world. It is all secured by one thing—good taste. She just knows what is right. Lobster Bisque, for instance, comes to the table as a bowlful, backed up with a tureen and ladle in case you would like more. I once drank three bowls of it. There is a seemingly simple dish of lamb's offal that is a masterpiece of timing and judgment; offal is always a good thing at the Angel. Joyce does a dish with salted ox-tongue, beets, and celeriac that uses the wonderful saupiquet sauce (see page 156) to great effect. And there will often be a Perry-Smith dish on the menu, such as the famous Salmon in Pastry with Currants and Ginger (see page 180) and the particularly idiosyncratic Rissoles à la Parisienne served with a cup of consommé and a glass of Marsala.

Here is the recipe for Gratin of Brains with Sorrel from The Carved Angel Cookery Book. *Joyce says that she usually buys ox brains since calves' brains are not easily obtainable in Dartmouth.*

GRATIN OF BRAINS WITH SORREL

2 oz sorrel, tough stalks snipped out, well washed and shredded
½ cup light cream
salt and pepper
2 calves' brains, cooked as in Cervelles aux Beurre Noir (see below)
½ cup fresh breadcrumbs

Preheat the oven to 475°F. Put half the sorrel in a blender with the cream and a little salt and pepper to taste, and blend to a creamy purée. Alternatively, chop half the sorrel finely and mix with the cream. Divide half the remaining sorrel among four small gratin dishes (about 6 inches in diameter). Arrange the brains on top and cover with the last of the shredded sorrel. Pour the sorrel cream over the top of each dish and scatter with breadcrumbs. Bake in the oven for 10 minutes or until golden brown. If the gratins look a little pale, finish browning them under a hot grill.

CERVELLES AU BEURRE NOIR

Perhaps I *should* be calling this "Brains in Black Butter," but there are some classic dishes that evoke for me a certain style that is French bourgeois to a T. I always associate a dish such as this with Paris—bistros, brasseries, and small neighborhood restaurants—so it seems correct to call it by its French name. It is the sort of offal dish that I always think about along with tête de veau, tripes, ris de veau à la crème, and langue de veau à la moutarde. It's the melting quality of the various sorts of offal that really gets me going. And, generally, one would find something perky in the way of a sauce or dressing to accompany them. The contrast is delicious.

2 calves' brains, cleaned of blood and nerves
salt and pepper
flour for dusting
3 tbsp peanut oil
½ cup butter
2 tbsp capers (preferably small ones), drained
1½ tbsp red wine vinegar
2 tbsp finely chopped parsley

For the court-bouillon

1 carrot, peeled and chopped
1 leek, trimmed and finely chopped

2 celery stalks, chopped
1 sprig of thyme
1 bay leaf
6 peppercorns
a dash of vinegar
salt
4 cups water

Cook all the court-bouillon ingredients together for 30 minutes. Strain into a clean stainless steel pan, add the brains, and poach gently for 15–20 minutes or until just firm to the touch. Remove to a warm plate, tilted to allow the excess liquid to drain off. Slice each brain in half lengthways down the natural divide of the two lobes. Season with salt and pepper and dredge lightly with flour.

Heat the peanut oil until it is very hot and sauté the brains briskly until golden brown all over. Remove from the pan, drain on paper towels to remove excess oil, and keep warm. Wipe the pan clean, add the butter, and heat until foaming and turning dark brown, but not actually black (it has always been called "black" butter, but one never actually burns it black). Return the brains to the pan, and baste with the butter for a few minutes over a moderate heat. Add the capers, sizzle, then add the vinegar and chopped parsley. Serve directly on hot plates, preferably straight from the pan.

SALAD OF CALVES' BRAINS WITH SAUCE RAVIGOTE

This is a very simple first course that can be further embellished with a little diced cucumber or small cubes of fried potato. Because the dish is so soft and silky, a little added texture can be nice. I happen to like it the way it is without any other intrusion. Of course, you could serve this as a main dish. If this is the case, then the only possible accompaniment is a dish of steaming hot boiled potatoes.

2 calves' brains, prepared as for Cervelles an Beurre Noir (see page 18)
1 tbsp chopped parsley

For the sauce ravigote

2 tsp Dijon mustard
1 tbsp red wine vinegar
salt and pepper
¾ cup peanut oil (or other flavorless oil)
1 tbsp capers, drained and coarsely chopped
2 sprigs of tarragon, finely chopped

1 tbsp finely chopped flat-leaf parsley
1 tbsp finely chopped onion

To make the sauce, whisk together the mustard, vinegar, salt, and pepper until well blended. Whisk in the oil in a thin stream, as if you were making mayonnaise. (If the sauce separates, whisk in 1 tbsp boiling water.) Stir in the capers, herbs, and onion, and leave to infuse for 30 minutes.

Meanwhile, poach the brains gently in the court-bouillon for 15–20 minutes or until just firm to the touch. Remove to a tilted warm plate to allow the excess liquid to drain off. Slice each brain in half lengthways, and then thinly slice each half. Arrange in a single layer on four warm plates. Carefully spoon the sauce over the brains and sprinkle with the chopped parsley.

DEEP-FRIED CALVES' BRAINS WITH SAUCE GRIBICHE

Although the main ingredients for this recipe are almost identical to those in Salad of Calves' Brains with Sauce Ravigote (see page 19), the end result is, of course, quite different. It would be a shame to leave this recipe out for fear of repetition, as it is one of the very nicest ways in which to prepare brains. The combination of fresh crusty breadcrumbs encasing the creaminess of the brains is superb.

2 calves' brains, prepared and cooked as for Cervelles au Beurre Noir (see page 18)
salt and pepper
flour for dredging
1 egg, beaten
8 tbsp fresh breadcrumbs
oil for deep-frying
1 bunch of flat-leaf parsley, picked into small sprigs
1 lemon, cut into 4 wedges, to garnish

For the sauce gribiche

2 tsp Dijon mustard
1 tbsp red wine vinegar
salt and pepper
¾ cup peanut oil (or other flavorless oil)
1 tbsp capers, drained and coarsely chopped
2 sprigs of tarragon, finely chopped
1 tbsp finely chopped flat-leaf parsley
2 hard-boiled eggs, peeled and finely chopped

To make the sauce, proceed exactly as for sauce ravigote (see page 20), substituting the chopped egg for the chopped onion. Cut the calves' brains in half lengthways, lightly season, and dip first in the flour, then in the beaten egg, and finally in the crumbs. Deep-fry at a temperature of 370°F for 4–5 minutes or until golden and crusty. Drain on paper towels while you plunge the parsley into the hot oil and deep-fry until dark green and crisp—this should take a few seconds. Do not be alarmed at the sound of the parsley hitting the oil, but do make sure that it is as dry as possible before you fry it, as this minimizes the spluttering. Sprinkle the parsley with salt while still hot, and drain on paper towels. Serve the brains on individual plates garnished with the deep-fried parsley and lemon wedges. Serve the sauce separately.

SAUTÉ OF CALVES' BRAINS WITH CILANTRO, CHILLIES, GINGER, AND GARLIC

2 calves' brains, prepared and cooked as in Cervelles an Beurre Noir (see page 18)
salt and pepper
flour
4 tbsp peanut oil
2 chillies, seeded (optional) and chopped
2-inch piece of fresh ginger, peeled and finely chopped
2 small garlic cloves, peeled and finely chopped
juice of 1 lime
2 tbsp Thai fish sauce (nam pla)
a pinch of sugar
1 small bunch of cilantro, leaves only, chopped
cilantro sprigs, to garnish

Slice the brains in half lengthways and then cut each half into five slices. Season lightly, dip in the flour, and fry the brains in hot oil until lightly browned on both sides. Drain on absorbent paper towels and keep warm. Add the chillies, ginger, and garlic to the pan, and fry briefly. Add the lime juice, 2 tbsp water, the fish sauce, sugar, and chopped cilantro. Arrange the brains on a plain white serving dish, spoon over the sauce, and garnish with the cilantro sprigs.

CÈPES

In my book there is no finer wild mushroom than the cèpe—also known as porcini, penny bun, *Boletus edulis*. If you are lucky you can find them fresh—picked by yourself, or in enterprising food shops in the autumn. Otherwise, it's either the dried or frozen variety.

The most common type of cèpe has a shiny, brown cap and a barrel-shaped stalk. Its texture is spongy yet firm. Watch out for stems that feel hollow, as this is an indication of worms being present.

As with many things, the simpler the cooking method used for cèpes, the better. My all-time favorite is to fry them in olive oil until crusty and golden brown, then, at the last minute, to throw in freshly chopped parsley and lots of garlic. Finish with a grind of pepper, a sprinkle of sea salt, and a squeeze of lemon, and you have one of the nicest things it is possible to eat. And the smell! Sometimes I think it is the smell of food that is the tastiest thing about it.

However, I shall not forget a dish I ate once at a hilltop restaurant near Portofino. Lunch took place on a terrace and a chef friend and I were the only customers, apart from the staff who were finishing their own lunch as we arrived. The coastal view from our table on a brilliant hot day was magical. A bottle of chilled local white wine and two glasses appeared from nowhere; knives and forks and two white plates followed. There was no menu, no mention of orders being taken, in fact nothing much was said at all. Food just started to appear.

The first dish was porcini. They were raw, sliced wafer-thin, and piled high together with shavings of Parmesan, and dressed with the finest olive oil and a little lemon juice. For us this was a new combination (for the lucky locals a seasonal delight, no doubt) that knocked our socks off. It was one of those rare moments when one discovers something that is sheer perfection.

Sadly, what looked set to become a lunch of a lifetime took a terrible nose-dive from then on. The finale was a slightly inebriated proprietor pushing a wobbly trolley toward us with offers of crêpes Suzettes . . .

Talking of porcini and Italians, the nicest combination of the two is to be invited to pick fungi in the Welsh forests, near Abergavenny, with Franco Taruschio of the celebrated Walnut Tree Inn.

FANFARE

Franco Taruschio

I have known Franco and his English wife, Ann, for nearly twenty years. Their simple white-washed inn in the rolling Welsh countryside is unique. Although only a few minutes outside the market town of Abergavenny, it is actually miles from anywhere, and for the past thirty years, regular customers have traveled many more miles to line up (literally) at the door of this extraordinary place.

Franco's cooking is a joy. I don't know of anyone's food that I look forward to eating more than his. It is really salivating stuff. In fact, the last couple of miles driven down those quiet country roads are given over to thoughts of plates of his amazing home-cured bresaola, the quite remarkable Vincis Grassi Maceratese (an eighteenth-century recipe involving layers of lasagne, prosciutto, truffle, and porcini), and huge platters of grilled seafood. It has been known for me to follow this with some torte with three liqueurs, the spumoni amaretti, and—ahem, and—the honey and brandy ice cream . . . I want to go there right now please.

CÈPE TARTS

Persillade basically means chopped garlic and parsley. It is a classic of Provençal cooking and is added to many sautéed dishes at the last minute, together with a few breadcrumbs to soak up any excess olive oil or butter. When added to fried cèpes, they become cèpes à la provençale, and if you are not wishing to bother with the pastry, then this dish is wonderful just as it is.

If you are lucky enough, like me, to have been foraging for fresh cèpes in Welsh forests, then these are the mushrooms to use for this dish. Obviously, these are not readily available in the shops! So, as an alternative, I would suggest either a combination of dried or canned cèpes (which are readily available in specialist food shops and some supermarkets) with large, black, flat mushrooms. Dried mushrooms are best because they have a much stronger flavor, and are easy to reconstitute.

This would be perfect for a light luncheon with an arugula salad and some thin slivers of Parmesan.

1 quantity pastry as made for Anchovy and Onion Tarts (see page 8)
1 lb fresh cèpes or 4 oz dried cèpes plus 8 oz flat mushrooms
½ cup butter
salt and pepper
1 bunch of flat-leaf parsley, leaves only
4 garlic cloves, peeled and chopped
1 cup dry breadcrumbs
grated rind of 1 lemon
1 egg, beaten
2 tbsp freshly grated Parmesan cheese

If you are using dried cèpes, cover with lukewarm water and leave to reconstitute for 20 minutes. Drain and gently squeeze dry with your hands. (Strain the soaking water and use it to make a soup or stock.)

Preheat the oven to 400°F. Roll out the pastry into four circles measuring about 6 inches across and ⅛ inch thick. Place on a floured plate and keep cool in the fridge. Slice the mushrooms thinly. Heat the butter in a large frying pan until just turning golden. Throw in the mushrooms and season with salt and pepper. Cook briskly until crusty and golden brown, driving off any moisture that builds up. Add the parsley, garlic, breadcrumbs, and lemon rind and mix thoroughly. Turn into a bowl and leave to cool. Remove the pastry circles from the fridge, brush the edges with beaten egg to a depth of ½ inch, and spread the mushroom mixture over the four circles up to the edge of the beaten egg. Sprinkle with the grated Parmesan and place on greased baking sheets. Bake in the oven for 15–20 minutes or until the pastry has risen around the edges and is thoroughly crisp underneath (check by lifting with a spatula). Serve piping hot.

CÈPE AND POTATO BROTH

This broth could be made entirely with dried cèpes, but if you have fresh, obviously use those. The dried ones will give a deeper and stronger flavor, as opposed to the fresh, which will be more subtle.

½ cup butter
2 onions, peeled and finely chopped
4 oz dried cèpes, soaked and drained (see page 24), or 1 lb fresh cèpes
salt and pepper
1 glass of dry white wine
2 cups strong chicken or game stock
2 potatoes, peeled and diced
1 small bunch of thyme and 1 sliver of lemon peel, wrapped together in cheesecloth
2 garlic cloves, peeled and chopped
1 small bunch of flat-leaf parsley, leaves only, coarsely chopped

Melt the butter in a pan, add the onions, and sweat until just turning golden. Add the cèpes, season with salt and pepper, and cook together gently for 10 minutes. Add the wine and allow to bubble away for a few minutes before adding the stock. Bring to the boil, then add the potatoes and the cheesecloth sack. Cover, and simmer gently for 30 minutes. Remove the cheesecloth sack, add the garlic and parsley, and simmer for a further 5 minutes. Pass the soup through a *mouli-légumes* or food mill (which gives a nicer texture than a blender), check the seasoning, and serve.

CHICKEN

There is chicken, and there is chicken. The French chicken, from Bresse, is the finest in the world. It is nurtured and cosseted like no other living creature (save, perhaps, the Japanese Kobe cattle, which are fed beer and given a daily massage).

The poulet de Bresse is a "controlled" breed in France and carries its own special criteria as to production and methods of rearing. In fact, it has its own *appellation contrôlée*, as wine does. Posh bird. V. I. P. (Very Important Poulet). It has a superb flavor, due to its diet and upbringing, and also because it is properly hung, like a game bird, to allow its flavor to develop.

Naturally, there are other fine farmyard-reared birds, in Britain and the United States as well as in France and elsewhere. And the better the bird, the better the dish cooked.

Well, up to a point.

A good cook can produce a good dish from any old scrawnbag of a chook. A poor cook will produce a poor dish—even from a Bresse chicken. I firmly believe this to be true. Take a boiling fowl, for instance; one of the toughest old birds that requires careful and controlled cooking. Poached gently for a few hours in water, with root vegetables, herbs, and a little wine, this classic French bourgeois dish is a delight. *Poule au pot* (hen in a pot) is its name, and it can be eaten just as it is; you could even anglicize it with a few dumplings, if you wished, flavored with tarragon, perhaps— chicken's favorite herb.

A boiling fowl is a hen that is often sold guts intact. Unless you are squeamish, it is interesting to discover within the cavity seven or eight partly developed eggs. These are yolks covered with a thin membrane, graded in size and queuing up like an egg-production line ready for laying. Traditionally, these are removed, beaten just like a normal egg, and used to enrich and thicken sauce or soup.

A dish I often make with poached chicken requires removing the bird from the stock, discarding the vegetables and herbs, and reducing the cooking liquid down to a quarter of its original. The egg yolks are then beaten with some cream, added to the liquid, and cooked gently until it thickens like a custard. I like to add lots of chopped parsley. Carefully cut up the bird, lay the pieces in a dish, and cover with this gorgeous, richly flavored parsley sauce. The only accompaniment necessary is some boiled potatoes.

Roasting a chicken is a joy for me; and if I am pressed to name my favorite food, then roast chicken it must be.

I would think that the nicest one I ever tasted was at Chez L'Ami Louis in Paris. The late M. Magnin used chickens from Les Landes—I think from his own farm but I am not sure—and roasted them to a divine juiciness and crispness. Today they are still as good as the first I ate twelve years ago.

At Chez L'Ami Louis, the roast chickens do have the advantage of being cooked in a wood-fired oven, their pedigree is fine, and so much butter is used. The resultant chicken is cooked almost to a state of chewiness—particularly at its extremities; the parson's nose, wing tips, and undercarriage where those secret "oysters" lie. These little nuggets are charmingly called "*les sots l'y laissent*," which, loosely translated, means "the bits that silly idiots leave behind." The name "oyster" presumably refers to their shape or color, or how they slip nicely out of the natural bone structure as if they were oysters being lifted from their shells.

Anyway, the chicken at Ami Louis arrives at your table sizzling hot in its well-worn Le Creuset, surrounded by its juices, and carved there and then. The only thing served with this is a plate piled high with pommes frites of the thinnest dimensions.

Roasting and poaching (you don't *have* to use an old boiler for poaching; a good tender chicken is delicious too) are my favorite ways of cooking chicken. Grilled small pieces or butterflied chickens (split in half and flattened) are delightful alternatives, particularly when cooked on a grill, having previously been marinated with herbs, garlic, olive oil, balsamic vinegar, lemon juice, or what you will. If it is not outdoor weather, then it is worth investing in one of those cast-iron ridged grills; without one it just isn't possible to achieve the searing heat that crisps and scorches the skin or flesh and gives it its distinctive taste and, of course, fabulous smell.

Incidentally, putting chicken, or anything else, save toast, under a radiant broiler or salamander is *not* grilling in my book. This is fine for giving the finishing touches to a dish to be glazed or au gratin. (A frightful word that often rears its ugly head in British menuspeak is the term "gratinated." It is horrid and should be banned.)

Can use Convelation over this for part of this [handwritten note, left margin]

ROAST CHICKEN

½ cup good butter, at room temperature
4 lb free-range chicken
salt and pepper
1 lemon
several sprigs of thyme or tarragon, or a mixture of the two
1 garlic clove, peeled and crushed

rub w/ olive oil, baste w/ butter [handwritten note, right margin]

Preheat the oven to 450°F. Smear the butter with your hands all over the bird. Put the chicken in a roasting pan that will accommodate it with room to spare. Season liberally with salt and pepper and squeeze over the juice of the lemon. Put the herbs and garlic inside the cavity, together with the squeezed-out lemon halves—this will add a fragrant lemony flavor to the finished dish.

Roast the chicken in the oven for 10–15 minutes. Baste, then turn the oven temperature down to 375°F and roast for a further 30–45 minutes with occasional basting. The bird should be golden brown all over with a crisp skin and have buttery, lemony juices of a nut-brown color in the bottom of the pan.

Turn off the oven, leaving the door ajar, and leave the chicken to rest for at least 15 minutes before carving. This enables the flesh to relax gently, retaining the juices in the meat and ensuring easy, trouble-free carving and a moist bird.

Carve the bird to suit yourself. I like to do it *in* the roasting pan. I see no point in making a gravy in that old-fashioned way with the roasting fat, flour, and vegetable cooking water. With this roasting method, what you end up with in the pan is an amalgamation of butter, lemon juice, and chicken juices. That's all. It is a perfect homogenization of fats and liquids. All it needs is a light whisk or a stir, and you have the most wonderful "gravy" imaginable. If you wish to add extra flavor, you can scoop the garlic and herbs out of the chicken cavity, stir them into the gravy, and heat through; strain before serving.

Another idea, popular with the Italians, is sometimes known as "wet-roasting." Pour some white wine or a little chicken stock, or both, or even just water around the bottom of the pan at the beginning of cooking. This will produce more of a sauce and can be enriched further to produce altogether different results. For example, you can add chopped tomatoes, diced bacon, cream, endless different herbs, mushrooms, spring vegetables, spices—particularly saffron and ginger—or anything else that you fancy.

For me, the simple roast bird is the best, but it is useful to know how much further you can go when roasting a chicken.

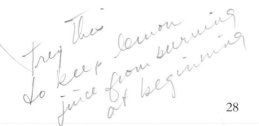

Try this to keep lemon juice from burning at beginning [handwritten note]

GRILLED BREAST OF CHICKEN WITH PROVENÇAL VEGETABLES AND AÏOLI

4 chicken breasts
a few sprigs of thyme
juice of 1 lemon
4 tbsp olive oil
salt and pepper
4 lemon wedges
watercress or parsley, to garnish (optional)

For the aïoli
2 egg yolks
2 large garlic cloves, peeled and crushed
salt and pepper
1½ cups olive oil
juice of 1 lemon

For the vegetables
1 large eggplant, sliced into rings
2 red bell peppers, peeled and seeded as for Pimiento Salsa (see page 149)
2 large zucchini, sliced diagonally
2 red onions, peeled and thickly sliced into rings
2 small fennel bulbs, thinly sliced
salt and pepper
olive oil

Put the chicken breasts in a shallow dish with the thyme, lemon juice, olive oil, and pepper.

To make the aïoli, first make sure all the ingredients are at room temperature. Traditionally, aïoli should be made in a pestle and mortar, but, failing that, a bowl and a whisk or, if you are not in the mood to be energetic (or are of a lazy persuasion), then an electric mixer will do. But no blender or whole eggs, please.

Beat together the egg yolks and the garlic with a little salt until thick. Start to add the olive oil in a thin stream, beating continuously. Add a little of the lemon juice and then some more oil. Continue beating, adding alternately more lemon juice and more oil until both are used up and you have a thick mayonnaise. Adjust the salt and add plenty of pepper. Cover and keep at room temperature.

To grill the vegetables and chicken, you need a cast-iron ribbed grill or skillet on the stove. This dish cannot be achieved with an overhead radiant broiler.

Put all the vegetables in a deep bowl. Season well and douse generously with olive oil. With your hands, mix all the vegetables together until evenly coated. This is a messy operation, but is the most practical method of ensuring even distribution of oil and seasoning. It doesn't really matter in what order you grill the vegetables. Fennel takes the longest and it needs to be charred more than the others, as this brings out its aniseed flavor. All the vegetables should be grilled on both sides and nicely blackened with crisscross stripes from the grill.

As each vegetable is cooked, transfer it to another bowl; it doesn't matter if they are warm or cold, they taste just as good either way. Taste one or two of them to see if they need more seasoning. Also, remoisten with a little more olive oil.

Remove the chicken breasts from their marinade and season with salt on the skin-side only (this helps the skin to crisp). Grill, skin-side down, for a few minutes, then turn 45 degrees and grill for a further few minutes. Turn over and cook for a few minutes more until bouncy to the touch and not quite cooked. Transfer to a hot plate and invert another plate on top to allow the meat to relax and lightly steam its way to becoming thoroughly cooked. This will take about 10 minutes.

Assemble the vegetables in the middle of a large oval platter, and arrange the chicken breasts attractively with the lemon wedges. Pour over any remaining juices from the chicken and vegetable dishes. Serve the aïoli separately. If you like you can pop bunches of watercress or parsley here and there for added color.

POULET POCHÉ À LA CRÈME WITH CRÊPES PARMENTIER

The definitive version of this Burgundian speciality is to be found at Georges Blanc in Vonnas, Burgundy, France. On more than one occasion I had wanted to try this dish instead of the more complicated or more novel dishes on the menu, but curiosity always got the better of me and I would plump for a *Menu Dégustation*—a six- or seven-course tasting menu that is supposed to represent the chef at his best. I am not sure about this. It appears to be good value and a balanced selection, but I feel, in the final analysis, that it is production-line cooking and not for me. However, I have to admit that on the two occasions I have eaten the *Dégustation* at Georges Blanc, it was delicious.

However, when finally I was grown up enough to choose such a mundane plate of food as boiled chicken in a cream sauce with potato cakes, the rather imperious and oh-so-confident (English) *sommelier* came out with an unforgettable phrase: "What do you want to choose that for! There is a little place just down the road that does a far better version at half the price." Thankfully, I wasn't put off and enjoyed one of the best dishes I have ever eaten.

The crêpe recipe is Grandmère Blanc's; the recipe for the chicken is not so grand Hopkinson.

For the chicken

4 lb chicken
3 carrots, peeled and cut lengthways
4 celery stalks, sliced into 3
3 leeks, trimmed and split lengthways
1 onion, peeled and studded with 3 cloves
2 bay leaves, a few sprigs of thyme and tarragon
peppercorns
salt
½ 750 ml bottle dry white wine
2 cups light cream
juice of 1 lemon

For the crêpe batter

1 lb 2 oz potatoes, peeled and cut into chunks
¼ cup milk
2 ½ tbsp all-purpose flour
3 eggs
4 egg whites
2 ½ tbsp heavy cream
salt and pepper
8 oz unsalted butter (melted, skimmed of froth, strained, leaving behind milky
residue to produce clarified butter)

To cook the chicken, put it in a large, deep flameproof casserole or large boiling pot with the vegetables, herbs, peppercorns, and 2 tsp salt. Add the white wine and sufficient water just to cover. Put on a high heat and bring to the boil, then skim the surface, which will have produced a gray scum. Turn down the heat to a mere simmer. More scum will appear from time to time, so skim the surface when necessary. Do not cover, though you may like to turn the bird over from time to time if portions of it are not submerged. Simmer for 1 hour.

Carefully lift out the chicken and place it on a large plate. Strain the cooking liquid into a clean saucepan and throw away the vegetables. Put the chicken back in 1 cup of the strained stock, bring back to the boil, then remove from the heat and cover. This is to keep the chicken warm and allow it to rest.

Reduce the rest of the stock until thick and syrupy, ending with about ½ cup. Add the lemon juice and the cream and boil to reduce again, gently, until the sauce is unctuous and the consistency of thin custard. (In fact, a wine merchant friend of mine always refers to this dish as "chicken in custard.") Check the seasoning and keep the sauce warm.

Meanwhile, to make the crêpe batter, steam the potatoes until cooked through. While still hot, put through the finest blade of a *mouli-légumes* or food mill into a bowl. Leave to cool. Mix together all the other ingredients, except the butter, in another bowl, and add to the potato. Pass the whole mixture through a sieve and check the seasoning.

To cook the pancakes, heat 1 tbsp of the clarified butter in a frying pan (preferably nonstick) until hot but not smoking. Use 1 tbsp of the batter per pancake, and cook three pancakes at a time. When the top of each pancake looks almost set, flip it over with a spatula, cook for a few seconds, then transfer to a warmed plate. Continue in this fashion until all the batter is used. Keep the crêpes in a single layer on an ovenproof plate in a warm oven.

The nicest possible way to present this dish is to place the whole chicken on a grand serving dish, arranging the crêpes attractively around the edge, and pouring the rich sauce over the whole bird. I don't believe this dish needs any further embellishment.

POULET SAUTÉ AU VINAIGRE

This very simple dish is a great favorite. Its success lies in the fact that there are very few ingredients other than a good chicken and excellent-quality vinegar.

When Michel Guérard first sent us his recipes via the *Sunday Times* magazine in the early 1970s, he included a recipe for Poulet Sauté an Vinaigre de Vin. It was a dish I cooked over and over again, I loved it so much. His version included Armagnac, Dijon mustard, tomato purée, garlic, white wine, chervil, and heavy cream. It is very good and very rich. I have to say, though, that today I prefer this more traditional version. But I thank him, and his translator Caroline Conran, for the introduction to his genius, which has inspired me and countless other cooks.

> 4 lb chicken, cut into 8 pieces
> salt and pepper
> ½ cup butter
> 2 tbsp olive oil
> 6 very ripe tomatoes, peeled, seeded, and chopped
> 1 cup best-quality red wine vinegar
> 1 cup chicken stock
> 2 heaped tbsp chopped parsley

Season the pieces of chicken with salt and pepper. Heat 4 tbsp of the butter and the olive oil in a flameproof casserole until just turning nut-brown. Add the chicken and fry gently, turning occasionally, until golden brown all over. Add the chopped tomatoes, and carry on frying and stewing until the tomato has lost its moisture and is dark red and sticky. Pour in the vinegar and reduce by simmering until almost disappeared. Add the stock, and simmer again until reduced by half. Remove the chicken to a serving dish and keep warm. Whisk the remaining butter into the sauce to give it a glossy finish. Add 1 tbsp chopped parsley, pour over the chicken, and sprinkle with the remaining parsley. Serve with plain boiled potatoes.

CHOCOLATE

I agree with the late Roald Dahl that the British chocolate bar is the best in the world. There is nothing to beat the gorgeous sickliness of a Mars bar, and, as a boy, I was seduced by the honeycomb center of a Crunchie. (I'm sure I wasn't alone in trying to make a deep hole in the honeycomb with my tongue, before the chocolate collapsed around it.) And I remember the effortlessness of eating a Milky Way or an Aero, and of being repeatedly surprised by the alarming speed with which one could consume a packet of Munchies, or one of those small, strangely shaped bars called Toffee Cup.

Somehow, the continental chocolate bars made by Nestlé, Lindt, Suchard, and others have never quite made it for me. Perhaps the ingredients are of a finer quality; the chocolate has an altogether more sophisticated (bland?) flavor. There are, of course, exceptions. Toblerone is one, and I have always had a soft spot for the miniature chocolate eggs manufactured by Suchard that are sold in plastic, foot-long tubes at Easter time.

However, setting all those mass-produced chocolate goodies apart, it has to be said that the great chocolate-makers of Belgium and France, who produce such pure, dark, and bitter blocks of black chocolate, are without equal anywhere. From this high-quality, cocoa-butter-rich stuff is made an altogether different type of sweet-meat: fabulously rich and powerful chocolates and pralines made with fresh cream and nuts; fragrant alcoholic combinations; fondant-rich nuggets of super sweetness; and mouth-coating, cocoa-covered truffles. It is only with this quality of chocolate that you can hope to achieve a good chocolate dessert or pudding. Never, never, never use that artificial stuff that calls itself "cooking chocolate" or "cake covering." A bar of plain Bourneville or Baker's is better than nothing and, in fact, I have made many impromptu hot chocolate puddings with a bar of this from the corner shop, but for more serious cooking with chocolate, it really is worth searching out the very best chocolate money can buy.

CHOCOLATE TART

For the pastry

¾ cup butter
½ cup powdered sugar
2 egg yolks
2 scant cups of all-purpose flour

For the filling

3 egg yolks
2 whole eggs
2 tbsp sugar
½ cup plus 2 tbsp butter
7 oz dark, bittersweet chocolate, broken into pieces

To make the pastry, put the butter, sugar, and egg yolks in a bowl (or food processor) and work together quickly. Blend in the flour, and work to a homogenous paste. Chill for at least 1 hour.

Preheat the oven to 350°F. Roll out the pastry as thinly as you can and use it to line an 8-inch tart pan. Bake in the oven for about 25 minutes or until pale biscuit in color, but thoroughly cooked through. Remove. Increase the heat of the oven to 375°F.

To make the filling, put the egg yolks, whole eggs, and sugar in a bowl and beat vigorously together, preferably with an electric mixer, until really thick and fluffy. Melt the butter and chocolate together in a bowl over a pan of barely simmering water, stirring until smooth. Pour into the egg mixture while just warm. Briefly beat together until well amalgamated, then pour into the pastry shell. Return to the hot oven for 5 minutes, then remove and leave to cool. Serve with thick cream.

SAINT-ÉMILION AU CHOCOLAT

I think it must have been during the 1960s that this wonderfully rich chocolate dessert started appearing on menus all over the place, particularly in the West Country of Great Britain. I am sure I am right in saying that George Perry-Smith, from the famous Hole in the Wall restaurant in Bath, was the initiator. The original recipe comes from Elizabeth David's *French Country Cooking*.

½ cup unsalted butter, softened
⅓ cup sugar

1 egg yolk
¼ cup plus 2 tbsp milk
8 oz dark, bittersweet chocolate, broken into pieces
12–16 macaroons or Italian *amaretti* cookies
a little rum or brandy

Cream the butter and sugar together until light and fluffy. Beat in the egg yolk. Heat together the milk and chocolate until melted and smooth. Allow to cool slightly, then add to the butter/sugar mixture and beat well. Arrange some of the macaroons in a soufflé dish or four individual ramekins, using just enough to cover the base. Sprinkle over some of the rum or brandy. Cover with a layer of the chocolate mixture, add a further layer of cookies, a little more rum or brandy, and another layer of chocolate. Depending on the size of your dish or dishes, carry on in this fashion until both cookies and chocolate are used up. Chill for at least 12 hours or overnight before serving.

MILK CHOCOLATE MALT ICE CREAM

The first time I ate this was on my first trip to California. It was in San Francisco, at Wolfgang Puck's fifth restaurant, called Postrio. In fact, the original recipe comes from Nancy Silverton, who now has a restaurant in Los Angeles called Campanile. Nancy was one of Wolfgang Puck's first pastry chefs and is an innovative cook in this field.

I think it is terrific to put together sickly rich things such as Horlicks, milk chocolate, and Bailey's Irish Cream, and to end up with a really smashing ice cream.

1 cup heavy cream
1 cup milk
6 egg yolks, beaten
2 oz Horlicks or malted milk powder
7½ oz milk chocolate, broken into small pieces
1½ tbsp Bailey's Irish Cream Liqueur

Heat the cream and milk together. Beat the egg yolks and Horlicks together, add the hot milk/cream mixture, and blend thoroughly. Return the mixture to the pan and heat gently until slightly thickened. Remove from the heat and add the chocolate, stirring until melted. Cool completely and add the liqueur, then freeze in an ice-cream machine following the manufacturer's instructions.

CHOCOLATE PITHIVIERS

For the crème pâtissière
1 cup plus 2 tbsp milk
1 vanilla bean, split lengthways
3 egg yolks
¼ cup sugar
3 tablespoons all-purpose flour

For the chocolate mixture
½ cup unsalted butter, softened
⅓ cup sugar
2 small eggs
4 oz ground almonds
4 tbsp unsweetened cocoa powder
½ tbsp dark rum
4 oz plain chocolate, chopped
1 quantity pastry as made for Anchovy and Onion Tarts (see page 8)
beaten egg, to glaze
confectioners' sugar, to dust

First make the crème pâtissière. Put the milk in a saucepan with the vanilla bean and heat gently to boiling point. Whisk together the egg yolks, sugar, and flour. Pour the hot milk into the egg mixture and whisk lightly together. Return the mixture to the saucepan and cook gently until it thickens. Pour through a sieve, discard the vanilla bean, and chill.

For the chocolate mixture, cream the butter and sugar together until light and fluffy. Add the eggs and beat again. Now add the ground almonds and cocoa powder. Beat again. Add the rum together with the crème pâtissière and finally fold in the chopped chocolate. Chill.

Preheat the oven to 400°F. Roll out the pastry to about ⅛-inch thick. Cut it into four 4-inch and four 6-inch squares. Place the smaller squares on a floured board. Using a large ice-cream scoop, place a scoop of the chocolate mixture in the center of each of the small squares of pastry. Brush the pastry edges with half the beaten egg, place the larger squares of pastry on top, and press down and around firmly, making sure there are no air bubbles.

Use a 4-inch round pastry cutter to cut the filled pastry squares into neat rounds. Discard the trimmings. Press and seal together the edges with a fork to form a decorative pattern. Brush the pithiviers with the remaining beaten egg and dust lightly with confectioners' sugar.

Place on a greased baking sheet and bake in the oven for 15–20 minutes or until the pastry is well risen, shiny, and golden brown. Remove from the oven, dust lightly with some more confectioners' sugar, and serve hot with thick cream.

CHOCOLATE BAVAROIS

3½ gelatin leaves
2 cups milk
12 oz dark, bittersweet chocolate, broken into pieces
5 egg yolks
1 cup heavy cream

Put the gelatin leaves in a bowl, cover with cold water, and leave to soften.

Heat the milk and melt the chocolate in it. Gently whisk together until smooth. Whisk the egg yolks and add them to the milk chocolate mixture. Cook over a gentle heat until thickened, like custard. Drain the gelatin and add it to the chocolate mixture while it is still hot. Whisk together well. Pass the mixture through a sieve into a cold bowl. Place over crushed ice and stir with a wooden spoon until starting to set. Lightly whip the cream until holding soft peaks, then carefully but quickly fold it into the chocolate. Pour into individual ramekins or a soufflé dish and refrigerate for at least 2 hours before serving with cold crème anglaise (Custard Sauce, see page 69).

PETIT POT AU CHOCOLAT

This is the richest little pot of chocolate you will ever eat. It is important that you allow a crust to form toward the end of the cooking—which may look as if you have overcooked them. Do not worry, as this, when cold, forms a chocolate crust that covers a cream of extreme intensity and velvet texture.

¾ cup heavy cream
½ vanilla bean, split lengthways
6 tbsp milk
4½ oz dark, bittersweet chocolate, broken into pieces
2 small egg yolks
1 heaped tbsp confectioners' sugar

Preheat the oven to 275°F. Warm the cream with the vanilla bean, whisk to disperse the vanilla seeds, then cover and leave to infuse for 30 minutes. Meanwhile, melt the chocolate in the milk. Beat together the egg yolks and sugar, add the chocolate milk and vanilla cream, and blend together thoroughly. Pass through a fine sieve and pour into little pots or ramekins. (This dish is often served in traditional porcelain custard pots.)

Bake in a bain-marie (water bath) in the oven for 45 minutes–1 hour or until slightly puffed up and spongy. Cool thoroughly in the fridge for at least 6 hours before serving.

CILANTRO

This is a herb I came to late in life. I had tried using it in stews, as is the style of Indian cooks, and found the resultant taste muddy and bitter. It wasn't until I discovered salsa, and some remarkably hot food in my initiation to Thai cooking, that its magical taste finally appealed to me. So much so, that on paying a visit to a favorite Thai café-cum-restaurant in west London, desperate for my hit of cilantro, and discovering that it hadn't yet been delivered, there seemed no point in staying for lunch.

I even find myself eating cilantro raw—whole clumps of it. I add it to far too many dishes, too often. I believe that cilantro should hardly ever be cooked and that if it is included in a hot dish, it should only be added at the very last moment. Its flavor is sharp, soapy, and metallic—not the most beguiling description but somehow it is a real spoiler for the taste buds. It seems to shout sharp and citrus and its flavor bursts open when combined with things spicy and hot-tasting. There is nothing like it. If *ever* I see a recipe again that suggests flat-leaf parsley as a substitute for cilantro, then I shall weep with frustration. There is no substitute. However, I know that there are many people who actively dislike its strident taste. And, incidentally, it is not a great partner to good wine.

Apart from that delicious salsa, I have also used cilantro most effectively in cold spiced cucumber soup; added it to a traditional mint sauce to be served with cold lamb cutlets; in creamy chicken salads with sesame sauce; and on a tomato salad with onions—let's give basil a rest for a while, shall we?

A friend gave me a recipe for a remarkably cooling chutney that was made with fresh coconut, green chillies, and huge amounts of chopped cilantro. It was sensational.

If you are ever lucky enough to find cilantro that still has its roots intact, there are two reasons for not discarding them. First, the roots allow you to keep the herb for a few weeks in your fridge. Simply immerse the roots in water in a glass jar, cover with a plastic bag, and secure the bag over the top of the leaves with a rubber band. The roots will carry on growing, and keep the cilantro as fresh as can be. Second, the roots actually have the most pungent flavor of all.

GREEN PASTE

This recipe makes about enough to fill an 18-oz Kilner or Ball jar (the ones with a rubber seal and a clamp). Stored thus, it will keep for up to three weeks in the fridge. It is not worth making less, as the processing of the paste is difficult with a smaller amount of ingredients.

3½ oz cilantro leaves, stalks, and roots
1½ oz mint leaves
8 garlic cloves, peeled
2 tsp ground cumin
1 tsp sugar
1 tsp salt
6 tbsp lime or lemon juice
5–10 green chillies, seeded if preferred (the seeds make the paste hotter)
½ cup cream of coconut

Purée all the ingredients together in a blender until smooth.

You could eat this paste with almost anything. It is particularly good as a chutney with grilled food, such as chicken, shellfish, rabbit, and, best of all, lamb. I like it so much that I often eat it on its own.

SALSA

To achieve the right balance for a salsa, there needs to be a good ratio of sweet/sour/hot/salt. It is very difficult to write an exact recipe, as it is more like a salad than a sauce, and the ingredients build themselves up on each other. I like mine with a hefty kick of chilli, but not so much that that is all you can taste. I prefer to seed the chillies, as this way you can use more chilli without the extra heat from the seeds. In salsa, I prefer the taste of green chillies rather than red. A rule of thumb is: the smaller a chilli, the hotter.

The fish sauce is a purely personal addition; I use it in place of salt.

8 well-ripened tomatoes, peeled, seeded, and coarsely chopped
1 red onion, peeled and finely chopped
a bunch of cilantro, leaves only, coarsely chopped
8 sprigs of mint, leaves only, coarsely chopped
juice of 3 limes
3 green chillies, seeded and chopped
½ tsp sugar
1 tbsp oriental fish sauce, such as nam pla (optional)
2 tbsp olive oil

Mix all the ingredients together in a bowl. Cover with plastic wrap and leave at room temperature for 1 hour before using.

Like Green Paste (see page 43), this partners with grilled food extremely well. A favorite combination is rare entrecote steak, chips, salsa, and a bowl of sour cream.

ORIENTAL SALAD

The idea for this recipe developed from traditional Thai salads, which make use of bean sprouts, noodles, mint and cilantro, chillies, onions, peanuts, and strips of other vegetables. It is a cooling salad to eat, though the herbs and chilli give it aromatic punch. To achieve the thinnest slices possible of carrot and cucumber, use a potato peeler.

1 small package rice noodles, cooked as per instructions, drained, rinsed, and cooled
8 oz bean sprouts
1 large carrot, peeled and thinly sliced lengthways
1 cucumber, peeled, cut in half lengthways, seeded, and thinly sliced lengthways
two 1-inch pieces of fresh root ginger, peeled, sliced, and cut into thin strips
a small bunch of cilantro, leaves only
6 mint sprigs, leaves only
3 large mild red chillies, seeded and sliced into thin strips
1 red onion, peeled and sliced into thin rings

For the dressing

1 tbsp toasted sesame seeds
2 tbsp rice vinegar
2 tbsp soy sauce
4 tbsp oriental fish sauce, such as nam pla
1 garlic clove, peeled and finely chopped
1 tbsp sesame oil
6 tbsp peanut oil

Mix the sesame seeds, vinegar, soy sauce, fish sauce, and garlic together in a bowl. Whisk in the oils.

In another large bowl, mix together all the salad ingredients thoroughly with your hands. Pour over the dressing, toss lightly, and leave to wilt slightly before serving.

This could be a light first course or, alternatively, an accompaniment to a dish such as Slow-Braised Belly Pork with Soy, Ginger, and Garlic (see page 158). You could also turn it into a light lunch dish by topping the salad with thin strips of grilled duck breast, cold roast chicken, pork, or rare beef. Deep-fried whole shrimp in breadcrumbs would be very sassy.

DIPPING SAUCE

This is based on a Vietnamese dipping sauce, but I have adapted it to include a lot more cilantro than the original recipe. I've also included mint. This sauce is extremely "moreish"—you keep wanting to have little tastes of it, all the time. It is perfect with deep-fried nibbly things—shrimp, strips of fish, onion, and eggplant, and is particularly good with breadcrumbed nuggets of calves' brains. As a dressing for cold shellfish (especially white crab meat), it has no rival.

a small bunch of cilantro, leaves only, finely chopped
6 mint sprigs, leaves only, finely chopped
4 small garlic cloves, peeled and finely chopped
4 small green chillies, seeded and finely chopped
1 heaped tbsp sugar
juice of 5 limes
8 tbsp oriental fish sauce, such as nam pla
½ cup cold water

Mix all ingredients together in a small bowl.

CILANTRO AND COCONUT SOUP

This soup is very much enhanced by the addition of the Thai stock (bouillon) cube, which is marketed under the name tom yum. All oriental grocers stock it, but it is not absolutely essential.

2 cups light chicken stock
1 tom yum cube
2-inch piece of fresh root ginger, unpeeled but chopped
6 spring onions, trimmed and finely chopped
4 small red chillies, seeded and finely chopped
2 lemongrass stalks, chopped
1 garlic clove, peeled and chopped
a large bunch of cilantro, leaves reserved, stalks and roots finely chopped
juice of 1 lime
3 tbsp oriental fish sauce, such as nam pla
1 can (14 fl oz) thin coconut milk
½ cup heavy cream

Heat together the chicken stock, tom yum cube, ginger, spring onions, chillies, lemon-grass, and garlic. Simmer gently for 30 minutes. Strain and blend with the cilantro roots and stalks, lime juice, fish sauce, and coconut milk. Return to the pan, reheat, and simmer gently for 5 minutes. Strain once more and return to the pan. Finely chop the cilantro leaves and add them to the soup with the cream. Warm through once more and serve.

COD

What a handsome fish the cod is, with its greeny gray skin that positively glistens when spanking fresh. The flesh is firm and sweet-smelling, and it reeks of the sea. Unfortunately, cod isn't always found in this condition.

In the past, cod has suffered a poor reputation. This is mainly due to some mean-minded fishmongers who have been quite happy to display tired, frozen fillets on their sad slabs, the water in the flesh weeping out over their plastic parsley.

The cooking of cod has also been misguided. All too often it is boiled or baked to death by an insensitive cook, or fried to a crisp by a careless fish-and-chip-shop cowboy. The perfect piece of cod, for me, is one that can be cut into lovely thick slices, dipped in seasoned flour, and pan-fried in foaming butter until golden, finally emerging crusty-coated and succulent. Another of my favorite ways with cod (see page 48) is to poach a whole fish in a tasty court-bouillon, as you would a salmon, and to serve it warm on a large dish surrounded by Mediterranean vegetables, with hard-boiled eggs and a big pot of aïoli. This is an alternative version of the Provençal classic, using fresh instead of salt cod. The texture of a fine cod cooked like this is a dream. The flakes of fish fall easily from the bone; glossy, opaque, and succulent.

LE GRAND AÏOLI

salt
12 young carrots, trimmed but unpeeled
8 oz fine green beans, or haricots verts, trimmed
12 large spring onions, trimmed
1 lb small red-skinned potatoes, scrubbed
8 small globe artichokes
juice of 1 lemon
1 quantity court-bouillon (see page 181)
4–5 lb cod, head removed, trimmed, and scaled
24 canned snails (optional)
4 hard-boiled eggs, peeled and halved lengthways
1 quantity aïoli (see page 29)
parsley and lemon wedges, to garnish
olive oil and coarse sea salt, to serve

Fill a large stainless steel pan with water and bring to the boil. Add plenty of salt. Add the carrots and cook until just tender. Lift out with a slotted spoon and reserve. Bring the water back to the boil and cook the beans for 3–4 minutes. Lift out with a slotted spoon and refresh in ice-cold water. Drain and reserve. Do the same with the spring onions. Cook the potatoes until tender in the same water. Lift out and reserve. Trim any tough-looking outer leaves from the artichokes, add them to the boiling water with the lemon juice, and boil for 20–30 minutes, or until a leaf pulled from the middle comes out easily. Drain the artichokes and reserve. Keep the cooking liquid hot, ready for reheating the vegetables. Do this either in a colander suspended over the water or in a steamer if you have one.

Bring the court-bouillon to the boil and add the cod. Bring back to the boil, then simmer for 5 minutes. Remove from the heat and leave for about 30 minutes, then lift the cod out. Place the fish on a large oval plate that will accommodate the fish as well as the vegetables. Wrap the whole plate in aluminum foil and keep warm in a very low oven. Meanwhile, reheat the vegetables and, if you are using them, heat the snails in a small pan.

To serve, arrange all the vegetables attractively around the fish. Intersperse with little clumps of parsley, the snails, the eggs, and the lemon wedges. Serve the aïoli and a bowl of coarse sea salt separately. Have a bottle of olive oil (preferably the one that you used to make the aïoli) on the table for dressing the vegetables.

This wonderful feast looks magnificent and is lovely eaten outside; I like eating it with plenty of cool, light red wine.

POACHED COD WITH LENTILS AND SALSA VERDE

Try to find the French lentils called lentilles de Puy for this dish, as their flavor is far superior to that of other lentils. They are slate gray in color and are becoming more widely available in supermarkets.

The combination of moist and succulent flakes of fish, the earthiness of the lentils, and the sharp punch of the sauce gives this dish a fine balance of flavors. This is one of the most satisfying plates of food I know, both for texture and flavor.

1½ lb cod, scaled, filleted, and cut into 4 pieces
juice of 1 lemon

For the lentils

8 oz lentilles de Puy, thoroughly washed and drained
1½ cups water
½ chicken stock (bouillon) cube
1 clove
1 bay leaf
1 small onion, peeled
salt and pepper

For the salsa verde

a bunch of flat-leaf parsley, leaves only
10 basil leaves
15 mint leaves
2 garlic cloves, peeled and crushed
1 tbsp Dijon mustard
6 anchovy fillets
1 tbsp capers, drained
½ cup extra-virgin olive oil
salt and pepper

To serve

1 lemon, cut into wedges
extra-virgin olive oil
sea salt
pepper
a few sprigs of flat-leaf parsley

First cook the lentils. Place them in a stainless steel or enameled saucepan, cover with the water, and add the bouillon cube. Push the clove through the bay leaf, then into the onion. Add the onion to the pan. Bring to the boil, then reduce the heat and simmer gently for 30–40 minutes or until the liquid has been absorbed and the lentils are tender. Season *now* rather than before, as salt added at the beginning of cooking can make the lentil skins tough. Keep warm.

Meanwhile, make the salsa verde. I usually make this in a food processor, but traditionally it is made with a pestle and mortar. In fact, some people find a pestle and mortar preferable, as it bruises and coaxes the juices out of the herbs and garlic, rather than pulverizing the living daylights out of them. However, I quite like the homogenization achieved in the processor. With the pestle and mortar method, the sauce is much more like a dressing.

Put the herbs, garlic, mustard, anchovies, and capers into the food processor with a few tablespoons of the oil. Process for a few minutes, occasionally stopping to scrape down what is thrown up against the sides of the bowl. With the machine running, add the rest of the oil in a thin stream, as if you were making mayonnaise; in fact, the finished sauce should look like coarse, green mayonnaise. Season with salt and pepper.

Poach the fish in lightly salted water, following the directions in Basque Chiorro (see page 105), but do not remove the skin. This is purely on aesthetic grounds, as I think the fish looks nicer unskinned.

To serve, place a portion of fish on each individual plate with a wedge of lemon. Pour a little olive oil over the fish, sprinkle with a little sea salt and a grinding of pepper, and tuck in a couple of sprigs of flat-leaf parsley. Serve the lentils and salsa verde separately.

DEEP-FRIED COD

Of course, you can deep-fry any fish, but to my mind, cod works best, and is quintessentially British. Sealed in by a crisp, golden batter, the flakes of fish cook to pearly white perfection. This batter recipe is the best I have ever come across. It retains its crispness like no other; perhaps it has something to do with the potato flour and the beer.

oil for deep-frying
four 6-oz cod fillets
seasoned flour for dusting

For the batter

1¾ cups all-purpose flour
6 tbsp potato flour (fécule)

1 bottle beer (½ pint)
1 egg yolk
2 tbsp oil
1 cup milk
salt and pepper

To make the batter, blend all the ingredients together, sieve, and leave to rest for 1 hour.

Heat oil for deep-frying to 350°F. Dip the cod in the seasoned flour, then immediately into the batter and deep-fry for 5–7 minutes, depending on the thickness of the fillets. Serve with french fries (see page 164), lemon, vinegar, watercress, tartar sauce, ketchup . . . or what you will.

POACHED COD WITH PICKLED VEGETABLE RELISH

This recipe comes from the *Chez Panisse Cookbook*. It is an inspired combination that contrasts soft and moist flakes of fish with a perky raw "chutney." The chutney should be made a good hour or more in advance so that the flavors may develop and mature.

1 quantity court-bouillon (see page 181)
1 lb cod fillet
olive oil and pepper, to serve (optional)

For the relish

3 tbsp finely diced carrot
3 tbsp finely diced red bell pepper
4 tbsp finely diced red onion
1 garlic clove, peeled and finely chopped
3 tbsp finely diced gherkins
4 tbsp finely diced green olives
1 tbsp finely chopped capers
5 anchovy fillets, finely chopped
1 tbsp red wine vinegar
½ cup extra-virgin olive oil
2 heaped tbsp finely chopped flat-leaf parsley
salt and cayenne pepper

Mix all the relish ingredients together in a large bowl. Taste after 1 hour, and adjust the seasoning if necessary.

Strain the court-bouillon into a clean pan and bring to the boil. Drop in the cod fillet, bring back to the boil, and switch off the heat. Leave for 10 minutes, then remove and skin the fish. Divide the relish among four plates, and carefully arrange the flakes of cod over the top. If desired, drizzle a little extra olive oil over the fish, and grind over some pepper.

BRANDADE DE MORUE

This is in my top-ten list of favorite things to eat. It uses salt cod, which is a little difficult to find, but if you have an enterprising local specialty food store, then you might be in luck. I have made it using fresh cod, but the final flavor lacks the characteristic pungency that you get with the real thing. The dish is a speciality of Provence, Nîmes in particular, where it is most often eaten at religious festivals, particularly Easter and Christmas Eve.

Always look for a nice piece of salt cod from a center cut, where the fish is at its thickest and most succulent. It must be soaked thoroughly, preferably under gently running water for 24 hours or so. Many recipes recommend removing the bones after cooking; I find it easier to wheedle them out with a small pair of pliers beforehand.

The olive oil for this dish should be of the finest quality.

1 large potato, weighing about 6 oz, peeled and cut into large chunks
salt
¾ cup plus 2 tbsp olive oil
¾ cup plus 2 tbsp milk
3 garlic cloves, peeled and crushed
1 lb salt cod fillet, soaked, drained, and boned
juice of 1 lemon
black pepper

To garnish

olive oil
12 slices of bread, cut diagonally from a baguette
black olives

Boil the potato in salted water until cooked. Drain and dry out in a warm oven. Mash while still hot, and keep warm. Heat the olive oil gently in a small pan. Put the milk and garlic in another small pan and heat until warm. Meanwhile, put the cod in a saucepan of cold water, bring to the boil, then switch off the heat. Leave for 5 minutes, then remove to a plate. Take off the skin and place the fish in a food processor. With the motor running, alternately add the olive oil and garlicky milk until a thick, sloppy paste is achieved. Pour in the hot mashed potato and quickly blend in. Don't overprocess the mixture once you have added the potato, as there is danger of it becoming gluey. Add the lemon juice and plenty of black pepper, but add salt only if necessary.

This is nicest served in a shallow bowl, forked up into a mound, and drizzled with a little olive oil, so that it trickles down the sides. Fry the bread slices in olive oil until golden brown, then arrange attractively with the black olives around the brandade.

This makes a substantial winter luncheon dish or a most antisocial late-night snack. As with the aïoli recipe (see page 48), the brandade goes particularly well with a glass of red French country wine.

CRAB

The Chinese cook a great crab dish. They chop the creature into four pieces—two claws, and the body split in half—and then throw it into hot oil with spring onions, ginger, soy sauce, and garlic. It is a complete mess when it arrives at the table but, as messes go, I know of no other I'd rather clear up. The Chinese also cook crab with chillies and black beans; equally tasty, equally finger-licking good.

If you are cooking crabs to pick out the meat afterward to use in a particular dish, then always choose large cock crabs as opposed to hens. The female crab is generally smaller but to distinguish between the two, if you are unsure, examine the flap on the underside; the female's is broader. More importantly, make sure that your chosen crab is heavy for its size; this indicates that there is plenty of meat inside and that the crab has grown to fill its shell.

I would boil a 4-lb crab for 20–25 minutes. (Cut the time by half for half the weight, and so on.) The water should be well salted. In his marvelous book *English Seafood Cookery*, Ricky Stein suggests water salted in the proportions of 5½ oz to 1 gallon. He says that this is roughly the salinity of sea water, in which he normally cooks his shellfish. He would. He has a plentiful supply just across the street from his restaurant, The Seafood, in Padstow. To simulate sea water, I would suggest using Maldon sea salt and a pinch of sugar.

Sometimes a crab will shed its claws as soon as it is put into boiling water. To prevent this happening, a practical and humane method of killing a crab is to insert a strong, sharp knife straight through the middle of the body underneath the flap. This severs the central nervous system and removes all tension. One final important step is to have ready a large container of iced water in which to plunge the crab the minute it comes out of the boiling water. This immediately stops the crab cooking and ensures noticeably moist flesh.

There is a surprisingly large amount of meat in a good weighty crab. It takes time and trouble to prise it out of every nook and cranny, but it is worth it if you like crab as much as I do. One way to prevent it seeming too tedious is to pick and eat at the same time, with a generous pot of mayonnaise on the side. This makes for an occasion that involves energetic participation with everybody wielding picks and claw busters.

CRAB VINAIGRETTE WITH HERBS

This dish uses mainly white crab meat with a small amount of sauce made from the brown meat. It is not really possible to take just a little of the brown meat to make the sauce, as all the ingredients that go with it have to be pulverized in the blender. I get very cross when I read recipes that ask you to blend together ridiculously scant quantities. If you've tried it, you will know that what happens is all the ingredients end up splattered against the sides of the blender. In this case, any sauce left over could either be turned into a mousse, set with a little gelatin, or added to soup made from the broken-up crab shell.

white meat from a cooked 3–4-lb crab
1 tbsp chopped mixed herbs, to include dill, tarragon, chives, parsley, and chervil
juice of ½ lemon
a pinch of cayenne
2 tbsp olive oil
salt

For the sauce

brown meat from a cooked 3–4-lb crab
1 tbsp ketchup
½ tbsp smooth Dijon mustard
½ tbsp horseradish sauce
juice of ½ lemon
1 tsp anchovy paste
2 tsp Cognac
salt and pepper
2 tbsp olive oil

Mix the white crab meat with the herbs, lemon, cayenne, and oil. Season to taste. In a blender, purée together all the sauce ingredients, except the olive oil, and pass through a fine sieve. Depending on the "wetness" of the brown meat, it may be necessary to thin the sauce with a little water. The ideal consistency should be like salad cream.

If you like neat plates of food, then divide the white crab meat into four portions and place in the middle of four plates, forming into circles with the help of a pastry cutter. Spoon the sauce in a swirl around the crab, and drizzle it with the olive oil. If you prefer less structured food, then serve the white meat in a bowl and the sauce separately.

CRAB TART

The combination of tomato, garlic, and saffron with any shellfish is a good one. When set into a rich egg custard tart, it is truly sublime. Crab works extremely well here, though any other sort of shellfish, or a mixture, can be most successful.

1 small can (approx. 14.5 oz) of Italian plum tomatoes, chopped
2 garlic cloves, peeled and chopped
1 bay leaf
1 small thyme sprig
salt and pepper
8-inch cooked pastry shell (see page 151)
1 cup heavy cream
½ tsp saffron threads
4 egg yolks
white meat, plus a little of the brown, from a 2-lb cooked cock crab

Preheat the oven to 350°F. Put the tomatoes, garlic, herbs, and seasoning in a saucepan and reduce to a thickish sauce. Cool, remove the herbs, and spread the sauce in the bottom of the pastry shell. Warm together 3 tbsp of the cream with the saffron and allow to steep for a few minutes. Beat together the egg yolks and the rest of the cream and add the saffron cream. Season. Loosely fold the crab into the custard and carefully pour into the tart shell. Bake in the oven for 30–40 minutes or until set and pale golden brown. Serve warm, rather than hot from the oven.

CREAM

There is nothing more luscious, more satisfying, more indulgent than a bowl of Jersey cream that has been untouched by methods of pasteurization. It is difficult nowadays to find an untreated pot of gorgeous yellow cream, but some enterprising farmers still produce the real thing. Even the mucked-about stuff has an allure that is undeniably luxurious, and it still tastes good.

I do believe, against all the odds, that cream will be with us for a long time yet, despite its well-known high cholesterol content. After all, who in their heart of hearts would want to be without crème brûlée, the best vanilla ice cream, or clotted cream on a scone with strawberry jam?

As a general rule, and in the following dessert recipes, pasteurized heavy cream is the type to use, and when it comes to cooking, it is not the difficult ingredient that it's cracked up to be. It is, however, helpful to understand a little bit about the composition and behavior of this and other creams.

Light cream I am not a fan of this. I think it must be artificially thickened because it is so white, and could not possibly be of this consistency without a stabilizer; it's the quantity of butter fat that makes cream thick and consequently more yellow.

Whipping cream I would suggest using this for making hot cream sauces. Its butter-fat content is lower and its composition thinner than heavy cream, and this gives it more time in a hot pan before it becomes too thick and consequently separates into oil and solids. If this does occur, however, I often throw in a splash of water, which, together with a bit of whisking, brings the sauce back in a trice.

What I find odd about whipping cream, though, is that it doesn't whip well! It's a complete misnomer; the butter-fat content is not high enough to support the air needed for a good whip. The result is often lackluster and floppy, and is inclined to separate and slip back to being runny again.

Heavy cream This cream is the best of all for whipping. It holds its body well and has a richness that you expect of sweet, whipped cream. However, I find it is often too rich for a hot sauce and can be temperamental.

Clotted cream I understand that clotted cream is made by heating heavy cream very, very slowly and skimming off the froth. It's delicious.

Crème fraîche The only sort of cream to be found in Europe. It is a shock the first time you try it because of its sharp taste. "Oh, it's off," people cry. I have never discovered the reason why this cream has been deliberately soured, but for something so rich, it is curiously refreshing and particularly good with chocolate things. I don't like cooking with it; it separates more easily than any cream I know.

Jersey cream Extra-thick, double-double, custard-yellow, untreated farm cream is quite the most glorious stuff. It really tastes like cream should, and for once the word "dairy" is the right description. The only thing I would do to this cream is eat it.

CRÈME CHANTILLY

Crème Chantilly is not just whipped cream; it must be flavored with vanilla, lightly sweetened, and very cold. Whipping cream is not the variety to use, as it breaks down too easily, so use heavy cream. To give lightness, crushed ice is added halfway through the whipping process. This may seem an odd thing to do but it helps (a) to keep the cream cold, and (b) the addition of a little water (melted ice) adds to the insubstantiality, which is the secret of a good crème Chantilly.

You may think it is a little old hat to include a recipe for this, but, like many other good cooking techniques and old-fashioned principles, the proper way of making crème Chantilly is often overlooked, and its preparation slap-dash. Crème Chantilly, carefully made, makes you realize just how good simple things can be.

1 cup heavy cream, chilled
generous ¼ cup confectioners' sugar
seeds of ½ vanilla bean
3 oz crushed ice

Before measuring out the ingredients, place a large, preferably stainless-steel, bowl in the freezer. The cream should also be very cold.

With a supple balloon whisk, beat the cream by hand (essential for good crème Chantilly) with the sugar and vanilla seeds until the whisk is just starting to leave a trail in the cream. Add the ice and carry on beating until the cream *just* holds its shape without flopping back. By this time the ice will have melted into the cream.

Kept in the fridge in its bowl the cream should hold itself for 2–3 hours without collapsing. The most perfect things to serve crème Chantilly with are warm fruit tarts, Chocolate Pithiviers (see page 38), warm poached apricots, plums, pears, etc.

FRUIT FOOL

"Soft, pale, creamy, untroubled, the English fruit fool is the most frail and insubstantial of English summer dishes" (Elizabeth David, *An Omelette and a Glass of Wine*). The perfect description. The fool is one of the few quintessentially English desserts that should not be tampered with. I have known it to be made with cream and custard but I don't think this is necessary. The perfect fool, for me, is just cream, fruit, and sugar. Rhubarb is my favorite, followed closely by gooseberry. Both use fruit that is cooked with sugar; other fools can be made by just puréeing soft fruits, such as strawberries and raspberries.

2 lb rhubarb, trimmed and coarsely chopped
1 cup sugar

grated rind of 1 small orange
1½ cups heavy cream

Preheat the oven to 375°F. Mix together the rhubarb, sugar, and orange rind in an ovenproof dish. *Do not add water.* Cover and bake for 45 minutes—1 hour or until the fruit is completely soft. Drain in a colander and reserve the juice. Purée the fruit until totally smooth, then chill the reserved juice and the purée until very cold.

Whip the cream in a large chilled bowl until the whisk forms ribbons. Carefully fold and stir in the rhubarb purée and some of the juice so the mixture is streaked, rather like a raspberry ripple ice cream. This is the way I like to do it because you get contrasts of pink, white, and crimson rather than homogeneous pink blancmange-like appearance.

FRANCIS COULSON'S STRAWBERRY POTS DE CRÈME

I first came across this recipe in a (sadly) forgotten book called *The Good Food Guide Dinner Party Book*. It was published in the early 1970s and culled recipes from restaurants around Great Britain that were included in the *Guide*. It still makes a good read and there are some real gems, from an era that was gently excited rather than fanatical about food.

One restaurant that has been in the *Guide* for an uninterrupted thirty-two years is the extraordinary Sharrow Bay Hotel in UIIswater in England's Lake District. It has been open for forty-four years, and Francis Coulson, who owns it with Brian Sack, has been there from day one.

8 oz strawberries, hulled
3 tbsp sugar
4 egg yolks
1 cup heavy cream
1½ tbsp Cointreau

Preheat the oven to 275°F. Purée the strawberries in a blender with the sugar and egg yolks. Pass through a fine sieve, then stir in the cream and the Cointreau, and mix well. Pour into individual ramekins and cook in a bain-marie (water bath) in the oven for about 1 hour. Check from time to time, as cooking times vary in different ovens; the texture of this custard should be just set and slightly wobbly in the center, and the custards will carry on cooking a little in their own heat. Leave to cool, then chill thoroughly for at least 6 hours. Serve with cold heavy cream poured on top so that each time you take a spoonful, the cream fills up the hole.

This is just as successful made with raspberries.

FANFARE

Francis Coulson

Francis Coulson loves cream. He always has, and I was once told, many years ago, the weekly Sharrow cream quota in high season. The exact quantity escapes me, but it was a high gallonage. I'm sure that it still is, judging by a fairly recent visit.

When arriving at teatime (and you should not consider a visit to Sharrow without taking tea at least once), tables of all shapes and sizes, inside and outside on the terrace, are groaning under the strain of fabulous cream cakes, sponges, chocolate things, the daintiest scones, and pots and pots of cream.

Everything is done properly at Sharrow Bay. Francis's extraordinary attention to detail combined with his genuine love of looking after guests, is what makes him a true hotelier. He never stops asking if you've had enough: "Would you like a little more?" "Do have another croissant," "Have you tried these brioches?" "You haven't finished your bacon."

He has never been affected by fashion. Take his dish of roast lamb, served with various traditional garnishes and a gravy that is described as being made "from the goodness of the lamb." This says it all.

CRÈME BRÛLÉE

Crème brûlée is one of the first things I ever made, aged about thirteen. The recipe came from one of those *Cordon Bleu* magazines that my mother used to collect. I stared apprehensively, though longingly, at the picture of crème brûlée in its large dish. It was before crème brûlée became the perfect restaurant dessert, served, for practical reasons, in individual pots. Traditionally, it was always served in a large dish. Its English name, Burnt Cream, is credited to Trinity College, Cambridge, and it has carried the name Trinity Burnt Cream ever since.

I am unsure as to when we all started calling it crème brûlée (I happen to like the name Burnt Cream). What I do know is that versions of it eaten in France are always too sweet. For me, the perfect crème brûlée has very little sugar in the custard itself, as the intensely sweet caramel more than compensates.

My own first effort was a sorry tale. I so desperately wanted to make it, but it did sound tricky, with instructions to stir gently for what seemed like an age. The recipe said to cook the custard until the mixture coated the back of a wooden spoon. To this day I have always thought this the stupidest advice, because when you make crème brûlée, the custard coats the back of the spoon even before you've started cooking it! It's a nerve-racking process because you are terrified of overcooking the mixture and of having to chuck out a pint of heavy cream. Anyway, I failed miserably because I was frightened of cooking the mixture too much and my caramel topping was a bit thick. So when I attacked it with a spoon, it was very alarming.

The lumps of caramel floated around and then instantly sank into my sploshy custard. The advice I give in the following recipe will help you make the perfect crème brûlée.

2 cups heavy cream
1 vanilla bean, split lengthways
5 egg yolks
1 tbsp sugar
2–4 tbsp demerara or raw brown sugar

Chill a 1¼-pint capacity, straight-sided, round, shallow dish, or four individual ramekins, in the freezer.

Heat together the cream and vanilla bean, whisking occasionally to disperse the vanilla seeds in the cream. Remove from the heat and leave to infuse for 10 minutes.

Lightly beat together the egg yolks and sugar. Strain in the cream and mix thoroughly. In a stainless steel or enamel saucepan, heat the custard over a very low heat, stirring constantly with a wooden spoon. From time to time, stop stirring to see if there is the odd tremor from the custard starting to heat. When this happens, take a whisk and beat energetically to disperse the heat throughout the custard. Resume stirring. The whisk may have to be used again. The custard is ready when you achieve an almost jelly-like consistency. Begin testing after about 10 minutes by removing the pan from the heat and drawing the whisk to and fro across the surface of the custard. Give a final energetic whisk and pour the custard into the ice-cold dish or ramekins. Leave to set in the fridge for at least 8 hours or overnight.

Preheat a broiler to its highest temperature. Spread the demerara sugar in an even layer over the surface of the custard and spray with a little water (this helps the sugar to caramelize). Place as near to the heat source as possible until the sugar has melted and caramelized. (Having said this, in recent years I have found that the most efficient way of doing this is to use a blowtorch. The magic of this is that you can direct the heat exactly where it's needed.)

Return the crème brûlée to the fridge for 30 minutes before serving.

RICE PUDDING

The texture of a good rice pudding is sublime. It must be creamy, yet set; light though not runny; almost mousse-like but not insubstantial. The very essence of its smell and flavor is intensely milky. The addition of pure vanilla I now think vital, although it is not an essential ingredient in most people's idea of rice pudding. I also think I would prefer to leave it out rather than use vanilla extract.

The secret of a good rice pudding is extremely slow cooking (my mother used to do hers in the bottom oven of the Aga stove). Patience is needed—it takes up to 4 hours to cook—and you must allow the skin to form naturally and never commit the cardinal sin of stirring it in. Round-grain rice is the one to use, as its natural starchiness helps toward a creamy texture.

Do remember that it takes a ridiculously small amount of rice to produce enough pudding. Don't be tempted to up the amount because you think it looks silly; it expands and overcooks to an excessive degree—that's the trick—and at the same time the milk reduces by half. Don't leave out the salt.

The best receptacle to use is a heavy, metal pan with two handles, also metal, so that you can start cooking the pudding on the stovetop and then transfer it to the oven. The technical reason for this is that you can bring the liquid and rice to the boil before it goes into the oven, then put it straight in the oven without transferring it to another dish, so maintaining the temperature and allowing the rice to continue cooking without a temperature drop. This results in a more even texture.

3 tbsp butter

¼ cup sugar

½ cup round-grain (short-grain) rice

3½ cups whole milk

½ vanilla bean, split lengthways

½ cup heavy cream

a pinch of salt

Preheat the oven to 275°F. Melt the butter in a flameproof casserole and add the sugar. Stir around and heat gently until gooey, like toffee. Add the rice and continue stirring until the rice looks puffy, pale golden, and sticky with sugar. Add the milk, which will seethe, and the rice/butter/sugar mixture will set into lumps. Fear not. Feel around with a wooden spoon and disperse the lumps because as the milk heats it will dissolve all in its path. Add the vanilla bean and squash it around a bit to release its little black seeds. Add the cream and the salt, and bring to the boil. Place in the oven and cook for 3-4 hours or until just starting to set and still *slightly* liquid-looking; as the pudding cools, it will finish cooking in its own heat. Serve very lukewarm, or cold if you like, but never hot.

CARAMEL ICE CREAM

To make this almost bitter, dark caramel ice cream, which a friend aptly describes as having an "adult" taste, you must be brave and take the caramel as far as you dare before it burns. Then, spectacularly, the cream is added, causing an almost volcanic eruption as the sugar and liquid seethe together as boiling butterscotch.

¾ cup plus 1 tbsp sugar

1 vanilla bean, split lengthways and broken into small pieces

¼ cup plus 2 tbsp heavy cream
1½ cups milk
8 egg yolks

Heat the sugar gently in a heavy-bottomed pan until melted. Do not stir during this time, though you might like to tilt the pan from time to time to help it on its way. Once it is completely melted and golden brown, add the vanilla bean and stir gently with a wooden spoon until the caramel is a deep mahogany color. Wait a moment longer or until you think the caramel might smell slightly burned, and then add the cream. Be careful of the eruption and quickly stir to quell the bubbles. Heat the milk, beat the egg yolks, and mix together. Add to the caramel/cream mixture and cook gently as if you were making Custard Sauce (see page 70), until just below boiling point. Whisk together, strain through a fine sieve into a cold bowl, and leave to cool. When cold, turn into an ice-cream maker and freeze according to the manufacturer's instructions.

VANILLA ICE CREAM

If there was one ice cream left in the world, I hope it would be this one. You can't beat good old-fashioned vanilla.

2 cups milk
1 vanilla bean, split lengthways
7 egg yolks
¾ cup plus 1 tbsp sugar
2¼ cups heavy cream

Heat together the milk and vanilla bean, and whisk vigorously as it comes to the boil, bashing and scraping the vanilla bean so that its seeds flow into the milk. Cover, remove from the heat, and allow to infuse for 30 minutes. Beat together the egg yolks and sugar, pour the flavored milk on to this mixture (including the vanilla bean), and mix well. Return the custard to a saucepan and cook gently as for Custard Sauce (see page 70). Strain into a cold bowl, add the cream, and leave to cool. When cold, turn into an ice-cream maker and freeze according to the manufacturer's instructions.

CUSTARD

My father once told me that Mr. Bird—of custard fame—used to drive a Rolls-Royce the color of his famous product. I suppose that indicates, more than anything else, that people rarely bother to put together a simple mixture of egg yolks, sugar, and milk to make their own custard. It is, after all, simplicity itself, and once you have the knack of knowing when to stop the cooking process before the eggs start to scramble, then custard will never come out of a carton again.

The following recipes are not necessarily based on custard sauce, as such; they consist more of a combination of eggs, cream, and milk with other things.

FANFARE

Margaret Costa

Margaret Costa wrote one of my all-time favorite recipe books. It is called The Four Seasons Cookery Book *and is long overdue for a reprint. It has a perfect formula— Spring, Summer, Autumn, Winter—and sticks to the brief admirably. There are concise and informative introductions, dotted about here and there with informal chatty recipes—more like ideas and suggestions, really—that address themselves to the subject in question. The more formal recipes that follow are easy to use and a joy to cook.*

Margaret Costa and her husband, Bill Lacy, had a restaurant called Lacy's on Whitfield Street, London. It was the first exciting restaurant I ever visited in the big city. I lunched alone (aged eighteen), was a little nervous, and had a ball. I remember the fabulous hot sesame-seed-encrusted bread (which was justly famous) and the very fine unsalted butter. I started my lunch with chilled avocado soup—very 1970s but very good—and followed it with turbot, cooked in chunks that were encased in a crusty brioche box together with chopped smoked salmon and a rich fennel sauce. For dessert I had Lacy's hot fruit brûlée, which consisted of exotic fruits topped with whipped cream and caramelized brown sugar. (In the mixture of fruit I thought the Chinese gooseberry the most exotic, later to be known as the ubiquitous kiwi fruit.)

Sadly, Lacy's has long gone, but Margaret Costa's wonderful book remains a testimony to her brilliance. One of my favorite recipes is the Lemon Surprise Pudding (see page 68). I could never tire of eating it. It has nursery food qualities about it; the soft sponge topping and the lemony custard beneath is a sublime combination. Eat it warm with thick cream.

LEMON SURPRISE PUDDING

¼ cup butter, softened
grated rind and juice of 1 lemon
⅓ cup sugar
2 eggs, separated
2 tbsp all-purpose flour, sifted
1 cup milk

"Cream the butter with the grated lemon rind and sugar. When it is fluffy, beat in the egg yolks; then stir in the sifted flour alternately with the milk. Add the juice of the lemon and fold in the stiffly beaten egg whites lightly but thoroughly. Bake in a moderate oven, 350°F for about 45 minutes, until the pudding is golden brown. Underneath the sponge topping there will be a creamy lemon sauce—this is the charming little surprise."

BREAD AND BUTTER PUDDING

I always feel that the custard in a bread and butter pudding should engulf the bread rather than the bread floating on top like a raft. I shall never forget those horrible school versions that looked like bits of old Spontex (the yellow ones) or sponges soaked in spotted milk—the spots being burned currants.

Bread and butter pudding *can* be the most delicious thing if it is made carefully from good ingredients. This version uses tea cakes. The idea came to me when I wanted to make a bread and butter pudding for a lunch party at home. I happened to have some tea cakes, albeit a bit stale, in my bread bin, so I thought I'd use those. It was a great success and the nicest thing about it is that the fruit and some spice is already there.

4 tea cakes, split and cut into half moons
½ cup butter, softened
2 whole eggs
3 egg yolks
1 cup milk
½ cup heavy cream
2 tbsp sugar
1 jigger of dark rum
a pinch of salt
a little extra sugar

Preheat the oven to 350°F. Lightly butter a deep oval porcelain dish. Spread the tea cakes with the butter and lay them in the dish slightly overlapping each other. Mix together the eggs, egg yolks, milk, cream, and sugar. Stir in the rum and salt. Carefully pour over the tea cakes and leave for 30 minutes or more for the bread to soak up the custard. Lightly sprinkle with the extra sugar and bake in the oven for 30–40 minutes or until just set and golden brown. Serve warm rather than hot, with thick cream.

CRÈME RENVERSÉE À L'ORANGE

This variation on a crème caramel theme came from my friend Gay Bilson in Australia. The first time I tasted it was while I was on holiday with her and some friends in southwest France. I had done much of the cooking on this holiday, and on the last night Gay decided that it was about time she had a turn in the kitchen. She made this exceptionally fine dessert in one big dish, which, when it was turned out, looked quite magnificent with an almost glassy sheen to the surface of its rich and golden caramel. The texture beneath, on the other hand, was almost the consistency of junket, it was so just-set. If you are at all worried or nervous about turning out something so delicate, then it can be made in individual ramekins. Naturally, the cooking time should be reduced if this is what you decide to do.

finely grated rind of 4 oranges
2¼ cups whole milk
⅓ cup sugar
2 whole eggs
4 egg yolks
generous ⅓ cup sugar

Put the orange rind, milk, and ⅓ cup sugar together in a stainless steel saucepan. Bring gently to the boil, then remove from the heat, cover, and infuse for 2 hours. Put the eggs and egg yolks in a bowl and pour on the orange milk. Mix lightly together, but don't allow the mixture to become frothy. Strain through a fine sieve, pressing down well on the orange rind to extract all the flavor. Let it rest for a few moments and skim the surface. Preheat the oven to 300°F.

To make the caramel, put the generous ⅓ cup sugar in a heavy-based saucepan or copper pan, add enough water to cover, and cook to a rich brown caramel. Pour into an ovenproof dish (with a capacity of about 1½ pints), making sure that the base of the dish is completely covered. When the caramel has set, gently pour on the milk mixture. Place in a bain-marie (water bath), making sure that the water comes at least two-thirds of the way up the sides of the dish. Cook for 1–1½ hours, checking from time to time to see whether the custard is set. When you think that it's not quite cooked—the center still looks a little runny—take it out and leave it, still in the bain-marie, for anything up to 30 minutes, by which time it should have set. Chill in the fridge for at least 6 hours.

When turning out, run a small, thin knife around the edge of the dish, place a plate over the top, and carefully invert the whole.

I have to say that I have eaten this dessert soon after it has come out of the oven, warm, with a spoon, straight in. Couldn't wait. I almost think it is better like this, but then you don't get the full visual effect of the dish.

CUSTARD SAUCE

It is unusual that the French, with all their chauvinism, should choose to credit this most wonderful sauce with an English title: crème anglaise. Classic crème anglaise does not have any other thickening ingredient than egg yolks. The consistency of a naturally egg-thickened custard is light and limpid, whereas one that has been helped to thicken with a little cornstarch or flour is okay but has a cloying texture that is more akin to the instant stuff. It is, of course, much easier to make because the flour acts as a stabilizer. For such things as trifle, where you need a custard that sets, then extra thickening is necessary.

2¼ cups milk
1 vanilla bean, split lengthways
6 egg yolks
generous ⅓ cup sugar

Heat the milk with the vanilla bean and whisk vigorously to disperse the little black seeds. Remove from the heat, cover, and leave to infuse for 30 minutes. Whisk together the egg yolks and the sugar until thick. Strain the infused milk into the egg mixture and whisk together thoroughly. Return to a saucepan over a gentle heat, and stir constantly but gently until the sauce has the consistency of thin cream. Whisk vigorously at this point to homogenize, then strain through a fine sieve into a cold bowl.

There is some debate as to the point at which the custard is cooked. As I have already mentioned (see page 62), the coating-the-back-of-the-wooden-spoon theory is not one I would recommend. If you feel brave enough, you should take the custard as far as you dare; the merest suggestion of a boil, i.e., the odd blip, will not spell disaster and, in fact, the reason for whisking vigorously at the end is to disperse parts of the custard that have started to cook into the parts that haven't. On occasion, I have found that if I think I have gone too far, and it looks as if all is lost and the custard has separated, an energetic blast in the blender has usually saved the day—the same applies to Crème Brûlée (see page 62).

CREMA CATALANA

I think the flavors in this custard are most unusual and absolutely delicious. However, some people to whom I have served it think it is disgusting. "Medicinal" has been suggested—perhaps it's the licorice flavor from the fennel seeds.

2¼ cups heavy cream
½ cup milk
1 tbsp crushed fennel seeds
1 vanilla bean, split lengthways
grated rind of 1 lemon
grated rind of 1 small orange
3 egg yolks
⅓ cup sugar

Preheat the oven to 275°F. Heat together the cream, milk, fennel seeds, vanilla bean, and lemon and orange rinds. Whisk as it comes to the boil to disperse the vanilla seeds, then remove from the heat, cover, and leave to infuse for 30 minutes.

Beat together the egg yolks and sugar until thick. Strain the infused milk/cream into this mixture. Whisk thoroughly and leave to stand for 10 minutes or so, as a froth will have formed and you should skim this off. Pour into four large ramekins, place in a bain-marie (water bath) of cold water, and cook in the oven for about 1 hour or until just set (still slightly wobbly in the middle). Chill thoroughly, for at least 8 hours or overnight, before serving.

PASSION FRUIT BAVAROIS

1 cup milk
½ vanilla bean, split lengthways
3 gelatin leaves
4 egg yolks
¼ cup granulated sugar
¾ cup plus 2 tbsp passion fruit purée
1 cup heavy cream
1 tbsp confectioners' sugar

Heat together the milk and vanilla bean. Whisk thoroughly as it comes to the boil to disperse the black seeds, then remove from the heat, cover, and leave to infuse for 30 minutes.

Put the gelatin leaves in a bowl, cover with cold water, and leave to soften. Beat together the egg yolks and granulated sugar. Strain the flavored milk into this mixture, and put back on a gentle heat, stirring constantly. Cook following the instructions for Custard Sauce (see page 70), then pour into a cool bowl.

Put the softened gelatin in a small pan with 2 tbsp water and heat gently until melted. Add to the warm custard and mix thoroughly. When the custard is cold, stir in the passion fruit purée, and either place the bowl over ice or put it in the fridge.

Lightly whip the cream with the confectioners' sugar. When the custard has started to set, fold in the lightly whipped cream and quickly pour it into either one large soufflé dish or four individual ramekins.

There are two ways in which to do this final process: if you have put the custard in the fridge it will set to a solid lump. This then needs to be broken down into manageable liquidity in either a blender or a food processor, before folding in the cream. If you use the bowl over ice method, then, from time to time, as the custard cools, draw a wooden spoon through the mixture until it has a jelly-like consistency, at which point you can fold in the cream. Either method is equally good, it just depends upon how much time you have. The end result, however, must be a thickish mixture that is still runny enough for the cream to be folded in.

ORANGE MOUSSE

This is also a bavarois (see Passion Fruit Bavarois, above), in fact, but it is made using only two leaves of gelatin, and it has a lighter texture than the passion fruit version.

The milk should be infused with the orange rind as well as the vanilla bean, and the orange juice should be added to the custard in place of the passion fruit purée. Otherwise, the method is exactly the same. These are the ingredients:

1 cup milk
½ vanilla bean, split lengthways
grated rind of 2 oranges
2 gelatin leaves
4 egg yolks
¼ cup granulated sugar
juice of 3 oranges
1 cup heavy cream
1 tbsp confectioners' sugar

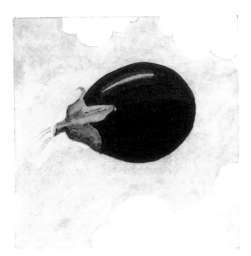

EGGPLANT

The eggplant is probably my favorite vegetable. I have an Australian friend who is as interested in them as I am. One January I went to stay with her and to herald my arrival she amassed at least fifty or sixty superb specimens on a giant palm leaf in the middle of the polished wooden floor of her Sydney livingroom. When I arrived, the early morning sun was streaming in on them through the windows. My efforts in return have been less glamorous. A T-shirt, a recipe, and I am working on a handbag for her fashioned from their skins. . . .

She calls aubergines "eggplants." It's a name I actually prefer. Both Americans and Australians call them eggplants, so I don't know why we British insist on referring to them by their French name.

There are hundreds of ways in which to prepare them. Their flavor is subtle and, to a certain extent, fugitive, so it is important to combine eggplants with strong flavors. They are an ideal match for pungent herbs, spices, and lamb. Tomatoes, basil, Parmesan, and garlic are also firm friends of the eggplant. As with many happy marriages in food, it only takes one other ingredient to set off a chain reaction. Therefore, eggplant/olive oil; olive oil/garlic; garlic/tomato; tomato/basil; basil/Parmesan, and so on.

I always find myself thinking of interesting things to do with eggplants. They give themselves easily to many cooking methods: grilling, roasting, stewing, or frying. When fried, their spongy flesh absorbs unlimited amounts of oil instantly. The Greeks always dip their slices in seasoned flour before frying to prevent this happening. It gives the slices a modicum of crispness for a while, though the flesh becomes flaccid on cooling.

I learned an important lesson about eggplants when I saw them being cooked in a Japanese restaurant. They were split in half and plunged into deep hot fat. The cut surfaces were instantly sealed and turned golden, allowing the inside to retain its natural juices and cream flesh. The surfaces were then slashed with a knife, and spread with a sweet soy bean paste and sesame seeds (see recipe on page 79). It's delicious.

I have never come to a conclusion about the "salting" question. Many recipes require eggplant to be salted and drained. Having cooked them on numerous occasions, salt or no salt, I haven't noticed any difference, *if* they are in peak condition. Incidentally, some eggplants contain a lot more seeds than others. This does not seem to have any bearing on age or bitterness, but less seedy ones have a better texture when cooked.

GRILLED EGGPLANT WITH A DRESSING OF OLIVE OIL, GARLIC, AND BASIL

This recipe was inspired by a request from Charles Carey—"The Oil Merchant"—to promote sales of his delicious lemon olive oil called Granverde Colonna. However, the recipe is equally successful made with a good-quality virgin olive oil.

12 garlic cloves (preferably new season garlic), peeled
salt and pepper
1 tbsp Dijon mustard
juice of 1 lemon
1 cup olive oil
2 large eggplants
extra olive oil for cooking
20 basil leaves, torn
lemon wedges, to serve (optional)

Put the garlic cloves in a small saucepan and cover with water. Bring to the boil and simmer for a minute or two, then strain. Put them back into fresh water with a little salt and cook until soft. Strain, and purée in a blender with the mustard and lemon juice. With the motor running, pour in the olive oil in a thin stream, as when making a dressing or mayonnaise. Empty into a bowl. (You may find that the amount of dressing made here is slightly more than you need for the amount of eggplant. However, the dressing keeps very well in the fridge for up to 3 weeks and would be delicious with many other things, such as grilled fish, poached eggs, or even spread on toasted baguette.)

Heat a ribbed cast-iron grill or a frying pan until very hot. Cut the eggplant into ¼-inch slices and season with salt. Brush the slices on both sides with olive oil and grill or fry until cooked and soft to the touch, but certainly golden brown and crisp. As you cook the slices, transfer them to a shallow oval dish or large plate. Arrange the slices in one layer, overlapping them as necessary.

Drizzle over the dressing, season with lots of freshly ground black pepper, and strew with the torn basil leaves. Serve with extra lemon wedges if desired.

FANFARE

Elizabeth David

Elizabeth David has inspired me, and countless others, more than any other cookery writer. She had a style of prose that is a joy to read and, at times, the description of a dish or a situation experienced is so evocative that it transports the reader from page to place. Of all her books, An Omelette and a Glass of Wine *remains my favorite—and that of my coauthor—because apart from the recipes, the stories and articles collected from* Vogue, Queen, *and* The Spectator *are, to this day, the finest works of food journalism ever written.*

I was fortunate enough to know Elizabeth toward the end of her life. This spiced eggplant salad was one of her favorite dishes.

SPICED EGGPLANT SALAD

This dish is inspired by Imam Bayeldi and uses similar ingredients. It is best served cold.

2 large eggplants
salt
½ cup olive oil
2 large onions, peeled and finely chopped
8 ripe tomatoes, skinned and coarsely chopped
1 heaped tsp ground cumin
1 heaped tsp ground allspice
¼ tsp cayenne
4 garlic cloves, peeled and finely chopped
2 tbsp currants
2 heaped tbsp chopped fresh mint
2 heaped tbsp chopped fresh cilantro

For this dish, I do think it makes a difference to salt the eggplant before cooking. Cut the eggplant into ½-inch cubes. Put them in a colander and sprinkle with 2 tsp salt. Mix together with your hands and leave to drain for 30–40 minutes.

Meanwhile, heat ¼ cup of the olive oil in a pan and fry the onions until golden. Add the tomatoes and spices. Stew gently for 5–10 minutes, then stir in the garlic and take off the heat. (I often find that adding the garlic too early on in any cooking process causes its flavor to disappear completely.) Stir in the currants.

Tip the eggplant into a clean dish towel and gently squeeze them dry. Put the remaining ¼ cup olive oil in your largest frying pan and heat until smoking. Add the eggplant and stir-fry briskly until thoroughly golden and cooked through. Stir in the onion and tomato mixture, and the fresh herbs. Tip into a bowl and leave to cool. Taste for seasoning and add more salt if necessary.

I often serve this with a bowl of plain yogurt, with more chopped mint added to it and pepped up with a little Tabasco.

CREAMED EGGPLANT

This is fabulous with roast or grilled lamb. If you are barbecuing over charcoal, then you could also cook the eggplant whole on the fire. It is advisable to prick them like a sausage prior to cooking, to prevent them bursting. The smoke from the fire lends a most distinctive flavor. If, however, you are cooking indoors, then the following recipe, using a roasting bag, is very good.

2 large eggplants, peeled and diced
1 cup olive oil
juice of 1 large lemon
salt and pepper
1 heaped tsp ground cumin
2 garlic cloves, peeled and crushed
1 tbsp sesame paste (tahini)

Put the eggplants in a roasting bag together with ½ cup olive oil, the lemon juice, salt, and pepper. Bake in the oven at 300°F for 1–2 hours or until completely collapsed (test by tweaking with your fingers). Tip the contents of the roasting bag into a blender, add the cumin, garlic, and sesame paste, and blend, adding the remaining olive oil in a thin stream. Check the seasoning.

Serve this dish hot or cold. I prefer it cold, either with something like the aforementioned lamb, or on its own as a first course with some crunchy bread and perhaps some pickled chillies.

EGGPLANT BAKED WITH HERBS AND CREAM

I first ate this dish at a restaurant called Hiély in Avignon, France. It is one of my very favorite restaurants and whenever I am in the vicinity I make a beeline for 5 rue de la République.

It is a fine dish, subtle in flavor and quite different from the other eggplant recipes in this chapter. This one turns out to be quite rich and does not rely on Mediterranean flavors.

In France, crème fraîche would be used, which has a sharpness that heavy cream does not have. Add a squeeze of lemon juice to the finished dish if you wish. Anyway, here is my version.

4 small eggplants
¼ cup olive oil
8 ripe tomatoes, skinned and coarsely chopped
salt and pepper
4 tbsp butter
2 garlic cloves, peeled and chopped
1 tbsp each of finely chopped tarragon, parsley, chives, and basil
1½ cups heavy cream

Cut the eggplants into ½-inch slices and fry on both sides in hot olive oil until pale golden. Drain on a paper towels and leave to cool. Season the tomatoes and cook in the butter for 5 minutes. Stir in the garlic and pour into a 2-inch-deep oval baking dish. Cover with overlapping slices of eggplant, and season lightly with salt and pepper. Stir the chopped herbs into the cream. Pour over the eggplant and bake in the oven at 375°F for about 30 minutes or until bubbling and lightly browned.

Serve with a crisp green salad dressed with lemon juice and walnut oil, mingled together with some garlic croûtons. A good accompaniment to grilled lamb chops.

GRILLED EGGPLANT WITH PESTO

2 eggplants
salt and pepper
½ cup olive oil
a large bunch of basil
3 garlic cloves
3 tbsp pinenuts, lightly toasted
3 tbsp grated Parmesan

Split the eggplants in half lengthways. With a sharp knife, make a crisscross pattern over the cut surfaces to a depth of 1 inch. Season lightly with salt and pepper and brush the surfaces with a little of the olive oil. Bake in the oven at 425°F for 20–30 minutes or until very soft.

Meanwhile, put the basil, garlic, pinenuts, and a little salt and pepper in a food processor. Work to a paste, then add enough olive oil to produce a loose-textured purée, similar to a thick vinaigrette. Pour into a bowl and stir in the Parmesan cheese. (Do not add the Parmesan to the processor, as over-working the cheese can cause the mixture to become gluey.) Spread the pesto over the eggplant and place under a hot grill until golden and bubbling.

VINEGARED EGGPLANT WITH CHILLI AND SPRING ONION

This dish is based on a recipe in the excellent *Foods from the Far East* by Bruce Cost, who owns a wonderful restaurant called Monsoon, in San Francisco. He serves some of the best Chinese food I have ever eaten, and he's not Chinese! His dish is called Sautéed Eggplant with Black Vinegar. I haven't been able to find any nice-tasting black vinegar, so I have substituted balsamic, which seems to work very well. Mr. Cost suggests serving the eggplant hot or at room temperature; I think room temperature or even cold is preferable.

1¼ lb eggplant
6 tbsp peanut oil
4 tbsp balsamic vinegar
2 tsp sugar
¾ tsp salt
3 tbsp finely shredded spring onions
½–1 tsp crushed dried red chilli (depending on your heat threshold)

Cut the eggplants into 1-inch chunks. Heat the oil in a frying pan until smoking, add the eggplant, and fry until well browned. Drain on paper towels.

Add the vinegar, sugar, and salt to the pan and bubble together. Throw in the spring onions and chilli, put back the eggplant, and stir carefully but thoroughly. Tip into a suitable dish and, if you like, decorate with a few sprigs of cilantro. Delicious on its own, or with cold roast lamb. And it makes brilliant picnic food.

GRILLED EGGPLANT WITH SESAME

This dish evolved by accident. Years ago I used to be a regular at Ikeda, a Japanese restaurant in London. A favorite dish was Nasu dengaku—eggplant grilled with miso paste and sesame. Recently I had some leftover peanut sauce, an uncooked dressing that is served with a cold Chinese chicken salad called Bang Bang Chicken, and some eggplant that needed using. I substituted the peanut sauce for the miso paste and, though it changed its characteristics, it worked like a dream. I suppose the idea came to mind because of the sweetness of both dressings, the sesame flavor, and, though I say it myself, an intuitive feeling for what goes with what.

Some Chinese cooks may say that this is a travesty of a Bang Bang Chicken sauce. All I can say is that it's delicious. The spiciness of the sauce is entirely personal; I have added fresh chillies in the past and found that they work just as well as Tabasco. But the joy of this version is that it is a pantry sauce and almost prepares itself. You may find, in fact, that you have far more sauce than you need. No worries. It keeps for ages in the fridge in a screw-top jar.

12 oz peanut butter
½ cup soy sauce
5 tbsp lemon juice
5 tbsp sesame oil
3 pieces of preserved (stem) ginger
3 tbsp preserved (stem) ginger syrup
8 shakes of Tabasco, or to taste
2 garlic cloves, peeled
½ cup cold water
2 eggplants, prepared and cooked as in Grilled Eggplant with Pesto (see page 78)
2 tbsp toasted sesame seeds

Put all the ingredients, except the cooked eggplant and sesame seeds, in a blender and process to a smooth paste. The consistency you desire is one of thick cream; add more water if necessary. Spread onto the cooked eggplants, sprinkle generously with sesame seeds, and place under a medium to hot broiler until all is nicely browned, even burned in places.

EGGS

The versatility of eggs is a constant source of amazement, and it upsets me sometimes when they are just taken for granted. The number of dishes that can be made from eggs, plus their many supporting acts, is, quite simply, magical. Without eggs, where would be our mayonnaises, hollandaises, béarnaises, custards, cakes, omelettes, or Yorkshire puddings? How would we make lovely clear soups, meringues, and jellies, without egg whites? And breakfasts, Sunday suppers, and picnics would never be the same again.

This section could easily be the longest if I allowed myself to run wild, so it should be said that these five recipes are tried and tested favorites that I would never tire of eating.

PIPERADE

Sometimes called Piperade basquaise, as it comes from that region of southern France on the Spanish border, this is essentially a dish of savory scrambled eggs. Although cooks pontificate about what is the definitive recipe, what is important is that a dish like this should reflect two things: the region, and what is available at the time. Obviously, one can't do without the eggs—and the better the eggs, the better the dish—but the other ingredients should be allowed the odd substitution or even be left out. After all, this is a simple affair and not something that requires precise detail.

8 super-thin bacon slices
olive oil for frying
2 slices of white bread, cut into tiny cubes
1 garlic clove, peeled and finely chopped
1 red bell pepper, roasted, peeled, seeded, and chopped
4 ripe tomatoes, peeled, seeded, and chopped
4 spring onions, finely chopped, or a small bunch of chives, finely chopped
8 eggs, beaten
chopped parsley or cilantro
salt and pepper

Grill or fry the bacon until done to a crisp. Drain and cool. Heat a little olive oil in a frying pan and fry the bread cubes until golden. Heat 3 tbsp olive oil in a separate pan and briefly fry the garlic, red pepper, and tomatoes. Add the onions or chives and eggs at the same time and cook gently, as for scrambled eggs. Stir in the croûtons and the parsley or cilantro and season. Serve on individual plates and garnish with two slices of bacon crisscrossed on each.

OEUFS EN MEURETTE

The first time I ever heard of this dish was when my mother told me how she was taken to The Berkeley by her cousin John when she was about eighteen. She said it was eggs in gravy and thought it disgusting. I love it.

1 750-ml bottle of Beaujolais
1 cup strong beef stock or canned beef broth
1 thyme sprig
1 bay leaf
1 small onion, peeled and chopped
1 tsp soft butter mixed with 1 tsp flour (beurre manié) for thickening

salt and pepper
4 thick bacon slices
2 tbsp butter
12 pearl onions, peeled
12 button mushrooms
1 garlic clove, peeled
8 bread slices, cut from a baguette and fried in olive oil
1 tbsp red wine vinegar
8 eggs
1 tbsp chopped parsley

Reserve a quarter of the bottle of Beaujolais and put the rest in a saucepan with the beef stock or broth, the thyme, bay leaf, and chopped onion. Cook over a high heat until reduced by three-quarters. Strain, then return to the pan and thicken slightly by adding the beurre manié in small pieces, whisking constantly over a moderate heat. Season and allow to simmer gently. Meanwhile, cut the bacon into small pieces and fry in the butter until golden brown. Remove the bacon, and fry the onions and mushrooms in the buttery bacon fat. Season and cook over a gentle heat, turning from time to time until cooked through. Keep warm with the bacon.

Rub the garlic clove over both sides of the fried bread croûtes and place the croûtes on four serving plates. Keep warm. Heat together the vinegar and reserved Beaujolais and poach the eggs. When cooked, lift out with a slotted spoon and place an egg on each croûte, allowing two eggs per person. Divide the bacon, onions, and mushrooms among the plates, spoon over the red wine sauce, and sprinkle with parsley.

SALADE FRISÉE AUX LARDONS

The essential part of this dish is adding the hot bacon and its fat straight into the salad, followed swiftly by the hot vinegar. There are two types of frisée (curly endive). One has quite tough, wildly curly leaves with the outer green ones being particularly bitter and unpleasant. These should be discarded. The other, sometimes called "spider" frisée, has much thinner, altogether more manageable leaves, and a milder flavor.

Have all the ingredients to hand, together with pans, frying pans, spoons, etc., before you start, as everything happens at the same time.

1 head of frisée, washed and picked over into small tendrils
salt and pepper
6 tbsp olive oil
vinegared water for poaching

4 eggs
6 thick bacon strips, cut into pieces
3 tbsp red wine vinegar
1 small baguette, sliced, rubbed with a garlic clove, cut into cubes, and fried in olive oil
1 heaped tbsp chopped flat-leaf parsley

Have the frisée ready in a roomy bowl and season lightly with salt and pepper. Have a frying pan heating through and bring the vinegared water to simmering point. Start to poach the eggs over a gentle heat. Meanwhile, fry the bacon in the hot olive oil until crisp and golden. Throw onto the frisée and stir in. Immediately add the vinegar to the hot frying pan and swirl around. Add this also to the salad. Mix in the croûtons and the parsley and divide among four plates. Place a poached egg in the middle of each. Sprinkle a little sea salt and a grinding of pepper over each egg and serve immediately.

EGGS FLORENTINE

I'm not too sure about the origins of Eggs Florentine. To many of us, it is a reminder of bistro cooking in the 1960s and 1970s, where it sat alongside chicken Kiev, Gnocchi a la Romana, and Coquilles St Jacques à la Parisienne. I wonder sometimes where the name comes from; after all, the combination of spinach and eggs crops up all over the place.

It is, however, absolutely delicious. My version makes the white sauce very tasty and rich with cream and I poach the eggs rather than cook them in the spinach.

¼ cup butter
1 lb spinach, picked over, thoroughly washed and dried
salt, pepper, and freshly grated nutmeg
4 eggs
vinegar
1 cup Parmesan, freshly grated

For the sauce

¾ cup plus 2 tbsp milk
2 cloves
1 small onion, peeled and chopped
1 bay leaf
salt and pepper
3 tbsp butter
3 tbsp all-purpose flour
6 tbsp heavy cream

To make the sauce, heat together the milk, cloves, onion, bay leaf, and seasoning. Remove from the heat, cover, and leave to infuse for 30 minutes or longer.

Melt the 3 tbsp butter in a saucepan, and stir in the flour to make a roux. Strain the milk into the roux and whisk thoroughly. Bring to the boil and simmer very gently over a low heat for a good 10 minutes. Strain again and adjust the seasoning, then stir in the cream and keep warm.

Melt the ¼ cup butter in a large saucepan until just turning nut brown. Put in the spinach, season with salt, pepper, and nutmeg, and stir-fry until limp and just cooked. Drain in a colander, pressing gently to extract excess moisture. Keep warm.

Poach the eggs in water with a little vinegar added. Meanwhile, divide the spinach among four shallow individual porcelain dishes or ramekins, leaving a space for the egg in each of them. Spoon in the eggs, top with the sauce, flash under a hot broiler or in a hot oven for a minute or two, and sprinkle each serving with plenty of Parmesan.

LACY'S OEUFS EN COCOTTE

This classic little dish of eggs used to be on the menu at Lacy's restaurant in London. It was called Oeufs en Cocotte Chez Nous—"the house way with eggs." It couldn't have been simpler, nor could it have been better. They used to serve two eggs (in those little brown and white dishes with handles). I always had three.

8 eggs
4 tbsp Meat Glaze (see page 204)

For the béarnaise sauce

2 tbsp tarragon vinegar
1 small shallot, peeled and finely chopped
½ tsp dried tarragon
2 egg yolks
½ cup plus 2 tbsp butter, melted
2 tsp chopped fresh tarragon
salt and pepper

In a small stainless steel or enamel pan, heat together the tarragon vinegar, shallot, and dried tarragon until the liquid has all but evaporated. Remove from the heat and cool. Add the egg yolks and whisk until thick. In a thin stream, add the butter, whisking all the time until the sauce is thick and glossy. Leave the milky residue that has separated from the melted butter behind as you pour the butter. Pass the sauce through a fine sieve and stir in the fresh tarragon. Season and keep warm.

Lightly butter eight ramekins and break an egg into each one. Season and place in a large shallow pan filled with enough hot water to come two-thirds of the way up the sides of the dishes. Simmer to poach the eggs, as it were, until they are set—the whites firm and the yolks runny. Heat the meat glaze and spoon it over the tops of the eggs to coat them completely. Top with 1 tsp of the béarnaise and serve. (You will find you have some sauce left over, but it is almost impossible to make smaller quantities of this.)

ENDIVE

M onsieur Yves Champeau of the Normandie Restaurant et Bar, in Birtle, Lancashire, England, would not countenance the fact that I detested the taste of endives—or chicory, as it is called in England, and witloof in Belgium. Aged sixteen, I had taken my first holiday job at the Normandie, to decide whether this was to be my chosen career—and also to see whether M. Champeau thought that it should be my chosen career. A memorable statement he made to my parents one night after they had eaten dinner was "I shell mek 'im or brek 'im." Encouraging words.

At lunchtime (for the staff and other members of the Champeau family, at 11 a.m.), a meal was put together and distributed to all parties. Hearing of my hatred for endives, M. Champeau decided that on this occasion I was to lunch with him and his wife, Toni (she was English and at the time I thought it comical that the husband should be called Yves and the wife Toni). It transpired that, unbeknown to me, a lunch consisting of pretty well every conceivable component of the chicory family had been prepared in my honor. There were braised endives; endive salad (the leaves raw with a mustardy dressing—this was the worst); a further salad of curly endives (frisée) with fried bread croûtons and garlic; and endives an gratin, for which some more previously braised endives had been wrapped in ham with sauce Mornay, dressed with cheese, topped with breadcrumbs, and browned under the grill.

It may come as no surprise to learn that I did actually come to enjoy these new tastes. I hadn't much choice. It is an adjustment of the palate that is necessary. Bitter is the taste of chicory—the French of yesteryear still miss it in their coffee—but the taste buds enjoy a "pucker" from time to time. Arugula—that most fashionable of salad leaves—is a prime example.

When cooking endive, it is absolutely essential that you do not use water. The endive itself is pretty well all H_2O. Also, you need lemon juice to counteract the bitterness. This may sound daft, but it is true.

The Normandie's braised endives were cooked in plenty of butter, which was heated until light brown before the endives were added, gently colored, seasoned, and finished with lemon juice. They were then covered and cooked in a moderate oven for a couple of hours. The resultant vegetable was golden brown, almost gooey, and had an aroma that was very agreeable.

M. Champeau knew his endives.

BRAISED ENDIVES

½ cup butter
8 small endives
salt and pepper
juice of 1 large lemon

Preheat the oven to 325°F. Choose a shallow, lidded pan that will accommodate the endives with little room to spare.

Melt the butter until just about to turn nut brown. Add the endives and turn down the heat. Season with salt and pepper and turn gently in the butter from time to time to coat all the surfaces and to color them lightly. Add the lemon juice, allow the endives to bubble, put on the lid, and cook in the oven for 2 hours. Halfway through the cooking, carefully turn each one over. The endives should be very soft and limp, the lemon juice completely evaporated, and the end result buttery and golden.

You may think 2 hours is too long, but an overcooked endive tastes much better than one that is underdone.

ENDIVES AU GRATIN

Sometimes called à la flamande, but this is disputable. Whatever its name, this dish involves wrapping braised endives (see above) in thin slices of cooked ham, and covering with béchamel sauce. It is a very comforting dish and, although I dislike the description, it could appear neatly under the heading "supper dish." I'm not quite sure why I dislike this description, but I think it is because there is an English tendency to put this type of dish into a category of scratched-together leftovers. Unhappily, this sort of recipe—its composition almost distorted beyond recognition—might well be found in some dreadful magazine under the title "Ham and Chicory Layer Bake."

In reality, it is a carefully constructed combination of ingredients that marry happily with each other, are well balanced, and produce a satisfying and substantial plate of food.

8 braised endives (see above)
8 small, thin slices of cooked ham
4 oz Gruyère cheese, grated
2 cups dry breadcrumbs

For the béchamel sauce

1¾ cups milk
4 cloves

1 large onion, peeled and chopped
1 bay leaf
salt and pepper
6 tbsp butter
6 tbsp all-purpose flour
½ cup heavy cream
freshly grated nutmeg

Heat together the milk, cloves, onion, bay leaf, and seasoning. Remove from the heat, cover, and leave to infuse for 30 minutes or longer. Melt the butter and add the flour to make a roux. Strain the milk into the roux and whisk thoroughly. Bring to the boil and simmer very gently over a low heat for a good 10 minutes. Strain again and adjust the seasoning. Stir in the cream and the grated nutmeg, and keep warm.

Preheat the oven to 375°F. Wrap each endive in a slice of ham, lay them in a buttered gratin dish, and pour over the sauce. Bake for 20 minutes. Remove from the oven and increase the temperature to 450°F. Sprinkle over the cheese and, following the line of each wrapped endive, sprinkle over the breadcrumbs. Cook at the top of the oven for a further 5 minutes or until golden and bubbling.

CREAMED ENDIVES

This is good with grilled fish and shellfish, particularly scallops.

4 large endives
6 tbsp butter
juice of 1 small lemon
salt and pepper
¾ cup whipping cream
1 tbsp finely chopped chives

Trim any damaged outer leaves and slice the endives into ¼-inch rounds, stopping before you get to the solid root base. Melt the butter in a frying pan, and heat until about to turn nut brown. Throw in the endives and fry briskly until lightly colored, then add the lemon juice and salt and pepper. Cook gently until any liquid has evaporated. Add the cream and cook gently for about 5 minutes or until the consistency is unctuous. Stir in the chives.

PICKLED ENDIVES

This is another wizard recipe inspired by Australia's Living National Treasure, Gay Bilson. She uses melon, I think, to pickle but I decided that the bitterness of endive combined with the sweet and sour marinade could be a winner. This is particularly good with all charcuterie—cured hams, salamis, smoked meats—and especially with cold roast duck or game.

1½ cups white wine vinegar
¾ cup plus 1 tbsp sugar
2 whole star anise
1 cinnamon stick, broken into 3 pieces
3-inch piece of fresh root ginger, unpeeled and thinly sliced
6 cloves
6 large endives, trimmed and cut lengthways into quarters

In a stainless steel pan, mix together all the ingredients, except the endives. Bring to the boil, then reduce the heat, cover, and simmer for 30 minutes. Place the endive pieces in a glass or stainless steel bowl. Pour the vinegar mixture over them and leave to cool completely. When cold, pack the endives carefully into preserving jars together with all the spices. Pour over the vinegar. Keep in the fridge. They can be eaten the next day, or will keep well for several weeks.

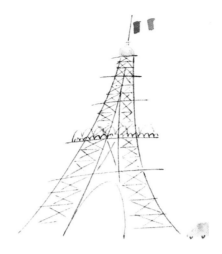

GARLIC

The very first job I was given to do as an apprentice at the Normandie Restaurant et Bar was to make garlic butter for the snails that were a permanent fixture on M. Champeau's menu. It was a particularly fine recipe that had been worked out to exacting proportions over many years. It involved a quite astonishing amount of garlic—more than I could believe possible.

At that time (1973), the machinery in the kitchen did not include a sufficiently large or efficient enough mixer with which to combine all the ingredients satisfactorily, so it was a "hands-in" job. One large bowl, all that garlic, parsley, breadcrumbs, seasonings, and enough butter to build a mountain. It was an interesting introduction to my chosen career, but a thought kept coming to me as I ended that first day: would I ever rid my hands of the smell?

Garlic frying is, without doubt, one of those smells that makes you want to eat instantly, rather like bacon grilling, onions frying, and hot chips with vinegar. The intoxicating aroma of garlic cooking in butter, or olive oil, is a salivating one, and I have a vivid memory of those snails appearing from M. Champeau's oven, sizzling and bubbling in garlic butter. Phew! That smell, off my hands at last and into those glorious snails.

Garlic is not all pungency and odor, however. Beautiful and creamy soft purées can be made from garlic, as can mellow sauces to serve with roast lamb, for instance. For this, the peeled cloves of garlic are blanched a couple of times in water and then braised slowly in flavorsome stock with wine and herbs. Liquidized with some of the stock, butter, or olive oil, and a little cream, the garlic is transformed into a velvety smooth sauce that would pacify the hardiest of garlic-haters.

One of the nicest seasonal things to look forward to is the arrival of new garlic in the spring. The heads are large and covered in a soft, greeny-white skin, as opposed to the more usual papery, parchment-like coating. These are, of course, the very same fresh bulbs that will be stored and dried for use later in the year. And the best, incidentally, is the pink-skinned garlic that usually comes from the south of France.

It was while reading a Chez Panisse recipe by Alice Waters that I first discovered that you could cook a whole head of new garlic.

FANFARE

Alice Waters

Single-handedly, Alice Waters created what is now known as Californian cuisine. Through a deep love and respect for ingredients, and the seasonal diversity of produce, she has influenced many cooks and restaurateurs.

I visited Chez Panisse in Berkeley, San Francisco, for the first time in February 1992. By this time, it was in its twenty-first year and, without beating about the bush, I ate, on two occasions, some of the finest food I have ever tasted. It had a wonderful freshness of flavor in what seemed to be effortless cooking. But of course it wasn't. I recall a stunning pizza made with chanterelles, some stewed clams with wine and herbs, and a green salad, the like of which I had never eaten before: "morning-gathered," "dew-fresh," "garden grown" for once meant just that.

We can all learn and inwardly digest Alice's beliefs and philosophies by reading her intelligent, original, and inspiring books.

BAKED NEW GARLIC WITH CREAMED GOAT'S CHEESE

8 heads of new season garlic
¾ cup olive oil
4 thyme sprigs
1 rosemary sprig
2 bay leaves
1 lemon, cut into 6 wedges
salt and pepper

For the creamed goat's cheese

6 oz goat's cheese (preferably rindless and not too ripe)
6 tbsp heavy cream
½ tsp dried chilli flakes (no seeds)
salt

Preheat the oven to 400°F. Slice off the tops of the garlic heads about a quarter of the way into the bulbs. Pack snugly into an ovenproof dish that will take them in one layer. Pour in the olive oil and tuck in the thyme, rosemary, and bay leaves. Give each wedge of lemon a gentle squeeze over the garlic, and then tuck them in too. Season with salt and pepper and put in the oven. Have a look after 10 minutes to see if the oil is bubbling. If so, turn the temperature down to 325°F and bake for a further 40–50 minutes. The garlic should bake slowly in order to give it a melting softness.

Meanwhile, mash the goat's cheese as smooth as possible and stir in the cream. Add the chilli to taste, and salt if necessary. Remove the garlic from the oven and allow to cool. Serve lukewarm, straight from the dish, with the goat's cheese in a bowl, a basket of toasted country bread, and bunches of watercress. The thing to do is to help yourself to a garlic bulb, ease out a clove, and smear it on the bread. Spread with goat's cheese and eat.

DEEP-FRIED GARLIC

These garlic cloves are so good that they could be eaten on their own as nibbles with drinks, but more often than not this is something I would serve with roast lamb, grilled duck breast, or steak. The garlic cloves are lovely tucked into a green salad, or a frisée salad with chunks of crisp duck confit. They are simplicity itself to make, and up to the time of frying they can be prepared in advance. The quantities in the recipe are for serving them as an accompaniment to another dish. Naturally, if you want to eat them on their own, you should cook more.

28 large garlic cloves, peeled
2 cups light chicken stock
seasoned flour for dusting
2 eggs, beaten
8 tbsp fresh breadcrumbs
oil for deep-frying

Put the garlic cloves in a saucepan and cover with cold water. Bring to the boil, then reduce the heat and poach for a minute or so. Drain and then repeat this process, using fresh water. Finally, cook the garlic in the chicken stock for about 10 minutes or until soft. Watch out for overcooking, as they can suddenly collapse. Carefully drain, reserving the stock for another dish (Garlic Purée or Garlic Sauce, for example—see below). Allow the garlic cloves to cool, then roll them in seasoned flour, then in beaten egg, and finally in the breadcrumbs. Handle them as little as possible. When in the flour and breadcrumbs, space the cloves well apart, and rotate and shake the dish or tray they are in, rather than touching them. Leave them in the breadcrumbs until ready to fry. Heat the oil, preferably in a deep-fryer, to 375°F, and cook the cloves for 1-2 minutes or until golden brown. Drain on paper towels and season lightly with salt.

GARLIC PURÉE AND GARLIC SAUCE

These two recipes are easily made by following the Deep-Fried Garlic recipe (see above) up to the stage of draining them from the chicken stock, and puréeing them with a little of the reduced stock and some cream. Butter (or olive oil) is the other ingredient to be added, both for flavor and richness, but also as a thickener and emulsifier.

28 garlic cloves, peeled
2 cups light chicken stock
1 tbsp Dijon mustard
1 tsp red currant jelly
½ cup butter, melted
juice of ½ lemon
salt and pepper

To make Garlic Purée, follow the instructions for poaching the garlic cloves given for Deep-Fried Garlic (see above). After cooking the cloves in the chicken stock, drain them carefully and reduce the stock by half. Put the cloves and ½ cup plus 2 tbsp reduced stock in a blender with all the remaining ingredients, and blend to a purée. Serve warm.

To make Garlic Sauce, repeat the above and add 1 cup heavy cream. Heat gently before serving.

SNAIL BUTTER

Unlike in my apprentice days at the Normandie, when my hands stank for days after making this butter manually, hopefully we all now have the use of kitchen machinery. This is the most intensely garlicky of butters but may be used for any number of dishes. It is important to include the breadcrumbs when preparing it for use with snails, or anything else that is going to be cooked in their shells in the oven, such as mussels or clams, as the crumbs help form a crust. However, if you are making this butter for melting over a grilled steak or fish, then omit the crumbs.

This recipe uses 1 lb of butter, which you may think is a lot. It is, but it will all be used up if you are preparing a dozen snails for four people. It is also easier to measure and mix the ingredients when making this amount. If you have some left over, roll it into a sausage shape, wrap it in foil, and store it in the freezer. It is one of the most useful things to have around.

2 cups unsalted butter, softened
2 oz peeled garlic, as fresh as possible, finely chopped
3 oz flat-leaf parsley, leaves only
½ cup dry breadcrumbs
¼ cup Pernod
1½ tsp salt
½ tsp black pepper
¼ tsp cayenne
5 drops of Tabasco sauce

Put the butter and garlic in an electric mixer and beat together. Blanch half the parsley briefly in boiling water. Drain, refresh under cold running water, and squeeze dry. Chop this and the remaining parsley as finely as possible. Add to the butter with the remaining ingredients and beat together until thoroughly blended.

GARLIC AND SORREL SOUP WITH PARMESAN CROÛTONS

This light and fragrant broth reminds me a little of avgolemono, to which beaten egg is added at the last minute. In this soup, chopped sorrel is introduced with the egg to retain its sharp taste and freshness. If you can find new season's garlic, use that. If not, use the freshest garlic you can find, preferably the sort with purple/pink skin.

4 heads of garlic
10 sage leaves
6 thyme sprigs
2 cloves
1 bay leaf
a good pinch of saffron threads
2 small dried chillies, crumbled
1 large onion, peeled and chopped
1 tbsp red wine vinegar
4 cups (1 quart) water
1 chicken stock (bouillon) cube
salt and pepper
1 large baking potato, peeled and finely chopped
2 eggs, beaten
2 handfuls of sorrel leaves, picked over, washed, dried, and coarsely chopped
2 tbsp olive oil

For the croûtons

1 small baguette, sliced, rubbed with a garlic clove, and cut into ½-inch cubes
3 tbsp olive oil
2 heaped tbsp grated Parmesan cheese

Separate the garlic cloves, don't peel them but bash them with the back of a heavy knife or cleaver. They only need to be lightly crushed, not smashed to smithereens. Put them in a stainless steel saucepan with the sage, thyme, cloves, bay leaf, saffron, chillies, onion, and vinegar. Add the water, stock cube, and salt and pepper. Bring to the boil, skim away any impurities that come to the surface, reduce the heat, and simmer for 30 minutes. Meanwhile, preheat the oven to 425°F. Prepare the croûtons by rolling the bread cubes first in the olive oil, and then in the Parmesan. Place on a wire rack that is resting on a baking sheet and bake in the oven for 10–15 minutes or until crisp and golden.

Add the potato to the soup, cover, and simmer gently for a further 30 minutes. Strain through a colander, pressing down on the solids to extract all their flavor. Return to a clean saucepan. Remove two ladlefuls of soup to a large bowl and, in a thin stream, pour in the eggs, whisking all the time. Set aside. Add the sorrel to the pan, stir in the egg liaison, and reheat gently, taking care not to let the soup boil. Pour into individual soup bowls and anoint each with a stick of olive oil. Serve the croûtons separately.

GROUSE

At the time of writing, "the glorious twelfth" is upon us and grouse is enjoying its short season. With the increase of imported produce and the availability of many foods, irrespective of season, it is nice to know that there are still some things left to look forward to.

There is nothing quite like a grouse, particularly those from the United Kingdom—mainly in Scotland and Yorkshire. Its flavor is like no other game bird. It lives on moorland and exists on a diet of heather and grubs (the French, if they can ever get their hands on a grouse, call it coq de bruyère—"heather hen").

There is a daft tradition among hotels and restaurants of competing to serve the first grouse of the season. This is a pity, as there will have been no chance for the bird to hang—which develops its pronounced flavor and increases tenderness—and it is always absurdly expensive to boot. Far better to wait. I think a grouse needs to be hung for four to five days.

For me, there is only one way to cook and serve grouse. That is, simply to roast it and to serve it accompanied by bread sauce, game crumbs, and red currant jelly. I like to serve it quite pink, on the bone, with the only extraneous garnish being a bunch of watercress. The only other dish that can evolve from a grouse is a rich soup made with the crushed carcasses.

ROAST GROUSE WITH BREAD SAUCE AND GAME CRUMBS

I always get my grouse "long-leg," which means with guts intact. It generally comes completely plucked and trimmed of all feathers. The advantage of it not being drawn is that it keeps longer and you can decide how "gamy," or "high," you want it.

Removing the innards is simplicity itself—not a pleasant job, but it only requires a small cut just behind the parson's nose. You then pop your finger inside and tug out the intestines, which should come away in one piece. Search through for the liver, but usually this remains in the cavity along with the heart. Remove and reserve these for cooking with a little brandy and some butter, to be spread on a piece of fried bread that will sit under the grouse when you serve it. The quantities given for the bread sauce may seem excessive. They are. I adore bread sauce.

As to the question of gravy, I don't bother. I have always found that with the brief cooking time that I insist on, hardly any juices seep out of the bird. There may be the odd crusty bit in the bottom of the roasting pan, and fat from the butter and bacon, but the bird itself is so moist and juicy that gravy seems incidental. If you insist on something, then you may like to rinse out the roasting pan with a little extra sherry, or if you had some poultry stock to hand, you could use that.

4 young grouse, cleaned
½ cup butter, softened
salt and pepper
8 thin bacon slices (optional)

For the bread sauce

1½ cups milk
6 tbsp butter
12 cloves
1 bay leaf, crumbled
1 thyme sprig
a good pinch of salt
1 small onion, peeled and finely chopped
3 tbsp heavy cream
2 cups fresh white breadcrumbs
pepper

For the game crumbs

¾ cup butter
3 cups fresh white breadcrumbs
½ cup medium dry sherry
salt and pepper

Begin the bread sauce in advance—if I am serving grouse for dinner, I make the infusion in the morning, but the sauce should be put together while the grouse is in the oven. Heat together the milk, butter, cloves, herbs, salt, and onion, bringing the mixture to just below boiling point. Simmer extremely gently for 10 minutes, then remove from the heat, cover, and leave to infuse.

To make the game crumbs (which can be made an hour or so before you are ready to eat), melt the butter in a large frying pan, and heat until just turning nut brown. Throw in the crumbs and stir-fry briskly. (I find a metal balloon whisk the best implement for this.) Continue stirring over a gentle heat until the crumbs are golden. Add a little more butter if necessary; the crumbs absorb copious amounts, and the end result should be crisp and buttery. Add the sherry to the crumbs and continue stirring over a gentle heat to evaporate the sherry out of the breadcrumbs, leaving the flavor behind. Irritatingly, adding the liquid forms the breadcrumbs into random lumps. The whisk is even more use here, as you have to break them up constantly. If you persevere, the crumbs will return to being golden and buttery. Season with salt and pepper, and keep warm.

To cook the grouse, preheat the oven to 425°F. Smear the softened butter over the grouse and season with salt and pepper. Lay two slices of bacon over each grouse, if using. Put the birds in a roasting pan and cook for a maximum of 15 minutes, basting frequently. The length of time really depends on the size of the birds, but it is a question of how springy the breasts feel when tweaked with your fingers—as an indication it feels like a shelled, hard-boiled egg. Leave the grouse to rest for 10 minutes or so in a warm place. This is actually the most important part of roasting anything and allows the meat to relax with the blood and juices intact. The bacon can either be kept warm and served alongside the grouse or very finely chopped and stirred into the game crumbs.

Meanwhile, strain the milk for the bread sauce into a clean pan. Reheat gently with the cream, and whisk in the breadcrumbs. Allow to thicken, and adjust the seasoning, adding plenty of black pepper.

The nicest way to present roast grouse is on a large white serving dish with a piece of fried bread spread with the liver (see p. 99) underneath each bird, and bunches of watercress tucked alongside. Serve the bread sauce and game crumbs separately in sauce boats, together with a bowl of red currant jelly.

GROUSE SOUP

fat and juices left from roasting 4 grouse, or ½ cup butter
4 thick bacon slices, chopped
2 carrots, peeled and diced
1 large onion, peeled and chopped
3 celery sticks, chopped
4 large flat mushrooms, as black as possible (this adds color), chopped
1 tbsp tomato purée
1 garlic clove, peeled and chopped
4 grouse carcasses, chopped
1 tbsp all-purpose flour
¼ cup brandy
½ cup port
1 cup red wine
3 cups strong chicken stock
salt and pepper
2 cloves
6 juniper berries, crushed
4 thyme sprigs
1 bay leaf
1 tbsp red currant jelly
2 tbsp pearl barley
½ cup heavy cream

Melt the grouse fat or butter in a large pan, add the bacon, and fry until crisp. Add all the vegetables, and fry until well colored. Add the tomato purée and stew it until it turns rusty brown. Add the garlic and the chopped grouse carcasses, and cook for about 5 minutes, stirring all the time. Stir in the flour and cook for a further 5 minutes. Add the brandy, port, red wine, and chicken stock, and bring to the boil, stirring constantly. Add the seasoning, spices, herbs, and red currant jelly, and simmer gently for about 1 hour. During this time remove any scum that appears on the surface. Strain the soup first through a colander (this gets rid of the big bits), then through a sieve into a clean saucepan. Add the pearl barley and simmer gently for 15–20 minutes or until the barley is cooked. Check the seasoning, stir in the cream, reheat, and serve.

HAKE

I think it is very sad that hake is so underrated and virtually unknown in these modern times. We used to eat it a great deal when I was a boy; baked in the oven with milk, sliced onions, and a bay leaf. The resultant liquor was then made into an old-fashioned egg sauce (see page 6). It was delicious.

But this lovely fish is hardly ever seen these days. It never seems to be on a restaurant menu, and rarely appears on the list at the fish-and-chip shop. And it's unusual to see it on the fishmonger's slab. For those who've never seen a hake, it is battle-ship gray in color, has a long, rather ugly, head, and is cylindrical in shape. Cod, its distant relative, has a similar bone structure around the head end but that's where the likeness ends. It is a pity that hake hasn't made a comeback in the way that cod seems to have done. Much of it, I understand, is exported to Spain.

The Spaniards adore hake (merluza) and cook it in a variety of ways. I have heard of a fisherman's soup that hails from Cadiz, Spain. Its Spanish name is Caldillo de Perro—"dog soup" (perro means "dog"!)—goodness knows why. The soup is made with young, small hake, Seville oranges, lemons, a lot of garlic, and some olive oil. It's a recipe I've never tried, but it sounds intriguing. The Spaniards' most famous method of cooking hake, though, is Merluza con Salsa Verde (hake with green sauce), which is made with parsley and peas, and is nothing like the Italian salsa verde, but is nonetheless delicious.

Hake fetches extraordinary prices in Spain, sometimes as much as you would pay for turbot or sea bass. I think the quality of hake is well worth paying a reasonable price for. Its texture is soft, and young fish are pale pink in parts. When cooked, the flakes of fish have a wetness about them, and a taste similar to that of cod.

I like to cook hake in cutlets, therefore on the bone (which is always more succulent), and one of my favorite methods is to press crushed peppercorns into the cut surface of the fish, lightly flour it, and then fry it in butter and olive oil. The surface becomes wonderfully crusty with the peppercorns, and then all that is necessary is to add a little brandy, a spoonful of light meat stock, and to finish this sauce with a knob of butter and a squeeze of lemon. Fishy steak au poivre in fact. Eat with some creamy mashed potatoes.

WARM HAKE WITH THINNED MAYONNAISE AND CAPERS

In Italy I was once served a dish of warm fillets of sea bass, lightly cooked and dressed with mayonnaise and some little flageolet beans. It was delicious. Made with hake, it can be just as good, certainly less expensive, and is perfect for a summer outdoor lunch.

4 lb hake, in a whole piece
1 quantity court-bouillon (see page 181)
1 small garlic clove, peeled and finely chopped
1 lb canned flageolet beans, rinsed and drained
2 large tomatoes, peeled, seeded, and finely chopped
2 tsp tarragon vinegar
2 tbsp olive oil
salt and pepper
1 tbsp capers, drained
extra tarragon leaves
cayenne (optional)

For the mayonnaise

2 egg yolks
1 tsp Dijon mustard
salt
a few dashes of Tabasco sauce
2 tsp (or more) caper vinegar
½ cup peanut oil
½ cup light olive oil
4 tarragon sprigs, leaves only, finely chopped

Poach the hake in the court-bouillon as for Poached Salmon with Beurre Blanc (see page 180), and keep warm. To make the mayonnaise, whisk together the egg yolks, mustard, salt, Tabasco, and vinegar. Pour in the peanut oil in the thinnest stream possible, then follow it with the olive oil, beating all the while until thick. Add the tarragon and set aside.

Mix together the garlic, beans, tomatoes, vinegar, and olive oil, season with salt and pepper, and warm through gently until hot but not boiling. Pour into a warmed deep white oval dish. Remove the skin from the hake, lift off the fillets and lay them neatly over the beans. Thin the mayonnaise with a little of the court-bouillon water to give it a coating consistency. Spoon over the fish fillets and sprinkle with the capers and a few tarragon leaves. Dust with a little cayenne, if you wish.

FILLET OF HAKE WITH HERB CRUST

This method of cooking suits hake very well. The succulence of the fish is important, as it is simply baked in a hot oven, with the minimum of oil or butter, until crisp.

4 heaped tbsp fresh breadcrumbs (brioche crumbs are particularly good)
2 tbsp chopped parsley
½ tbsp chopped tarragon
½ tbsp chopped dill
1 tbsp chopped chives
grated rind of 1 lemon
1 garlic clove, peeled and finely chopped
four 6-oz hake fillets, skinned
salt and pepper
all-purpose flour for coating
1 egg, beaten
olive oil
1 quantity Beurre Blanc (see page 181), to serve

Preheat the oven to 425°F. Mix together the breadcrumbs, herbs, lemon rind, and garlic. (This is best achieved with a whisk. You may find that there is more than you need, but it is difficult to make with less. Use up in a dish of fried potatoes.) Season the fish fillets with salt and pepper and dip one side of them only first into the flour, then into the beaten egg, and finally into the herb and breadcrumb mixture. Lay on a buttered baking sheet, and if there are any bald spots, fill in with more of the breadcrumb mixture. Drizzle with a teaspoon or so of olive oil. Bake in the top of the oven for 10–15 minutes or until golden and crusty. Serve on warmed plates with the Beurre Blanc.

BASQUE CHIORRO

This recipe originates from Constance Spry and has been a great favorite for many years. I have adapted it slightly by omitting the flour, which I find unnecessary. For the oil, Constance Spry suggests "good" oil; of course these days this would mean olive oil. When her book was written, you could probably only buy olive oil in tiny bottles, from Boots the chemist. The recipe uses a huge amount of garlic, plenty of spice, and some red wine. Hake, and perhaps cod, are about the only fish that can stand up to it.

3 large onions, peeled and finely chopped
6 tbsp olive oil

2 tbsp finely chopped garlic
1 heaped tsp tomato purée
2 tsp hot paprika
a pinch each of cayenne and ground mace
2 wineglasses of red wine (16 oz)
1 cup water
1 bay leaf
salt and pepper
juice of 1 lemon
1½ lb hake, scaled, filleted, and cut into 4 pieces
12 bread slices cut from a baguette and fried in olive oil until golden brown
1 tbsp chopped parsley

Fry the onions in the olive oil until golden. Add the garlic and fry for a further few minutes without browning. Add the tomato purée and spices, and cook gently until rusty brown. Pour in the red wine and allow to bubble for a few minutes. Add the water and bay leaf, and season with salt and pepper. Cover and simmer very gently for 45 minutes.

Ten minutes before the sauce is ready, bring to the boil some lightly salted water with the lemon juice added. Put in the four pieces of fish, bring back to the boil, and switch off. Leave for 5 minutes, then lift the fish out on to a hot plate. Allow the excess water from the fish to drain away by tilting the plate. Skin the fish, and transfer carefully to a large, shallow terra cotta dish. Cover with the sauce and arrange the croûtes attractively around the edge. Sprinkle liberally with the chopped parsley.

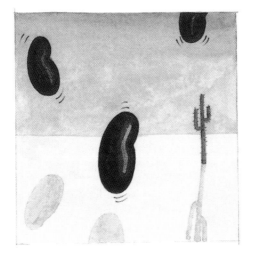

KIDNEYS

I first remember eating kidneys on a Sunday morning at home. My father would put a dish of chopped ox kidney in the bottom of the Aga stove on Saturday night and they would be ready for breakfast by Sunday morning. It was the most natural way of doing things, as far as I could see, and they would be served up on fried bread along with, perhaps, some bacon or sausage, as a tasty treat for the weekend.

Ox kidney costs next to nothing, and it is a pity that it is, more often than not, only used for steak and kidney pudding. I am very fond of kidneys cooked in all sorts of ways and like each and every variety. When choosing pork chops, I always scour the butcher's window for the ones that still have a piece of kidney attached. Gently braised pork kidney is one of the most delicious pieces of offal I know. It is difficult to find on its own, no doubt due to lack of demand, and is sadly underrated.

When spring lamb is in season, I am always on the lookout for its kidneys, which are sold fresh and still in their suet jackets. They are at their sweetest and most tender at this time, and I have to say that, in my opinion, they are an infinitely finer thing than the lamb itself. These kidneys can be picked up for very little and four would make a substantial meal for one person, costing not much more than a few dollars. So, search them out and roast or grill them still wrapped in their fat.

Veal kidneys, on the other hand, are luxury food. It is debatable as to whether they are the best in every way; a carefully cooked lamb's kidney is just as tender, though the veal kidney certainly has the more delicate flavor. Like lamb, veal kidneys usually appear with a suet cladding and can be given similar treatment. But, unfortunately, as they have to pass through a rigorous health check, more often than not, it is a careless procedure, and the kidneys are wrenched from their secure suet shell by thuggish examiners. If you are ever lucky enough to come across a kidney from locally reared veal, then you should find your kidney intact. Furthermore, I am a great advocator of home-reared veal. It often has a finer and more attuned flavor than the sometimes pappy, over-milk-fed stuff. Home-reared is usually darker, and though it may not be as tender, it tastes much, much better.

If your veal kidney has been mutilated and cannot be roasted intact, then there are plenty of other cooking methods available to you. By far the most successful way of cooking kidneys is to slice them on the cross-section (still with a little suet left inside), and to sear them very briefly on a cast-iron, flat griddle. Griddles are terrific, by the way, and are used for things like Welsh cakes and drop scones. They sit directly over the heat—preferably gas—and have a myriad of other uses, so try to find one, perhaps in an old-fashioned ironmongers. A slice of kidney takes literally seconds to cook, and should be pink and rosy within and lightly charred without. This method leaves you enormous scope for interesting and endless embellishment. A classic accompaniment that never ceases to please is béarnaise sauce (see page 85).

ROASTED LAMBS' KIDNEYS WITH CABBAGE
AND MUSTARD DRESSING

It is important that the lambs' kidneys used in this dish are fresh (frozen ones are horrible, anyway), because you need their cladding of suet. The roasting of the kidneys can take place in its entirety on the stovetop, if you like, which means you don't have to heat the oven. For the mustard dressing, use the recipe in Leeks Vinaigrette (see page 121).

6 tbsp butter
1 large onion, peeled and thinly sliced
1 large Savoy cabbage, cored and thinly sliced
1 garlic clove, peeled and chopped
salt and pepper
10 lambs' kidneys in their suet
1 quantity mustard dressing (see page 121)
1 tbsp chopped parsley, to garnish

Melt the butter in a large pan and sweat the onion until pale golden. Add the cabbage and garlic, season, cover, and stew gently, stirring occasionally. Keep warm.

Heat a heavy-duty, preferably cast-iron, frying pan until hot. Season the kidneys with salt and pepper and put directly into the hot pan. A certain amount of smoky sizzling will go on, but don't be alarmed, as this will subside as the kidneys start to roast. In any case, turn the heat down slightly after a couple of minutes, but not so low that the kidneys start to boil in their own juices rather than roast. You should only need to turn them once and the whole process should take no longer than 10–15 minutes—perhaps more if you like your kidneys well cooked. Allow to rest in a warm place for about 5 minutes before slicing in half and laying, cut-side up, in an attractive fashion on top of the cabbage mixture. Drizzle with the mustard dressing and garnish with the chopped parsley.

GRILLED VEAL KIDNEYS WITH ROSEMARY
AND ANCHOVY BUTTER

Kidneys treated this way can be topped with all sorts of different butters. Favorite ones that I have used in the past have included Montpellier Butter (see page 6), lime, ginger, and cilantro butter, mixed herb and garlic butters, red wine butter, and others made with mustard and horseradish. But my favorite of all is this anchovy one.

2-oz tin of anchovies, drained of oil
juice of ½ lemon
1 cup butter, softened
1 large garlic clove, peeled and finely chopped
1 rosemary sprig, leaves only
black pepper and salt
2 veal kidneys, suet removed and trimmed of any excess fat and membrane
olive oil for brushing
watercress and lemon wedges, to garnish

Purée together the anchovies, lemon juice, butter, garlic, rosemary, and pepper. Check for salt. Pass through a sieve if you prefer to discard the rosemary leaves (some people find them an irritation, as they get stuck in teeth, etc.). Spoon the butter onto a piece of foil, and roll up into a sausage shape. Chill in the fridge until firm.

Heat a flat griddle until very hot. Cut the kidneys into ½-inch slices, removing excess core if you wish, though I usually leave it in. Season lightly with salt and pepper, and brush with a little olive oil. Grill briefly on each side for no more than 45 seconds–1 minute, or a little longer if you like them well cooked, but they do toughen up. Divide the kidneys into four servings and cut the butter into thin slices. Top each slice of kidney with a piece of butter and garnish with watercress and lemon wedges.

SAUTÉ OF VEAL KIDNEYS WITH SHALLOTS, SAGE, AND BEURRE NOISETTE

This is the sort of dish that can be put together in no time and would work just as well with liver, sweetbreads, brains, or any other light meat that can be cooked quickly.

2 veal kidneys, suet removed and trimmed of any excess fat and membrane
6 tbsp butter
1 tbsp olive oil
salt and pepper
3 large shallots, peeled and finely chopped
18–24 sage leaves
2 tbsp red wine vinegar
6 small spring onions, mostly green, finely sliced diagonally

Cut the veal kidneys into small pieces respecting their natural divisions. Remove any unwanted sinew or fat. Spread the pieces of kidney out on a plate. In a large and not-too-heavy frying pan, or a wok if you prefer, heat 2 tbsp butter and the olive oil until foaming. Season the kidneys with salt and pepper and throw into the pan. Sear briefly before tossing and turning in the butter and oil for a very short time until the kidneys have taken on a little color, but are not overcooked—they need to be rare, as they are going to be reheated. Turn the kidneys into a colander over a plate and leave to drain. Return the juices to the pan, add the shallots, and cook gently for about 10 minutes or until golden brown and gooey, adding a little more butter if necessary. Remove from the pan with a wooden spatula and add to the kidneys. Wipe the pan clean with a paper towel and heat the remaining butter in it until golden brown, i.e., beurre noisette. Throw in the sage leaves and fry until crisp, being careful not to burn them or the butter. Turn off the heat, lift out the sage leaves, and place them on paper towels. Lightly salt them. Reheat the butter and return the kidneys and shallots to the pan. Stir-fry for a few moments, and pour in the vinegar. Sizzle for a few seconds, then add the finely sliced spring onions. Spoon onto a heated serving dish, top with the sage leaves, and serve piping hot with mashed potatoes.

LAMB

Having lived in western Wales for several years, I have come to the conclusion that Welsh lamb is by far the best. I have never bothered to find out why, but I suppose it comes down to mountains, sweet grass, plenty of rain (as I remember), breeding, and, I think most important, being well-fattened. I remember buying roasts of lamb from my butcher, one Glyn Owen of West Street, Fishguard, and noticing a rich cladding of pure white fat on the best end that was as thick as a suet crust. As a matter of course, a lattice of caul fat was stretched over legs of lamb; not something you see done nowadays, except by some country butchers.

The lamb I like best is known as a "hogget." It's late-season lamb, as opposed to spring lamb, is halfway to mutton, I suppose, and tastes fantastic. It is very "meaty," strong-flavored, and, I guess, not to everyone's taste. I, for one, am nonplussed by the enthusiasm for new-season lamb. First, I abhor the ridiculous pre-Easter prices and, quite frankly, find the flavor often nonexistent in exchange for tenderness.

I love mint sauce, too. And red currant jelly. And crisp fat from a shoulder (the best-tasting roast meat I can think of, save beef) that has been cooked for several hours, until the meat is of such melting texture that it can virtually be eaten with a spoon. Further pleasures from roasts such as this include squashing second helpings of roast potatoes into that half-congealing mixture of lamb fat, gravy, and mint sauce . . . don't try and tell me you don't know what I'm talking about.

My mother cooks an ace neck of mutton stew with pearl barley. How I love pearl barley. Have you ever tried cooking it in the style of Italian risotto? It is extremely good, particularly if you use lamb stock for the liquid, plenty of buttery onions, a little white wine, and a sprig of rosemary for added flavor. Neck of mutton stew is one of those forgotten dishes that deserves revival. Such comforting stews are so easy to prepare; it's just that we've forgotten how to find the time to make them in today's convenience-food-orientated world. Some ready meals from supermarkets are particularly good and I applaud the quality. But, and it's a big but, I wonder whether the easy availability of convenience foods will eventually lead to the demise of the talented home cook who might unknowingly be good at, and enjoy, preparing a neck of mutton stew?

The first recipe in this section uses one of the very cheapest cuts of meat it is possible to buy—breast of lamb. Only a week before the death of Elizabeth David, I finally prepared Breast of Lamb Ste-Ménéhould. I first came across it in *An Omelette and a Glass of Wine* and had always wanted to cook and eat it. Elizabeth had become a good friend, and I was a great admirer of her writing. I only wish I could have cooked it for her, as I know it was one of her favorites. We would have drunk a bottle of old Rhône wine with it. Maybe two . . .

BREAST OF LAMB STE-MÉNÉHOULD

This is a remarkable dish because it uses the least glamorous part of the lamb and makes it into something so good that it knocks your socks off. The way in which it is cooked removes any notion that this over-fatty cut is going to be indigestible or greasy. The end result is supremely comforting and very savory.

I think it fitting to give this recipe exactly as it appears in *An Omelette and a Glass of Wine*. The piece was originally written for an issue of *The Spectator*, dated 11 August 1961—hence the reference to the cost of lamb at Harrods at that time.

"One of the breadcrumb-grilled dishes I like best is the one called Breast of lamb Ste-Ménéhould. It is very cheap (breast of English lamb was 8d a pound at Harrods last Saturday—one often finds a cheap cut cheaper and of better quality in a high class butchery than in a so-called cheap one, and 2½ lb was plenty for four), but I am not pretending it is a dish for ten-minute cooks. It is one for those who have the time and the urge to get real value out of cheap ingredients. First you have to braise or bake the meat in the oven with sliced carrots, an onion or two, a bunch of herbs, and, if you like, a little something extra in the way of flavoring such as two or three ounces of a cheap little bit of bacon or salt pork, plus seasonings and about a pint of water. It takes about two and a half to three hours—depending on the quality of the meat—covered, in a slow oven. Then, while the meat is still warm, you slip out the bones, leave the meat to cool, preferably with a weight on it, and then slice it into strips slightly on the bias and about one and a half to two inches wide. Next, spread each strip with a little mustard, paint it with beaten egg (one will be enough for 2½ lb of meat), then coat it with the breadcrumbs, pressing them well down into the meat and round the sides. (I always use breadcrumbs which I've made myself from a French loaf, sliced, and dried in the plate drawer underneath the oven. I know people who think this business of making breadcrumbs is a terrible worry, but once the bread is dried it's a matter of minutes to pound it up with a rolling pin or with a pestle— quicker than doing it in the electric blender.)

"All this breadcrumbing finished, you can put the meat on a grid over a baking dish and leave it until you are ready to cook it. Then it goes into a moderate oven for about 20 minutes, because if you put it straight under the grill the outside gets browned before the meat itself is hot. As you transfer the whole lot to the grill pour a very little melted butter over each slice, put them close to the heat, then keep a sharp look-out and turn each piece as the first signs of sizzling and scorching appear.

"The plates and dishes should be sizzling too, and some sort of sharp, oil-based sauce— a vinaigrette, a tartare, a mustardy mayonnaise—usually goes with this kind of dish."

I think this sort of recipe makes you want to cook it straight away. It really is very easy and I urge you to try it. Serve the lamb with some mashed potatoes.

ROAST LEG OF LAMB WITH ANCHOVY, GARLIC, AND ROSEMARY

Lamb and anchovy, odd though it may seem, were made for each other. I think I am right in saying that this roast lamb is a continental classic—I have certainly seen it in both France and Italy.

4-lb leg of lamb
two 2-oz cans anchovies
a small bunch of rosemary
4 large garlic cloves, peeled and sliced lengthways into 3 pieces
6 tbsp butter, softened
black pepper
½ 750 ml-bottle white wine
juice of 1 lemon
a bunch of watercress, to garnish

Preheat the oven to 425°F. With a small sharp knife, make about 12 incisions 2 inches deep in the fleshy side of the leg. Insert a piece of garlic, half an anchovy, and a small sprig of rosemary into each incision. Push all of them right in with your little finger. Cream the butter with any remaining anchovies and smear it all over the surface of the meat. Grind over plenty of black pepper. Place the lamb in a roasting pan and pour the wine around. Tuck in any leftover sprigs of rosemary and pour over the lemon juice. Put in the oven and roast for 15 minutes.

Turn the oven temperature down to 350°F and roast the lamb for a further hour, or slightly more, depending on how well-done you like your meat. Baste from time to time with the winy juices. Take the meat out of the oven and leave to rest in a warm place for at least 15 minutes before carving.

Meanwhile, taste the juices and see if any salt is necessary—it shouldn't be because of the anchovies. During the roasting process the wine should have reduced somewhat, and mingled with the meat juices and anchovy butter to make a delicious gravy. If you find it too thin, then a quick bubble on the burner should improve the consistency.

When it comes to good food smells, this is one of the best, because as you slice the lamb the waft of garlic, rosemary, and anchovy hits you head on. Once again, mashed potatoes are good with this.

MARINATED AND GRILLED LAMB CUTLETS WITH HUMMUS, OLIVE OIL, AND CILANTRO

Whenever I visit a Greek restaurant, I invariably find myself with a craving for some hummus and a charcoal-grilled lamb kebab. Initially, I would do the usual thing and start with the hummus and go on to the grilled kebab. But once, a little while back, my finishing off the hummus coincided with the arrival of the kebab, and I couldn't resist dipping one into the other, along with some pickled chillies. The combination was every bit as good as the more traditional lamb chops, mint sauce, and mashed potatoes.

12 lamb cutlets, nicely trimmed
2 tbsp olive oil
3 tbsp balsamic vinegar
3 dried chillies, crumbled
1 tsp crushed cilantro seeds
½ tsp ground cumin
½ tsp ground ginger
juice of 1 lemon
pepper
1 red onion, peeled and cut into rings

For the hummus

10-oz can of chickpeas, drained and rinsed
juice of 1 lemon
1 large garlic clove, peeled and crushed
1 tbsp tahini (sesame seed paste)
½ cup olive oil
salt
Tabasco sauce
½ tsp ground cumin

For the garnish

a small bunch of fresh cilantro
olive oil
cayenne
lemon wedges

Put the lamb cutlets in a shallow dish. Mix together all the other ingredients, except the red onion, to make a marinade. Pour over the cutlets and mix well, turning the cutlets around so they are evenly coated. Tuck in the rings of red onion, cover with plastic wrap, and marinate for at least 12 hours or overnight.

To make the hummus, blend the chickpeas with the lemon juice, garlic, tahini, and a little water, to form a paste. Pour in the olive oil in a thin stream, as if you were making mayonnaise. (Add more or less than the ½ cup olive oil, depending on how creamy you want the hummus.) Season with salt, Tabasco, and cumin, spoon into a bowl, and set aside.

Season the cutlets and cook them fiercely on a cast-iron ribbed grill or, failing that, in a hot frying pan (an overhead radiant broiler is an inefficient cooking medium for these cutlets) until well charred, slightly burned, but still pink in the middle. Obviously, if you prefer them well-done, cook for a little longer.

Put a swirl of hummus in the middle of each of four hot plates, and attractively lay three lamb cutlets on top of each. Tuck in some sprigs of cilantro, drizzle with olive oil, dust with a little cayenne, and serve with the lemon wedges.

ROAST BEST END OF LAMB WITH EGGPLANT AND BASIL CREAM SAUCE

This dish is equally good hot or cold, depending on the time of year. In fact, in summer months, rather than roasting, I have poached the meat until medium rare in a savory bouillon, and left it in the stock to cool. In this case, rather than serving the hot eggplants as an accompaniment, I have substituted Spiced Eggplant Salad (see page 76), but still served the same cold basil sauce.

2 eggplants, cut in quarters lengthways through the stalk
salt and pepper
olive oil
3 rosemary sprigs
4 garlic cloves, unpeeled and lightly crushed
1 lemon, cut into 4 wedges
a little oil for roasting
2 best ends or racks of lamb, chined and trimmed

For the sauce
a bunch of basil, leaves only
10 mint leaves
4 tbsp aïoli (see page 29)
2 tbsp meat glaze (see page 204)
½ cup heavy cream
1 tsp red wine vinegar

Put the eggplant pieces in a colander, sprinkle with salt, and leave for 1 hour. Rinse and dry.

Preheat the oven to 425°F. Put the eggplant pieces on a piece of aluminum foil large enough to wrap around the eight quarters with lots to spare. Season with pepper, drizzle over the olive oil, and tuck in the rosemary sprigs and garlic cloves. Squeeze the juice from the lemon wedges over the eggplants and leave the skins in the foil. Fold the foil over to make a parcel and crimp the edges tightly. Place on a baking sheet at the bottom of the oven.

Lightly oil and season the two racks of lamb. Put the racks in a heavy roasting pan and cook on the stovetop until the meat and fat are golden and sealed. Place in the top of the oven 15 minutes after the eggplants went in, and roast for 20–25 minutes, basting two or three times. Remove both the eggplants and the lamb from the oven at the same time and leave to rest in a warm place for 10–15 minutes before carving or opening the parcel.

To make the sauce, purée all the ingredients, except the cream and vinegar, together in a blender until completely smooth. Whisk in the cream but only stir in the vinegar just before serving, as it can discolor this lovely green sauce. (I like to serve the sauce cold over hot lamb—like mint sauce—but then I have always thought that cold sauce with hot food is delicious. Similarly, I like hot things with cold food; hot potato salad with cold ham, or scrambled eggs with smoked salmon, for instance.)

To serve the lamb, carve each best end into chops—there should be seven or eight on each—and arrange on a large serving platter. Open up the foil parcel, being careful not to allow the juices to escape, and arrange the wilted eggplants attractively alongside the lamb. Serve the sauce separately.

LEEKS

The softy of the onion family. As a rule, I only use the white parts—although the green tops can seem attractive for their color, their flavor is coarse and their texture tough. They should be saved for the stockpot.

Leeks, for me, make the finest quiche. Poor old quiche. What a shame that this delicious dish had its reputation ruined by the wine-bar boom of the 1970s, when it became popular as an easy money-spinner. Thick, soggy pastry, or worse, whole-grain (does anybody *really like* whole-grain pastry?), meager fillings, and a complete lack of seasoning.

Many years ago, on an early gastronomic tour (aged seventeen with a battered Mini Clubman), I had lunch at a restaurant called the Cleeveway Hotel outside Cheltenham, England. The cook there was a chap called John Marfell—a George Perry-Smith (see page 179) apprentice. He used to cook a leek quiche of sublime quality and richness, using plenty of heavy cream and lots of egg yolk. I hope that he has not since become tired of cooking classics such as this.

I am particularly fond of cold leeks. And it seems a shame that, just as the summer arrives—when you want to eat Leeks Vinaigrette and drink Vichyssoise—leeks develop woody centers and go out of season. Having said that, the blurring of the seasons and increased imports mean that most vegetables, including leeks, are now available most of the year.

It is the simplicity of a dish like Leeks Vinaigrette that makes it so good. Embellishments such as a soft-boiled or poached egg can be nice, or an anchovy or two could be considered, but that is a matter for you. As to the vinaigrette, there is a type of dressing I always refer to as Parisien or Lyonnais. It goes with bistro or brasserie food—sharp and strong, gutsy and rich. The flavor of olive oil is too fruity; it needs a tasteless oil such as peanut or vegetable, and the other ingredients should include a good Dijon mustard, red wine vinegar, and a little water to help the emulsification process. What I really love is the creamy texture you end up with; this is best achieved in a blender.

Incidentally, this dressing is also excellent on warm potatoes, hot Lyonnais sausages, frisée salads with crisp bacon and croûtons, and salade de museau—a type of brawn or pressed pig's head—which the Parisians and the Lyonnais are potty about. And me too.

LEEKS VINAIGRETTE

I was always taught to refresh leeks in cold water for this dish. I now think differently. It may make the green part of the leek greener, but you lose much of the flavor into the water while they cool. I sometimes think we do too much blanching, with vegetables here, there, and everywhere being flung into iced water to set the color and arrest the cooking; it all gets a bit cosmetic.

It is easier to make a large quantity of this dressing than a small one. It can be stored in the fridge for a few weeks.

16 leeks, about thumb thickness, trimmed and washed, 1 inch green on each
salt and pepper
2 tbsp smooth Dijon mustard
2 tbsp red wine vinegar
1–1½ cups peanut or other flavorless oil
2 hard-boiled eggs
1 tbsp snipped chives

Put the leeks into fast-boiling, well-salted water and cook until tender. Drain, and allow to cool naturally. Put the mustard, vinegar, and salt and pepper in a blender. Add 4 tbsp water and blend together. With the motor running, pour in the oil in a thin stream until homogenized. If you think the dressing is too thick, thin with a little more water. The ideal consistency is that of thin salad cream or dressing.

Slice the leeks lengthways and arrange in a serving dish, cut-sides uppermost. Drizzle with the dressing and grate over the hard-boiled eggs. Sprinkle with the chives and serve with some crusty bread.

LEEK TART

The secret of a good leek tart is to sweat the leeks in plenty of butter for as long as possible until they are completely soft and wilted.

½ cup butter
8 leeks, trimmed, split lengthways, washed, and thinly sliced
salt and pepper
4 egg yolks
1½ cups heavy cream
4 tarragon sprigs, leaves only, finely chopped
One 8-inch pastry shell (see Red Pepper Tart, page 151), baked blind
Melt the butter in a large pan and add the leeks. Season with salt and pepper and cook

over a low heat, stirring occasionally, until thoroughly soggy. This could take up to 1 hour. Cool.

Preheat the oven to 350°F. Beat together the egg yolks, cream, tarragon, and seasoning and add to the leeks. Stir well. Pour into the pastry shell and bake for 30–40 minutes or until set and golden brown.

Occasionally, I have introduced a few spoonfuls of freshly grated Parmesan into the custard. It adds an extra savory quality.

LEEKS WITH CREAM AND MINT

This could either make a simple first course or a light lunch dish to be eaten with some brown bread. This sort of dish is what marrying flavors is all about.

1½ cups whipping cream

8 leeks, about thumb thickness, trimmed, washed, and
cut diagonally into ½-inch slices

salt and pepper

4 ripe tomatoes, peeled, seeded, and cut into thick slices

1 tbsp butter

4 mint sprigs, leaves only, coarsely chopped

½ garlic clove, peeled and finely chopped

Preheat the oven to 375°F. Bring the cream to the boil and simmer to reduce by one-third. Cook the leeks in fiercely boiling salted water for 3–4 minutes, then drain well. Divide the leeks and tomatoes equally among four lightly buttered, individual, shallow ovenproof dishes. Add the mint and garlic to the reduced cream and season with salt and pepper (the cream will reduce slightly more during baking, so be sparing with the salt). Ladle over the leeks and tomatoes and bake in the oven for 20 minutes or until the top is scorched with golden brown flecks.

VICHYSSOISE

I adore good Vichyssoise, but how many times do you get a tasteless bowl of cream with a few chives on top? It is the simplest of soups to make and requires next to no effort, although it has to be said that after blending, it really is worth passing the soup through a very fine sieve to achieve a wonderfully smooth result.

6 leeks, white parts only, trimmed and sliced

3 cups light chicken stock

2 potatoes, peeled and chopped
salt and pepper
1 cup heavy cream
a small bunch of chives, snipped

Simmer the leeks in the chicken stock, covered, for 20 minutes. Add the potatoes, salt, and pepper and cook for a further 20 minutes. Blend until smooth, then strain through a fine sieve, cool, and add the cream. Correct the seasoning and chill thoroughly. Serve in ice-cold bowls and garnish with chives.

LIVER

O f all the varieties of offal we eat, the liver is used from more creatures than any other. Calf, lamb, pig, duck, chicken, game—both furred and feathered—and one of my most favorite, monkfish. It has a similar consistency to that of foie gras in a fishy way, and is almost as rich. If you are ever lucky enough to come across some, grab it quick. It's fabulous. It is relatively easy to find in France, particularly in large city markets—ask for *foie de lotte*.

Liver from beef is not really worth trying; in fact I don't think I have ever eaten it. I am sure it is far too tough and probably quite bitter. Calves' liver, on the other hand, along with their kidneys, is highly prized (and highly priced). Lambs' liver is good and tasty, but requires careful preparation and cooking to avoid ending up with shoe-leather and memories of school lunches. Chicken livers are a marvelous vehicle for numerous dishes, and their versatility is endless. They marry themselves neatly to so many good things: pasta and potatoes; little savory toasted things; on skewers or deep-fried and in various salads—one of my favorites being frisée, bacon, croûtons, poached egg, and sautéed chicken livers. If deep-frying, dip them first in flour, then in beaten egg, and finally in fresh breadcrumbs. These are marveous dipped into runny garlic mayonnaise or béarnaise sauce. And then there is everybody's favorite—chicken liver pâté. That is, of course, everybody's favorite after foie gras.

Now, I know that this is a controversial subject, but I do believe in the freedom to eat what you wish to eat, or not eat, as the case may be. Life is becoming more and more restricting as it is. This most extraordinary of livers, from either duck or goose, is made by force-feeding the bird with corn until its liver is dramatically increased in size. When cooked, the result is a staggeringly rich liver of unquestionably delicious taste.

CALVES' LIVER VENETIAN STYLE

My friend the wine merchant Bill Baker says that the Fegato alla Veneziana at Harry's Bar in Venice is the best that he has ever tasted, and it is important that the pieces of liver are the size of postage stamps and almost as thin. Sadly, I have not eaten the Fegato at Harry's, but I have taken Mr. Baker's advice, and at least got the shape right.

3 mild Spanish onions, peeled and very thinly sliced
5 tbsp vegetable oil
8 exceptionally thin slices of calves' liver, cut into small squares
salt and pepper
1 tbsp chopped parsley
2 tbsp red wine vinegar

Cook the onions in 3 tbsp of the vegetable oil until completely cooked through and soft. They may take on a little color during this time but it doesn't matter; the most important thing is that they cook slowly, which can take up to 30 minutes. In a large and not-too-thick frying pan or wok, beat the remaining 2 tbsp vegetable oil until smoking hot. Season the calves' liver with salt and pepper, and toss briefly in the hot oil for about 20 seconds. Drain in a colander. Add the onions to the pan and similarly toss briefly in the oil until golden brown and slightly scorched in parts. Return the liver to the pan with the parsley and, finally, stir in the vinegar. Serve without delay and not without mashed potatoes.

N.B. The final cooking of this dish—that is after the initial cooking of the onions—should not take more than about 1 minute.

RICHARD OLNEY'S TERRINE OF POULTRY LIVERS

I like this terrine for its simplicity and understatedness. Many pâtés and terrines that one encounters these days are overworked and elaborate, forsaking a savory taste in favor of pretty layers or bland mousse. This could never be the case with any of Richard Olney's recipes. Allow me to elaborate . . .

FANFARE

Richard Olney

One of my most memorable meals was enjoyed at the home of Richard Olney in the south of France—the more unfashionable end, near Toulon, southern Provence really. He lives at the end of an almost impossibly steep road. He settled there from his native America in 1951 and I would guess that he may find it sad that the panoramic views from his hilltop home are not quite what they were. (It's not that unfashionable.)

I arrived for lunch after a death-defying drive on the back road from St. Tropez—large buses, not much road—in a nervous state and in need of a drink. Domaine Tempier rosé was very forthcoming while we watched Richard cook a fish soup made from very small Mediterranean fish. It is a real pleasure to watch very good cooks cook, to see things done properly and without any apparent effort. The real joy, of course, is in watching someone with a talent for doing something very well deriving much pleasure in its execution.

Lunch was a simple affair that began with the fish soup and was followed by a salad and then some Reblochon cheese in, naturally, fine condition. However, salad is a different thing in the Olney home. Here, the small salad leaves were collected from Richard's garden just before lunch. Among this day's pickings, I remember arugula, little romaine lettuces, and pourpier (purslane), with herbs such as basil and hyssop. There was some onion too, I think, and perhaps a little garlic. And a superb vinaigrette that was made from his own vinegar and local olive oil. But what I remember most of all was the sliced boiled eggs—hard-boiled but with just a hint of softness at the yolks' center. Strewn over these were hyssop flowers. These are bright blue, have a more delicate flavor than the herb itself, and look stunning against the deep yellow yolks—just the prettiest thing. I gave a silent cheer when this salad was put on the table.

Richard Olney was not a professional cook in the normal way of things. However, he was, in my opinion one of the greatest writers on food and wine. His last two books were on wine, one on Yquem and the other on the Domaine de la Romanée Conti. I wonder whether, in fact, it was wine that was Richard's passion, with food as an essential accompaniment.

However, it is his writing on food that has given me the most pleasure and inspiration. Both the French Menu Cookbook and Simple French Food are classics and compulsory reading for all. Methodic descriptions are told in such a gentle way that the result and taste of the final dish becomes perfectly obvious to the reader. He nudges you along so that you get it right. Read this recipe and you will see what I mean.

"This terrine should be prepared the day before it is served, but, unlike many, it does not keep remarkably well, and once cut into, it should be consumed within a day or so.

1 tsp mixed dried herbs (herbes de Provence, for instance)
2 heads of cloves (the tiny ball attached to the extremity of each clove)
1 garlic clove
1 healthy handful of fresh white breadcrumbs
1 onion, finely chopped
1 tbsp unsalted butter
6 oz fresh pork fat, chilled
1 lb poultry livers, trimmed of greenish stains and white nervous tissue, chopped
1 egg
1 tbsp finely chopped parsley
salt and pepper
2 bay leaves

"Reduce the mixed herbs and clove heads to a powder in a stone mortar. Add the garlic clove and pound to a paste. Add the breadcrumbs and mix together so that the garlic thoroughly impregnates the whole. Put aside.

"Cook the chopped onion gently in butter for 10 minutes or so, or until it is yellowed and soft.

"Remove enough thin slices from the pork fat to line the bottom and the sides of the terrine and to cover the surface, once filled; cut the rest into little cubes.

"With the exception of the slices of pork fat and the two bay leaves, combine all the ingredients in a large mixing bowl, working them thoroughly together with both hands, squeezing the mixture repeatedly, through clutching fingers, until it is completely homogeneous. Taste for salt and pepper.

"Line the bottom and sides of the terrine with slices of pork fat, pressing them to ensure their adhering, pour in the liver mixture, tap the bottom of the terrine two or three times against a wooden surface to settle its contents, place the bay leaves on the surface, and lightly press the remaining pork fat slices on top. Cover the terrine (if it does not have a lid, fit over it a piece of foil) and poach it in a bain-marie, either in the oven (the terrine placed in a larger, deep pan, hot water poured in to immerse it by two-thirds) or on top of the stove (in a tightly covered saucepan large enough to contain the terrine, filled to two-thirds the terrine's height with hot water), without allowing the water to boil, for 1 hour.

"Place the terrine on a platter, to collect any juices that run over the edge, and remove the lid or foil. (Don't be alarmed at the quantity of liquid in which the contents seem to float—it is made up of gelatinous juices that will solidify in the terrine, and of fat that will solidify on the surface.) Place a board or a plate just the size of the terrine's opening on the surface, with a weight of about 2 lb on top—a can of conserves, for instance. The weighting lends a firm, close texture to the body, without which it would be impossible to slice and serve the terrine neatly. When cooled, remove the weight and put the dish to chill. Serve it in slices directly from the terrine, the border of pork fat removed from each slice or not, as preferred."

DUCK LIVERS, CRÊPES PARMENTIER, AND ONION MARMALADE

This is duck livers with two of my favorite things: soft, light potato pancakes, first eaten at the restaurant Georges Blanc in Vonnas, and the wonderful, now ubiquitous, onion marmalade from Michel Guérard's book *Cuisine Gourmande*.

The recipe for the onion marmalade will fill a whole jar and can be kept in the fridge to serve with all sorts of dishes: terrines, cold meats, game dishes, etc. If you want to make enough just for this dish, then halve the recipe.

1 batch Crêpes Parmentier (see page 30)
8 perfect duck livers (or 1 lb chicken livers), any green bits scraped off, and trimmed of all nervous tissue

salt and pepper
2 tbsp olive oil, if grilling, or 2 tbsp clarified butter (see page 31), if frying
1 tbsp snipped chives

For the onion marmalade

½ cup butter
1½ lb onions, peeled and thinly sliced
1½ tsp salt
1 tsp pepper
½ cup sugar
7 tbsp sherry vinegar
2 tbsp grenadine cordial (in my view, optional)
1 cup plus 2 tbsp coarse red wine

First make the onion marmalade. Heat the butter in a saucepan until it becomes nut brown. Throw in the onions, season, and add the sugar. Cook very slowly for 30–45 minutes or until the onions are dark brown. Add the vinegar, the optional grenadine, and the red wine. Cook for a further 30 minutes, stirring occasionally, until the mixture is a deep mahogany color and the butter has separated out from the onion mass and is floating on top. Cool slightly, pour into jars or other suitable containers, and cool thoroughly before putting in the fridge. The butter will settle on the top and can be removed.

Cook the Crêpes Parmentier as described on page 31, and keep warm. Gently warm 3 tbsp onion marmalade but do not allow to become too hot. Heat either a cast-iron griddle or a heavy-bottomed frying pan until very hot. If grilling, put the duck livers in a bowl, season, and add the olive oil. With your hands, mix them together so that they are evenly coated. Carefully put on the griddle and cook for about 1 minute on each side, more if you like them less pink. Put on a warm plate and allow to rest.

If frying, melt the clarified butter in the pan and heat until hot. Cook the livers for the same length of time and allow to rest for 5 minutes or so. The resting is important, particularly with something like liver, as when the livers come off the grill or out of the pan, the outside bit is well cooked and the inside is rare. The resting period allows the two to merge together into a uniform pink.

To assemble, put a pancake on each plate and spread each one with the warm onion marmalade. Slice the livers horizontally and pile up on each pancake. This is for aesthetic reasons, as the pink slices of liver look nicer than two dark brown lumps. Sprinkle with the chives and serve.

OLIVE OIL

The first time I made mayonnaise, the olive oil I used came from Boots the chemist. It was a small bottle, pretty tasteless, and quite clearly not meant for culinary purposes.

I wonder why it has taken us so long to become interested in using olive oil. Elizabeth David wrote about its wonderful qualities forty years ago, and since then we have traveled to Spain, France, and Italy for holidays and enjoyed its sunny, fragrant taste. But it is only in the past five or six years that our use of olive oil has become a matter of course. It has also become a bit of an obsession. There are people demanding to know whether the oil is first pressing, or is it virgin? Is it *extra*-virgin and cold-pressed? Is it filtered? Does it have a vintage? Is it time to introduce an appellation? And, if so, who should control it? And, anyway, who made the oil? Which *tree* did the olives come from, and who picked them? Please understand that I am very fond of olive oil, and respect its qualities, but it is, after all, just something that happens to be very nice to cook with.

Wherever you go, it seems that someone wants to dribble a bit of that golden green liquid over your food. It's just not on. I went to a place once where a terrine of duck foie gras (one of the richest and fattiest things it is possible to eat) was served with a slick of olive oil poured over it. There is even a restaurant in London's West End named after a brand of it.

The interest in simple and rustic Italian food must be a major cause of its popularity. Olive oil is healthier, I suppose, than butter, but that is not an issue here; I like the taste of both and would not substitute one for the other. One might think that they do in Italy. Well, they don't. If a dish needs butter, it gets butter; if it needs olive oil, it gets olive oil. It's a question of region too.

Olive oil marinates meat or fish to a melting richness and performs miraculous transformations of texture and flavor on many ingredients. But, when it comes to making mayonnaise, I find it overbearing to use just olive oil. Elizabeth David would have disagreed with me. She talked about its ointment-like consistency—which is a fine description—because when made this way that is exactly what it looks like. My preference is for a 60/40 combination of olive oil and peanut oil (or another flavorless variety). This cuts down the richness and helps with the homogeneity.

The exception to this is when making the wonderful garlic mayonnaise called aïoli, which is found in the south of France, particularly Provence. This must be made only from olive oil (see page 29). And, incidentally, in that part of France, olive oil is called beurre de Provence. That's regional nomenclature for you. The following recipe for mashed potatoes uses beurre de Provence rather than butter.

OLIVE OIL MASHED POTATOES

I have to admit that the inspiration for this delicious purée comes from nowhere near Provence. I found a recipe for creamed new potatoes with olive oil in *Cuisine Spontanée* by Frédy Girardet. He has a restaurant in Switzerland, just outside Lausanne. Made with new potatoes, it is a quite different thing from our idea of soft, fluffy mashed potatoes. New potatoes produce a silkier and creamier texture, but you don't want to eat too much of it. However, made with Jersey Royals, the flavor is quite extraordinary.

> 2 lb russet potatoes, peeled and cut into chunks
> salt and pepper
> ½ cup whole milk
> 2 garlic cloves, peeled and crushed
> 1 rosemary sprig
> 1 thyme sprig
> 1 cup virgin olive oil

Boil the potatoes in salted water. Meanwhile, heat together the milk, garlic, rosemary, and thyme, then remove from the heat, cover, and leave to infuse. Drain and mash the potatoes—I use a *mouli-légumes*—and put them in the bowl of an electric mixer fitted with a paddle rather than a whisk. Strain the flavored milk through a fine sieve, add the olive oil, and gently reheat. Switch the mixer on at a low speed and add the milk mixture to the potatoes in a steady stream. When all the liquid has been added, adjust the seasoning with salt and pepper. Turn the mixer speed up and beat until you have a smooth, glossy purée.

This is very good with roast meats, particularly veal and lamb. But the first time I ever made it, it went with rabbit.

SAUCE VIÈRGE

There is no point in making this unless you have sun-ripened tomatoes, which actually taste of tomatoes, and the finest quality olive oil. To call it a sauce is a slight misnomer—it is more like a dressing.

> 4 very ripe tomatoes, peeled, seeded, and chopped
> 1 tbsp red wine vinegar
> salt and pepper
> 2 small garlic cloves, peeled and thinly sliced
> 1 small shallot, peeled and finely chopped
> 1 small bunch of basil, leaves only, torn into pieces
> ½ cup olive oil

Use a white porcelain dish for making this sauce, as it looks best. Mix together the tomatoes, vinegar, salt and pepper, garlic, and shallot. Leave to macerate for 30 minutes. Stir in the basil and olive oil, and serve with grilled sea bass.

VINAIGRETTE

Vinaigrette is very easy to make. Once you've made a batch, put it in a screw-top jar in the fridge and it will keep for several weeks. So this recipe is for a large quantity; in fact, it is more successful to make a lot rather than a little.

½ cup red wine vinegar
1 tbsp smooth Dijon mustard
salt and freshly ground white pepper, to taste
½ cup walnut oil
1 cup olive oil

In either a blender or an electric mixer, beat together the vinegar, mustard, salt, and pepper. Mix together the oils and, with the machine running, add them to the vinegar solution until homogenized.

ONIONS

I have sometimes thought that the phrase "take one onion" would be a good name for a recipe book. How many savory recipes are there that do *not* use onions? Their harmonious flavor pulls together good stews, rich and satisfying soups; roasted around a joint of meat, they lend their essential flavor to a fine gravy. Cooked whole on their own with seasoning, a pinch of sugar and a little stock, then roasted in the oven, they produce one of the great kitchen smells of all time. Sometimes the skins are left on, sometimes not. Although the skin insulates the flavor within, taking off the skin produces a gooey and scorched outside. And who doesn't love the aroma of burnt onion?

Thinly sliced onions, braised slowly in copious amounts of butter, a splash of white wine and wine vinegar, with cream added at the end, is my idea of a perfect winter accompaniment to a roast leg of lamb. Alternatively, the mixture can be puréed to produce the classic sauce soubise.

A recently discovered method of cooking onions (along with other vegetables discussed elsewhere) is to slice them thickly and grill them on a cast-iron ribbed infrared grill. Once again, that slightly burned smell, produced by the onion's natural sugar content, is intoxicating. With this method, the onion slices need no oiling, nor does the grill. They produce their own natural crust, but you have to be patient, as lifting them too early in the cooking process spells disaster. (This applies to all grilling.) Red onions are the best variety for this. They look good with their black stripes and just need to be thrown into a bowl, seasoned and dressed with a little balsamic vinegar and olive oil, and finished off with a handful of chopped parsley.

Almost guiltily, I have a real craving for deep-fried onion rings from time to time, even frozen from a package if desperate. But they are very easy to prepare. Simply dip the rings in flour, beaten egg, and breadcrumbs, or in a batter, and drop into deep hot fat until they turn crisp and golden brown. They are absolutely fabulous with steak tartare.

ROAST ONIONS

The best size of onion for this recipe is a small to medium one, weighing about 2–3 oz. I have read some recipes for roast onions where you don't peel them. This is okay, but what happens then is that the onion steams inside the skin and doesn't actually roast. The flavor is quite nice in the end, but if you peel the onion first you get a marvelous caramel, helped with a little sugar, from the onion's natural juices.

½ cup butter
16 onions, peeled
2 tbsp white sugar
4 tbsp red wine vinegar
1 cup beef stock (I have successfully used a can of beef broth)
salt and plenty of black pepper

Preheat the oven to 400°F. In a large roasting pan or frying pan that will go in the oven, melt the butter until just turning brown. Put in the onions, sprinkle over the sugar, and stir and turn constantly over a medium heat until thoroughly coated and starting to color. This will take several minutes. Add the red wine vinegar, which will seethe and splutter. Turn up the heat and reduce until almost evaporated. Add the stock or broth, bring to the boil, and taste the liquid before adding a little salt. (Use salt sparingly—as the stock or broth reduces, its saltiness will intensify.) Grind on plenty of pepper and transfer to the oven. Cook for about 30 minutes or until almost all the liquid has disappeared and the onions are a deep mahogany. Serve at once.

It almost goes without saying that these are extremely good with any roast— particularly lamb.

GRILLED RED ONION RELISH

This recipe is inspired by a Californian idea rooted in spicy Mexican dishes like salsa (see page 43). It was only a few years ago that I discovered salsa. It has certainly broadened our culinary horizons and should not be dismissed as a passing fashion. After all, the Mexicans have been making it and eating it for hundreds of years.

A good basic salsa can be made with chopped red onion, tomatoes, fresh cilantro, lime juice, and chillies.

4 large red onions, peeled and thickly sliced
salt
1 tsp sugar

2 large green chillies, seeded and chopped
2 tbsp roughly chopped cilantro
juice of 2 limes
3 tbsp olive oil

Grill the onion slices on a ribbed infrared grill until scorched with black stripes on both sides. Transfer to a bowl, season with salt, and add all the other ingredients. Mix together with your hands, separating the rings of onion as you do so. Leave to marinate for at least 1 hour before using. Excellent with barbecued steak or pork chops.

ONION TART

This is a classic among tarts. My idea of the perfect onion tart is one from which the filling oozes out when you cut into it. You may be surprised at the amount of onions given in the recipe, but the secret is their long, slow cooking before adding them to the tart shell. I have, on occasion, added other ingredients, such as thyme or sage, little bits of chopped, smoked bacon, and chopped anchovies. My mother used to make a jolly good cheese and onion tart using Lancashire cheese crumbled into the mixture, but I prefer the purity of onions alone.

For the pastry

¼ cup butter, cut into cubes
1 scant cup all-purpose flour
1 egg yolk
a pinch of salt

For the filling

½ cup butter
4 large onions, peeled and thinly sliced
salt and pepper
4 egg yolks
1 cup heavy cream

To make the pastry, quickly work the butter into the flour. Add the egg yolk, salt, and enough water to form a firm dough. Chill for 30 minutes.

Preheat the oven to 350°F. Roll out the pastry as thinly as possible and use to line an 8-inch flan tin (make sure it is a deep one). Prick the bottom, and bake in the oven for 15–20 minutes or until straw colored and cooked through.

Meanwhile, melt the butter in a large saucepan, add the onions and a sprinkling of salt, and stew very gently, covered to begin with, without browning. When very wet and sloppy, remove the lid and carry on cooking on the same heat, stirring from time to time, until as much of the liquid as possible has evaporated. This can take up to 1 hour. Pour into a bowl and cool.

Mix the egg yolks with the cream, and add to the onions with plenty of pepper. Adjust the salt if necessary before pouring into the pastry shell. Try to make sure that you fill the tart as high as you dare—depending on the juices from the onion, you may have a little of the custardy liquid left over—but do try to get it all in. Half-filled tarts are always disappointing.

Bake in the oven for 30–40 minutes or until set and lightly browned.

CREAMED ONIONS WITH ROSEMARY

3 large Spanish onions, peeled and very thinly sliced
½ cup butter
salt and pepper
½ cup white wine vinegar
½ cup dry white wine
3 rosemary sprigs
1½ cups heavy cream

Sweat the onions gently in the butter with salt on a very low heat until very soft and mushy—this could take an hour or so. Add the vinegar and reduce until evaporated. Add the white wine and reduce gently by two-thirds. Add the rosemary sprigs and the cream, and a generous grinding of pepper. Cook gently for a further 10 minutes or so, until thick and creamy.

You may find that a pinch of sugar improves the balance of flavors. Excellent with really porky sausages, and mashed potatoes. And applesauce.

ONION SOUP

An easy way to make the most delicious onion soup is to take the recipe for Creamed Onions with Rosemary (see above) and to change direction halfway through. Creamed Onion Soup is one of my all-time favorites; it is sweet and rich and intensely savory, and, like all cream soups, it cries out for croûtons.

3 large Spanish onions, peeled and very thinly sliced
½ cup butter
salt and pepper
¼ cup white wine vinegar

1 cup dry white wine
2 cups light chicken stock
1 cup heavy cream
croûtons, to serve

Follow the recipe for Creamed Onions with Rosemary until just before adding the rosemary. Add the chicken stock and simmer for 30 minutes. Blend until smooth, then put through a fine sieve, add the cream, and reheat gently without boiling. Serve with plenty of croûtons.

PARMESAN

Let's get one thing quite clear: Parmigiano Reggiano is the only cheese of its type to qualify for the title "Parmesan." All other granular types of cheese—which may have similar taste and texture—are collectively called "grana."

Parmesan is made in and around Parma and is unique. The finest cheeses are aged for about four years and can develop a crumbly and buttery texture like no other cheese. Parmesan is made from unpasteurized skimmed milk and cooked until the curd has separated. The whey is fed to pigs, which, in turn, provide us with prosciutto di Parma. Aren't we lucky.

It may come as a surprise that not all Parmesan has to be grated. Moreover, it is often preferable to eat it in thin slivers (made using a potato peeler) over a salad or atop the ubiquitous carpaccio. When in peak condition, it is a wonderful cheese to eat on its own, or after dinner with some ripe figs or cherries or, better still, pears.

A well-matured Parmesan develops a sweet and tangy quality when in its prime and can be broken off into chunks with the fingers. It should not be cut, but eased off in a chunk with a special stubby knife designed for the purpose. Any knife will do, of course, but it's nice to use the correct implement. When it comes to grating Parmesan, Reggiano is the finest one to use, but (and expense comes into this in a big way) good quality grana is quite respectable and a good deal cheaper.

Parmesan, for me, is like a seasoning; it is not so much something that you cook with, more something you add after cooking. As we all know, its sweet, salty taste transforms a simple dish of pasta that has been turned in butter. A risotto Milanese is incomplete without Parmesan. The saffron, onion, chicken broth, and rice come together to form a glorious, unctuous mass once the cheese is stirred in.

Similar things happen to a bowl of soft polenta. This Italian peasant staple has become a fashionable dish in recent times, but it seems that although many of us, including me, love it, just as many hate it. Perhaps it is reminiscent of school semolina pudding. Who knows? If salt instead of sugar, and fresh Parmesan instead of jam, had been handed around in the cafeteria, things might have been different.

Shellfish risottos do not require Parmesan; fish and cheese do not go well together. Lobster thermidor is a disgusting dish. I also don't understand the addition of cheese to fish soup. There are times when personal taste is not necessarily the issue. Is it possible that some revered and age-old combinations are simply not right?

I once worked in a restaurant where I was asked to cook a dish called Délices de Sole Parmesan. It consisted of pieces of Dover sole dipped in Parmesan and bread-crumbs and fried in butter with bananas. I was quite new to the cooking game at the time, but even then I thought this was a bit rum.

PARMESAN FRITTERS

It is essential to have a deep-fryer for this recipe, or a clean immersible frying basket at least. This is a nice, old-fashioned little dish, and the sort of thing that everybody likes: creamy cheese inside and a crisp crust without.

½ cup butter
1 scant cup all-purpose flour
1½ cups hot milk
6 tbsp freshly grated Parmesan
freshly grated nutmeg
2 egg yolks
salt
¼ tsp cayenne
3½–4oz fresh mozzarella, chopped into small cubes
oil for deep-frying
flour for coating
2 eggs, beaten
fresh breadcrumbs for coating
parsley sprigs, to garnish (optional)
extra Parmesan, for dusting
lemon wedges

Melt the butter in a saucepan, stir in the flour, and make a roux. Add the milk, stirring constantly to make a smooth, thick sauce. Do give the sauce time to cook properly; as with all flour-based sauces, the taste of flour must be cooked out, so keep stirring to prevent scorching and sticking. The sauce must be very thick, as it has to set firm enough to be cut into squares when cold. Stir in the Parmesan and nutmeg. Remove from the heat, allow to cool for 10 minutes, and then stir in the egg yolks and seasoning. Stir in the mozzarella carefully to avoid breaking up the cubes. Spread the mixture in a lightly oiled baking pan—a jelly roll pan would be ideal. Cover with plastic wrap and put in the refrigerator for at least 4 hours, overnight would be even better.

Heat the oil in a deep-fryer to 375°F. Sprinkle some flour on a plate, put the beaten egg in a shallow dish, and spread the breadcrumbs on another plate. Cut the cheese mixture into roughly 1-inch squares. With floured hands, carefully dip each cheese square first into the flour, then into the egg, and finally into the breadcrumbs. Place the squares on a tray covered with waxed paper. When all the squares have been coated, fry them in batches in the hot oil. The size of your frying receptacle will determine the number of fritters you can cook at any one time. I would suggest five or six, but on no account overcrowd the pan. They should take no longer than a minute or so, but golden brown should be the final result. As each batch is fried, drain well before putting on paper towels and keeping hot in a low oven. If using, deep-fry the sprigs of parsley for a few seconds, drain, put on paper towels, and sprinkle with salt.

Arrange the fritters on a white dish, sprinkle with the extra Parmesan, strew with the parsley, and tuck in the lemon wedges.

CRISP PARMESAN CRACKERS

These very thin, fine crackers are delicious served with beef consommé or as an accompaniment to a very good dry martini.

For 15–20 crackers

6 tbsp all-purpose plain flour
3 oz slivered almonds
3 oz Parmesan cheese, freshly grated
3 tbsp butter, melted
1 egg white, beaten with a pinch of salt
extra Parmesan and cayenne, for dusting

Preheat the oven to 400°F. Sift the flour into a bowl and stir in the almonds, Parmesan, and melted butter. When thoroughly mixed, fold in the egg white and form into a dough. Flour a suitable surface and roll out the dough as thinly as possible. With a 3-inch pastry cutter, cut the pastry into circles and put on a well-greased baking sheet. Bake for 7 minutes or until pale golden. Remove immediately with a spatula and place on a wire rack to cool. Dust with Parmesan and a little cayenne while still warm.

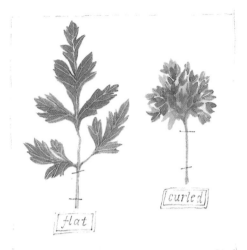

PARSLEY

I shall never forget a children's story I was told when I was little:

Once upon a time there was a dear old lady who lived in a chocolate box cottage at the end of a leafy lane. Her garden was a riot of beautiful flowers and shrubs, which she tended and cosseted with love and care from dawn till dusk.

At the end of each day, after her chores, she would trip down to the bottom of the garden for a natter with the fairies and pixies who, quite naturally, lived there. They loved the old lady and all the flowers that she grew in her garden, for it was their playground.

Time passed and, as is the way of things, the old lady died and some horrid city folk moved in to her lovely cottage. They didn't want flowers in their garden, they wanted to fill it full of vegetables. So, out came the nasturtiums, the lupins, cornflowers, and roses. No more hollyhocks, lavender, Canterbury bells (the fairies use them for hats, you know), or forget-me-nots. In their place went cabbages, carrots and sprouts, rutabagas, potatoes, and horrible old turnips, together with row upon row of parsley. And this particular parsley grew and grew in huge bunches all over the place.

Well, as you can imagine, the fairies and pixies were none too pleased about this, so they decided one night to cause a little mischief. There was a full moon and plenty of light and one by one they scampered up and down the rows of parsley, pinching it as they went with their spindly little fingers, over and over and over again, until they could pinch no more.

And that, dear reader, is how we come to have curly parsley.

The flat-leaf variety of parsley is infinitely finer and has much more flavor than the "pinched" stuff. The problem is, though, that few people realize just how much of it is needed. For example, white sauce with a few flecks of green floating in it is not parsley sauce. For a small panful, I would use a whole bunch (see Salmon, page 182). A wonderful soup can be made from it, requiring many more bunches, and is one of the nicest soups I know. Parsley stuffings are delicious, too. For instance, little forcemeat balls, dense with parsley and chopped lemon rind, are a wonderful partner to braised rabbit or a potted hare.

I've even used parsley as a vegetable. Gently stewed in a little butter for a few moments with a sliver or two of garlic, it is very good with grilled chicken. For this, however, you do have to use the curly variety, as, irritatingly, the flat type sticks to the sides of the pan and doesn't absorb the butter well. You need the curly type of parsley if you want to deep-fry it, too. I adore deep-fried parsley. It is simplicity itself to prepare. Just drop some well-dried sprigs into hot fat for a few seconds. (One of those electric deep-fryers with a basket is ideal.) Lift the parsley out, drain it on paper towels, and sprinkle with salt. It's a shame you don't see it used as much as you used to, accompanying old favorites such as fresh whitebait and goujons of sole. Surely dull dishes without their hive of deep-fried parsley?

POTATO PURÉE WITH PARSLEY

This purée is fabulous with fish. It puts one in mind of a really good fish pie, fish cakes, and, of course, any poached fish with parsley sauce. Essentially, this recipe turns simple mashed potatoes into something quite special. It is very appealing to look at and its taste is so good that you could almost eat it on its own (I have).

2 lb potatoes, peeled and cut into large chunks
salt and pepper
2 bunches of flat-leaf parsley, leaves only
½ cup butter
½ cup milk
½ cup heavy cream
½ garlic clove, peeled and crushed

Cook the potatoes in boiling salted water until tender. Drain, mash, and keep warm in a covered stainless steel or enameled pan.

In another pan of fiercely boiling water, blanch the parsley leaves, refresh in cold water, drain, and reserve. Heat together the butter, milk, cream, garlic, and seasoning. Pour into a blender with the parsley, and blend together while still hot. (It is important that the liquids are hot; cool dairy produce when agitated has a tendency to separate.) Add this parsley purée to the warm potato and whisk together thoroughly.

GAY BILSON'S PARSLEY SALAD

My friend Gay Bilson serves this as an appetizer at her restaurant, Berowra Waters Inn, in Sydney, Australia. It is one of the best things I have ever eaten. All at once it is refreshing, sour, and salty—everything that you could need to sharpen the appetite. The little biscuits that go with it are perfection.

There is enough for twenty-five people in this recipe, but only enough to serve as a small taster, which, at the restaurant, is served along with a complimentary glass of Bollinzer. So, for a first course at home, halve the recipe, but it is so good as an appetizer with drinks, I would always use it for that.

For the salad

4 oz finest quality fleshy, black olives (Gay suggests Ligurian)
4 oz flat-leaf parsley leaves, coarsely chopped
4 oz red onion, peeled and finely chopped
2 oz Italian salted capers, rinsed

2 large garlic cloves, peeled and finely chopped
20 large anchovy fillets (preferably pink Spanish anchovies)
grated rind of 2 lemons
black pepper
½ cup olive oil
lemon juice, to taste
thin slivers of Parmesan cheese

For the biscuits

2 cups bread flour
1 tsp salt
½ tsp cayenne
½ tsp baking powder
½ cup water
1 tsp soft butter

For the salad, coarsely chop the black olives and mix together with the parsley, onion, capers, and garlic. Chop the anchovies into small pieces, mix with the lemon rind, plenty of black pepper, and olive oil, and mix into the other ingredients. Add lemon juice to taste, spoon onto a flat dish, and finish with thin slivers of Parmesan.

To make the biscuits, put all the ingredients, apart from the water and the butter, into a food processor. Heat the water and butter together and pour into the machine with the motor running, until it forms a ball. Leave the mixture to rest for 30 minutes. Using a pasta machine, roll the pastry out on the thinnest setting (usually 7) and cut into manageable lengths. Cut into 2-inch-wide rectangles and deep-fry at a temperature of 360°F until puffed up like poppadoms. Drain on paper towels and serve with the salad.

PARSLEY SOUP

When Lindsey Bareham was compiling her soup book (*A Celebration of Soup*), she was also reviewing restaurants for the *Sunday Telegraph*. I was lucky enough to be invited along as her companion on several occasions, and this often involved some long train journeys.

Soup recipes, more than any other, come easily to me and it was a happy collaboration whilst thundering up and down the English countryside. This parsley soup's destination was Exeter—en route for Gidleigh Park and The Carved Angel in Dartmouth—and now, having given her this recipe, I am having it back for my book. And ironically, as it's turned out, written with her assistance.

6 tbsp butter
2 large leeks, white parts only, sliced
2 big bunches of flat-leaf parsley, stalks and leaves separated, stalks chopped
1 large potato, peeled and chopped
2½ cups light chicken stock
salt and pepper
½ cup heavy cream

Melt the butter in a stainless steel or enameled saucepan and sweat the leeks and all the parsley stalks gently, uncovered, for 20 minutes. Add the potato, chicken stock, and salt and pepper, and simmer for a further 20 minutes.

Coarsely chop the leaves of one bunch of parsley and add to the soup. Simmer for 2 minutes. Meanwhile, blanch the leaves of the other bunch of parsley in fiercely boiling water for 30 seconds. Drain and refresh immediately under cold running water, then gently squeeze dry in a tea towel.

Blend the soup with the blanched parsley to make a vivid green purée. Pass through a fine sieve into a clean pan, add the cream, reheat, and adjust the seasoning.

PEPPERS

I used to think that Italian cooking was just veal, pasta, and tomatoes. I thought spaghetti boring, veal a tasteless meat (usually pan-fried in soggy breadcrumbs), and all that was ever done to tomatoes was to turn them into insipid sauces.

However, a turning point was eating Piedmontese peppers for the first time at Franco Taruschio's Walnut Tree Inn near Abergavenny in Wales. This, along with his home-cured bresaola, his fresh pasta, good olive oil, and fine Parmesan, was a revelation. The recipe for the peppers originally came from Elizabeth David's *Italian Food*, so thanks to her and Franco, and the peppers, Italian cooking became a voyage of discovery for me.

Roasted peppers create such a marvelous smell that you almost wish you could bottle it. They are best cooked over a wood fire or a grill, the juices collecting inside while the skin blackens and blisters. Red peppers are the finest and sweetest, yellow second-best, and, for me, green, white, and purple are frankly not worth the bother. The only time I ever use green peppers is for Gazpacho (see page 152).

PIEDMONTESE PEPPERS

4 red bell peppers
salt and pepper
4 garlic cloves, peeled
8 ripe tomatoes, peeled and seeded
½ cup olive oil
16 canned anchovies, drained

Preheat the oven to 425°F. Split the peppers in half lengthways, and remove the cores and seeds. Season the insides lightly with salt and generously with pepper. Slice each garlic clove thinly and distribute among the four peppers. Place a tomato inside each pepper half, again season with pepper and a little salt. Place in a roasting pan, pour the olive oil over each pepper, and roast in the oven for 30 minutes. Lower the oven temperature to 350°F and cook for about another 45 minutes or until the edges of the peppers are slightly burned, and somewhat collapsed.

Remove the peppers from the oven and allow to cool before placing the anchovies in a crisscross pattern on each pepper. Place on a plain white serving dish and spoon the juices over each pepper. It is essential to serve some good crusty bread for mopping-up purposes.

PIMIENTO SALSA

This relish is very good with all sorts of grilled food, particularly steak, lamb cutlets, and fish steaks such as cod or tuna. It is also excellent with poached eggs.

2 large red bell peppers
2 green chillies, seeded and chopped
2 large ripe tomatoes, peeled, seeded, and coarsely chopped
1 medium red onion, peeled and finely chopped
1 small bunch of cilantro, leaves picked and chopped (if your cilantro has roots, include these)
1 small bunch of mint, leaves picked and chopped
4 tbsp olive oil
½ tsp salt

Put the peppers under a hot broiler, turning from time to time until they are scorched and blackened all over. To facilitate peeling, place the hot peppers in a cold pan, cover, and leave for 20 minutes. (Some people do this in a bag; I think this method is less hassle.) Peel, core, and seed the peppers, then chop finely. Mix with all the other ingredients, and leave to macerate for 1 hour before use. Serve at room temperature.

ROULADE OF PEPPERS AND EGGPLANT

This clever and spectacularly good dish came to me via a chef who used to work for Gay Bilson at Berowra Waters Inn in Sydney. When serving this dish in the past, I have accompanied it with items such as fresh mozzarella cheese, creamed and puréed goat's cheese, or even some garlic mayonnaise. It's good to serve some sort of toasted bread, spread perhaps with puréed anchovy or any of those "Mediterranean-type" pastes—tapenade, anchoiade, or sun-dried tomato. There seems to be an endless variety of these on the supermarket shelves in little glass jars.

4 red bell peppers
2 large eggplants, stalks removed
olive oil
salt and pepper
30 basil leaves, torn into bits
3 garlic cloves, peeled and thinly sliced
balsamic vinegar

Roast, peel, and seed the peppers as described in Pimiento Salsa (see page 148). Meanwhile, slice the eggplants lengthways as thinly as possible. Heat olive oil in a large frying pan to a depth of about ¼ inch until very hot but not smoking. Add the eggplant slices and fry until golden brown on both sides, adding more oil if necessary. Remove the slices and drain on paper towels as you proceed.

On a spacious work surface, lay out a large sheet of plastic wrap. In the middle, make a rectangle with the eggplant slices, taking care that they overlap each other slightly. Season lightly with salt and pepper. Evenly distribute the basil leaves and slivers of garlic over the eggplant slices. Sprinkle lightly with balsamic vinegar and cover with the pieces of pepper.

By lifting the edge of the plastic wrap, carefully form the ingredients into the shape of a jelly roll, taking care not to trap the plastic wrap inside. Tuck the leading edge of the wrap underneath the formed roll, twist the ends together like a Christmas cracker, and turn in opposite directions. This will tighten and firm up the roll. Refrigerate for at least 6 hours, preferably overnight.

To serve, take a sharp serrated knife and cut, with plastic wrap intact, into slices at least 1 inch thick. Using a fish slice, carefully transfer each slice to individual serving plates. Only now should you remove the collars of plastic wrap.

ROWLEY'S VINAIGRETTE OF RED PEPPERS AND ANCHOVY

Rowley Leigh is chef at the excellent Kensington Place in London. He is also a good chum and it was at his home that I first ate the original version of this dish. It is simplicity itself to prepare, and of all the dishes on Rowley's menu it's the one I never tire of—he says I never eat anything else.

4 red bell peppers, roasted, peeled, halved, and seeded (see Pimiento Salsa,
page 149), taking care to collect all their juices
salt and pepper
3 tbsp red wine vinegar
9 tbsp olive oil
4 hard-boiled eggs, peeled
8–10 anchovies
2 tbsp capers, drained
2 tbsp chopped parsley

Arrange the peppers and their juices in a plain white dish. Season with salt and pepper, and spoon over the vinegar and olive oil. Chop the whites of the hard-boiled eggs and sprinkle over the peppers. Arrange the anchovies attractively in a crisscross pattern, sprinkle over the capers, and sieve the egg yolks on top. Strew with parsley and serve.

RED PEPPER TART

For the pastry

1 scant cup all-purpose flour
4 tbsp butter, cut into cubes
1 egg yolk
a pinch of salt

For the filling

4 red bell peppers, roasted, peeled, and seeded (see Pimiento Salsa, page 149)
½ cup heavy cream
6 egg yolks
1 garlic clove, peeled and chopped
salt and pepper

To make the pastry, add the butter to the flour and rub in. Add the egg yolk, the salt, and enough water to form a firm dough. Chill for 30 minutes.

Preheat the oven to 350°F. Roll out the pastry as thinly as possible and use to line an 8-inch tart or flan pan. Prick the bottom with a fork, and bake in the oven for 15–20 minutes or until pale golden brown and cooked through.

Meanwhile, purée all the filling ingredients and pass through a sieve. Pour into the pastry case and bake at 325°F for 30–40 minutes or until set.

GAZPACHO

In my version of this famous Spanish soup, I purée all the ingredients to a fine consistency. I then add the main vegetables, i.e., peppers, onion, tomato, and cucumber, afterward, together with croûtons and some chopped mint.

Half the olive oil is puréed into the soup, the rest is stirred in later, which gives it a nice oily sheen. Also, the reason for using partly ice, as opposed to just water, allows the soup to be made very much at the last minute, as it is instantly chilled.

6 tbsp red wine vinegar
1 cup water
1 cucumber, peeled and chopped
1 small red bell pepper, cored, seeded, and chopped
1 small green bell pepper, cored, seeded, and chopped
1 lb very ripe, full-flavored tomatoes, peeled and chopped, or 7 fl oz
passata (commercially made strained tomatoes)
2 garlic cloves, peeled and chopped
1 small onion, chopped
8 drops of Tabasco sauce
2 mint sprigs, leaves only
1 tbsp tomato ketchup
salt and pepper
1¼ lb ice cubes
1 cup olive oil

For the garnish

3 tbsp finely chopped mixed peppers, onion, tomato, and cucumber
croûtons made from 2 slices of white bread, cubed and fried in olive oil
8 mint leaves, chopped

Purée all the soup ingredients together, apart from half the olive oil. Pass through a coarse sieve, pressing down well on the vegetables. Stir in the reserved olive oil.

Pour into a chilled glass bowl, tip in the chopped vegetables and the croûtons, and sprinkle on the mint and serve.

CHILLED PIMIENTO SOUP WITH BASIL

4 red bell peppers, roasted, peeled, and seeded (see Pimiento Salsa, page 149)
2 cups light chicken stock
6 large ripe tomatoes, peeled and seeded
1 large garlic clove, peeled and crushed
½ cup olive oil
2 tbsp balsamic vinegar
15–20 basil leaves
1–2 small fresh red chillies, seeded
salt

In a blender, purée all the ingredients, reserving six basil leaves. Pass through a fine sieve into a large white bowl and chill thoroughly. When serving, place an ice cube in each bowl (I like to do this because it keeps the soup cold as you eat it), and garnish with the reserved basil, torn into shreds.

PORK PIECES AND BACON BITS

I have always found that if you want to eat the tastiest and most interesting pieces of pork, then you should go to a Cantonese restaurant. They do belly pork in many different ways: slow-roasted with soy; roasted until the skin is like sandpaper; braised in stock with garlic and aniseed; and various one-dish "hot-pots" where pieces of meat are cooked with oysters, eel, bean curd, pork kidney and liver, and many other ingredients too numerous to mention. In China, every bit of a pig is used.

The same goes for France. A charcuterie is one of my favorite places to dip into on travels in that country. I can't resist looking at the trays of porky things such as museau (sliced pork brawn, or "head cheese" as the Americans call it), pork chops that have been made into a confit, smeared with fat and ready to be added to a pot of haricot vert beans and braised in the oven. Myriad sausages, both dried as in salamis and saucisson sec, and others, such as cervelas and saucisson de Lyon, which will be boiled and served with lentils or hot potato salad. Then there are the dried hams, such as jambon de Bayonne, freshly cooked boiled hams, and knuckles of cured pork for choucroute. And there are always those lovely slabs of poitrine fumée, a smoked bacon that bears no resemblance to our lackluster, watery, ready-sliced, pre-packed version. This poitrine fumée is marvelous stuff. I only wish you could buy it outside of France because its smoky flavor is so pungent, and its texture is firm with an equal proportion of meat and fat that produces the best crisp bacon you will ever eat.

The Italians call this bacon pancetta. It appears in two forms. One is exactly like poitrine fumée, and the other is unsmoked and comes in a long sausage. Its center is like the lean part of back bacon (the loin) and rolled round it is the belly. It has a deep and strong cure—like bacon used to have—and is, once again, dry and meaty with just the right amount of fat. This sort of bacon is perfect for putting into a beef stew or a coq au vin. The smell of it frying in its own fat is one of the best. You can find this in good Italian grocers.

It is a shame that here in Britain we actually haven't progressed further than roast pork with sage and onion stuffing and applesauce, and sausages. I know that there are artisan pork butchers dotted around here and there—particularly in the West Country—but they are very few and far between. There used to be good-quality, homemade brawn in any self-respecting butcher's shop, but not so much now. Have we become so sophisticated and health-conscious that we only like our pork in neat little fillets or a well-trimmed chop? Even more perversely, you will find a hearty and gutsy dish that has been over-refined so that it, too, loses its identity. Recently, on a visit to a smart new restaurant in London's West End, I ordered a dish of braised pig's head. What was odd was that the only parts of the head served were a small piece of cheek, a little tongue, and some brain. It came in a neat little bowl with some admittedly good gravy, but where was the ear and some of the lovely fatty skin?

A SAUCE TO SERVE WITH BOILED HAM

In *French Provincial Cooking* by Elizabeth David, I first came across the dish *Le Saupiquet des Amognes*. Mrs. David describes it as a "sauce piquante à la crème served with slices of ham fried in butter." She also goes on to say that it is a sauce "which is one well worth knowing." I agree. It is nicely old-fashioned, being a very rich sauce that is (a) thickened with flour and butter—very unfashionable—and, (b) uses lots of cream— very unhealthy. The dish originates in Burgundy, particularly around the region of Morvan, which is noted for its ham dishes.

The sauce is also particularly good with boiled salted ox or calves' tongue (see page 223).

4 shallots, peeled and finely chopped
6 tbsp white wine vinegar
3–4 juniper berries, crushed
6 tbsp white wine
2 tbsp butter
1 rounded tbsp all-purpose flour
1 cup strong beef stock
(use the recipe for Meat Glaze on page 204, and use the
stock before the final reduction)
¾ cup plus 2 tbsp heavy cream
salt and pepper

In a stainless steel or enamel pan, boil together and reduce the shallots, vinegar, juniper berries, and white wine until nearly all the liquid has been driven off.

Meanwhile, melt the butter in another pan, add the flour and make a roux. Heat the beef stock and add to the roux, using a whisk. Cook gently for a few minutes, then add to the reduced shallot mixture. Bring back to the boil, add the cream and seasoning, and allow to simmer very gently for 5 minutes or so. Strain through a fine sieve, check the seasoning, and the sauce is ready.

PROSCIUTTO WITH WARM WILTED GREENS

This recipe comes from *Chez Panisse Cooking* by Paul Bertolli with Alice Waters. The greens in question can be young spinach leaves, arugula, frisée, or, if available to you, Chinese greens, such as bok choy.

¼ tsp salt
2 tbsp red wine vinegar
1 large shallot, peeled and finely chopped
1 garlic clove, peeled and very finely chopped

pepper
4 tbsp olive oil
3 large handfuls of greens (about 9 oz), washed and dried
12 very thin slices of prosciutto

Dissolve the salt in the vinegar, stir in the shallot and garlic, add pepper to taste, and stir in the olive oil. Put the vinaigrette in a stainless steel bowl or wok large enough to hold the greens comfortably, and place over a low heat. Add the greens, toss them continually with a pair of tongs or two forks for about 1 minute or until they are slightly wilted but have not gone entirely limp. Remove from the heat, and working directly from the bowl, place a small mixture of greens loosely on each prosciutto slice. Roll up and serve while still warm.

OLD-FASHIONED PORK TERRINE

The texture of this terrine is vastly improved if it is hand-chopped with a large knife. It may be grated using the large-holed disk of a grater, but the result is not as good. This feeds many more than four people—probably about twelve in fact; making a terrine for four people is not practical.

12 oz pork fatback
2 lb shoulder of pork
8 oz lean bacon in one piece, rind removed
8 oz pork liver
2 tbsp butter
2 small onions, peeled and finely chopped
1 cup fresh white breadcrumbs
1 wineglass of dry white wine
3 tbsp brandy
4 garlic cloves, peeled and finely chopped
2 tbsp chopped flat-leaf parsley
10 sage leaves, finely chopped
½ tsp ground allspice
2 tsp herbes de Provence
2 level tsp ground black pepper
2 tsp salt

Preheat the oven to 325°F. Cut 4 oz of pork fatback into thin slices and use them to line a 3-pint dish, reserving two or three slices for the top. (The shape of the container is up to you. It could be the traditional oval terra cotta dish with a lid, or the neater rectangular porcelain or orange cast-iron type made by Le Creuset.) Having done this, cut the remaining fat into small dice. Do the same to the pork shoulder, bacon, and liver. Put them all together on a chopping board. Using a large knife, mix thoroughly by further chopping until all three ingredients are a uniform mass. Place in a large bowl.

Melt the butter in a frying pan and cook the onions until pale gold. Cool and add to the meat together with all the other ingredients. Take a small amount of the mixture and fry in a little oil until cooked through. Allow to cool and taste for seasoning. Pack the mixture into the terrine and cover with the reserved slices of pork fat. Put the lid on (or cover with aluminum foil) and cook in a bain-marie using a deep enough roasting pan so that the water will come three-quarters of the way up the dish. Cook in the oven for about 1½ hours.

Remove from the oven, lift out of the roasting pan, and pour away the water. Return to the empty pan and uncover. The terrine will have slightly shrunk away from the edges and be surrounded by meat juices and fat. Insert a thin skewer into the middle of the terrine, hold it there and count to five, then hold it against your bottom lip. If it is hot, *not warm*, then it is cooked. Allow to rest for 10 minutes.

If the lid of the terrine is suitable, then invert it and weight it down to press the terrine. If not, then a small piece of wood cut to fit the top of the terrine, wrapped in plastic wrap and then foil, may be used instead. Press for at least 30 minutes, during which time juices and fat will have come to the surface or poured over the edge of the dish. If it is the latter, then return these juices to the terrine. Replace the lid, allow to cool completely, then put in the fridge. Wait for 3 days before consuming. Eat with crusty bread and gherkins.

SLOW-BRAISED BELLY PORK WITH SOY, GINGER, AND GARLIC

Braised belly pork given this treatment ends up as a wondrously tender and melting piece of meat. The recipe has evolved from various ideas, with both European and Asian influences. Most of the time it ends up slightly different from the time before, with a lot of trial and error, but that's the fascination of cooking.

The right thing to serve with this would be some briefly fried spinach or, if you happen to live near an oriental supermarket, then get some bok choy (Chinese greens) and some egg noodles.

4 pints water
4 lb belly pork, in one piece, rind and bones intact
¾ cup dry sherry or sake
3 star anise
2-inch cinnamon stick
15 thin diagonal slices of fresh root ginger

½ tsp (or less) dried chilli flakes
1⅓ cups good-quality soy sauce
1 tbsp red currant jelly
6 tbsp balsamic vinegar
30 garlic cloves
6–7 spring onions, trimmed and thinly sliced into shreds
cilantro sprigs
1 large red chilli, seeded and cut into thin strips

Bring the water to the boil in a shallow pan that the pork will fit into quite snugly, but with a few gaps to spare. Put in the pork and when it comes back to the boil, remove any scum. Add the sherry or sake and simmer for 30 minutes. Add the spices, ginger, chilli flakes, soy, red currant jelly, and balsamic vinegar. Bring back to the boil and simmer, covered, on a very low heat or in a very low oven for 2–3 hours, carefully turning the meat from time to time. Add the garlic after 1 hour of cooking.

When a thin skewer inserted into the meat offers absolutely no resistance, then the meat is cooked. Gently remove onto a serving dish along with the pieces of ginger and garlic, and keep warm. Reduce the sauce until of a syrupy consistency but watch out for excess saltiness due to the soy sauce, so keep tasting.

Spoon the sauce over the meat and strew with the spring onions, cilantro sprigs, and chilli. The meat can be eaten with a spoon, the bones will just slip out and the fat and rind will be lusciously soft and melting.

PETIT SALÉ AUX LENTILLES

This is a French country classic, though I suppose one could say that boiled bacon and split peas would be our English version. To cheat, it would be perfectly acceptable to buy some good-quality bacon in a piece, and to use that instead of salting your own.

4 lb belly pork, in one piece, rind and bones intact
1 quantity Brine (see page 224)
12 oz Puy lentils (the brown ones are a perfectly good alternative)
12 small carrots, peeled
20 pearl onions, peeled
12 tender celery sticks, cut into 3-inch pieces
2 bay leaves
3 cloves (stuck into the carrots or the onions)
2 thyme sprigs
¼ cup butter

salt and pepper
2 tbsp chopped flat-leaf parsley

For the sauce

Dijon mustard
½ cup heavy cream

Soak the pork in the brine for 3 days, then drain and place in a large pot. Cover with cold water, bring to the boil, and drain again. Put the pork back in the pot and cover with 3 pints water. Poach gently for 30 minutes. Add the lentils, vegetables, herbs, and spices, and continue cooking on a very low heat, stirring from time to time, for a further 1 hour or until the lentils and vegetables are tender. Remove the pork and keep warm. Stir the butter into the hot lentils for added richness, check the seasoning, and stir in the parsley. Pour into a warmed deep oval serving dish, slice the pork, leaving the bones intact, and lay on top. Serve with a little mustard sauce, made by simply whisking the mustard into the heavy cream.

POTATOES

You only have to look through *In Praise of the Potato*, by Lindsey Bareham, to find lots of ideas for the humble tuber. If a whole book can be written on the subject of potatoes, I had better restrict myself somewhat.

It is difficult to say what preparation appeals to me most when cooking potatoes. Mashed comes directly to mind, particularly when made with fruity olive oil instead of butter. The olive oil idea came from *Cuisine Spontanée* by Frédy Girardet. His recipe uses new potatoes, which I think is odd, but I thank him for the tip. Also, I adore that triumph of French inventions, the gratin dauphinois, and, of course, simple pommes frites.

Lindsey suggests that Arran Comet, Maris Peer, Ulster Sceptre, Desirée, King Edward, Maris Piper, and Pentland Dell are the best varieties for frites. Whichever type you decide to use, the other most important step is wash, wash, wash. Removing the starch from the potato allows it to crisp more easily; otherwise you will end up with a limp affair soon after initially feeling crisp.

There is much debate about which is the best oil to use. Where I come from in Lancashire it was always beef dripping. In Belgium it is reputed that horse fat is used for making what are considered to be Europe's finest chips. Peanut oil is probably the most successful universally available oil.

I almost cannot contain my excitement when the first tiny Jersey Royals arrive. Just boiled for a few minutes with a sprig of mint and lashings of butter, they are to me a treat in the same class as caviar and truffles. Incidentally, these two luxuries probably go better with potatoes than with anything else.

Roast potatoes made from big King Edwards (always cut across the widest section lengthways) are a nibbler's delight. My all-time favorite leftover is a lukewarm crusty-edged roast potato spread with fresh horseradish that is so pungent it makes your nose run.

And another fond memory is of a roasted potato cake called Pommes Bernaise at the restaurant Chez L'Ami Louis in Paris. I tasted it eleven years ago on a first visit to Paris. A Parisian friend, called Hubert, took me there for Sunday lunch. He had first been taken there by his father in the 1930s. As far as he could remember, this potato cake had not changed one bit in all that time. The proprietor, Monsieur Magnin, sadly, died four years ago. He was ninety-three and was one of the best "rôtisseurs" (roast cooks) I have ever come across. I would say that M. Magnin's roast chicken, cooked in a wood-fired oven, and this potato cake, are what this book is all about.

Remember, when cooking potatoes, to treat them with respect. They haven't always had their fair share of that.

ROAST POTATOES WITH OLIVE OIL, ROSEMARY, AND GARLIC

The secret of this is to parboil the potatoes as far as you dare and to use enough olive oil so that the potato has enough of it to "oven-fry" rather than roast.

2 lb russet potatoes, peeled and cut into 1-inch chunks
salt and pepper
2 heads of garlic, broken into cloves, peeled and bruised
1 cup pure olive oil (not virgin)
a few rosemary sprigs
1 tbsp red wine vinegar

Parboil the potatoes in salted water until they are pretty well cooked through, and drain carefully by lifting them out with a slotted spoon into a tray. Preheat the oven to 450°F. Dry out the potatoes in the oven if necessary before roasting. Meanwhile, blanch the garlic cloves in boiling water for 10 minutes, and drain.

Heat a heavy-bottomed ovenproof dish or large frying pan with a metal handle that will fit in the oven. Pour in the olive oil and heat until hot but not smoking, add the potatoes, and season with salt and pepper. Allow them to soak up and be coated with the oil but give them the minimum of handling. Add the garlic and tuck in sprigs of rosemary. Put in the oven and roast for about 30–40 minutes, turning the potatoes over from time to time. The end result should be golden brown nuggets of crunch with a gooey potato inside; the garlic cloves will have puffed up, will have a crisp skin, and will be equally gooey. Drain the potatoes in a colander and leave to allow excess olive oil to seep out. (This can be used again like dripping.) Tip the potatoes into a hot serving dish and spoon over the vinegar.

Depending on your oven and the dish you are cooking them in, the time needed can vary considerably, so go by instinct and taste rather than exact instructions. But then, that's what good cooking is all about.

POTATO CAKES

My mother makes really good potato cakes. They are sort of misshapen, soft, gooey, and floury. They are at their best eaten on a Sunday afternoon, melting in front of the fire in their pool of butter. It should be winter, about 5 p.m., dark outside, and a Marx Brothers film has just finished on the television.

1 lb dry mashed potato
1 scant cup all-purpose flour, sifted
salt and pepper
oil or clarified butter for frying
up to 8 tbsp extra butter

Lightly mix together the potato and flour, and season generously. With floured hands, form the mixture into little cakes about 2½ inches in diameter. Heat the oil or clarified butter, preferably in a nonstick pan, and fry until golden brown on both sides. Don't overcrowd the pan, so do them in batches. Keep warm in a low oven, adding flecks of butter here and there so that they soak it up. Serve with plenty of napkins.

Another potato cake you might enjoy is the one called Crêpes Parmentier, which you will find in the chicken chapter (see page 31). It is more like a pancake and is a marvelous base for all sorts of toppings and embellishments.

FRENCH FRIES

Good fries are not possible unless you fry them twice. The initial blanching in oil is purely for cooking the potato throughout without coloring it. You could, in fact, boil your fries in water and then fry them, which would produce wonderfully fluffy and moist fries. However, this is not really practical, as most fries, because of their shape and thinness, would collapse into the water. The time between the initial blanching and the final brief frying in hot oil can be a few hours, so any worry about making fries and the imagined bother involved, can be forgotten.

4 large russet potatoes, peeled

peanut oil for deep-frying

salt

Depending on whether you like your fries thin or thick, cut the potatoes lengthways into the appropriate thickness. Then wash under cold running water until the water is clear and rid of all starch. Drain in a colander and leave to dry before frying.

In a suitable pan or an electric deep-fat fryer, heat the oil until it has reached 300°F. Do allow yourself plenty of oil, as the more you have in the pan, the less the temperature will drop when the fries are down! (This also applies to boiling green vegetables—the more fiercely boiling water you have surrounding asparagus, for instance, the quicker it will come back to the boil and the greener will be the asparagus.) Put in the fries—don't overcrowd—and fry for 6–7 minutes. Lift one out and check it with your fingers. It should be soft right through. If not, then give them another minute or so. Lift out the basket and allow to drain. Increase the temperature of the oil to 360°F, and continue cooking for between 30 seconds and 2 minutes. This time variance depends very much on the type of potato available at different times of the year. Certain potatoes just will not crisp, so see the suggestions on page 161, or ask your greengrocer which are best.

POTATO SALAD

A good potato salad comes very high on my list of favorite things to eat. Equally, a bad potato salad is one of the most disgusting. As with all things that are simple to prepare, they are not thought out with enough care because of their very simplicity, and therefore become slapdash.

There are two important things to remember when making potato salad: use waxy potatoes of even size, preferably new, even more preferably Jersey Royals or red or white new potatoes, and dress the potatoes while they are hot.

If the potatoes are Jersey Royals, then scrape off their skins before cooking; if they are another variety, and perhaps imported, then boil them in their skins but peel after cooking. There is nothing worse than eating a new potato with its skin on. People say it is better for you and more healthy. Nonsense, it's just laziness. Good imported new potatoes for this salad are varieties such as La Ratte and Belle de Fontenay. And, if you are lucky enough to come across them, the Pink Fir Apple.

1½ lb waxy potatoes
salt and pepper
4 mint sprigs
1 tbsp smooth Dijon mustard
2 tbsp red wine vinegar
6 tbsp vegetable oil
2 tbsp olive oil
a small bunch of spring onions, trimmed and finely chopped, or a bunch of chives, snipped

Boil the potatoes in well-salted water with the mint. Meanwhile, make the dressing by whisking together the mustard, vinegar, and seasoning, and whisking in the oils. Drain the potatoes and, depending upon which potato you are using, peel them or not. If the potatoes are very small, i.e., marble-sized, then leave them as they are. If they are walnut-sized, then slice them in half at their longest point. While still hot, dress the potatoes together with the spring onions in a large enough bowl that will allow maximum movement for even distribution of the dressing. Eat lukewarm.

POTATO, TOMATO, AND BASIL SOUP

This soup comes from the marvelous *Greens Cook Book* by Deborah Madison. It is excellent made with Jersey mids, when the price has dropped, as they give the best flavor. Do not be tempted to make this soup with maincrop (old) potatoes—it doesn't work. The recipe mentions that water is fine for the liquid, and don't be alarmed about the vinegar, it's quite remarkable how it transforms the taste of the soup.

¼ cup butter
2½ pints water
1 large white onion, peeled and finely chopped, or 2 bunches of spring
onions, trimmed and finely chopped
1 bay leaf
5 thyme sprigs
1½ lb new potatoes, washed and coarsely chopped
1 tsp salt
1 lb ripe tomatoes, skinned, seeded, and finely chopped
4 tbsp olive oil
a small bunch of basil, leaves only
red wine vinegar, to taste
pepper

Melt the butter in a large pan with a little of the water, and add the onion, bay leaf, and thyme. Stew over a low heat for a few minutes, then add the potatoes and salt. Cover and simmer for 5 minutes. Pour in the rest of the water and bring to the boil. Cook until the potatoes are falling apart. Pass the soup through a *mouli-légumes* and return to the pan. In a separate saucepan, fry the tomatoes with a little seasoning in 1 tbsp of the olive oil, and cook until their juices have evaporated and the tomatoes have thickened slightly. Whisk them together to make a semi-smooth sauce, and add them to the potato soup. Purée the basil, a splash of vinegar and salt, then add the remaining olive oil to make a dressing.

Serve the soup in individual bowls with a spoonful of the basil purée floating on top and a generous grinding of pepper. If the soup thickens between the time it is made and served, thin it with additional water or, if you prefer, a little cream.

RABBIT

My mother used to make a mean rabbit pie. This was wild rabbit, only available from the market occasionally and usually in the winter months. While it was cooking away in the Aga stove, it smelled much like hare and tasted like it, too, because of the cloves, juniper, and booze that cooked with it. But it was a real tasty bunny—none of those imported Chinese pieces, which were the only other choice then. These days, however, it is possible to obtain better quality farmed rabbits. They don't taste anything like wild ones but are none the worse for that. These are prepared and eaten in quite a different manner.

Wild rabbits are tough but flavorsome. Tame ones are fleshy, have pale, pinky-white meat, and require briefer cooking especially if sautéed or grilled. Also, they can happily be gently braised resulting in a melting pot of goodness. Any good rabbit, wild or tame, can also produce a fine pâté or terrine.

The best farmed rabbits I have tasted are French ones. And the first one I cooked was while holidaying in Provence with my friend Gay Bilson. We were the guests of Terence and Caroline Conran and were dispatched by Terence to Arles market early one morning to buy lunch. Terence said, "Get some rabbits. They are extremely good and we can grill them over olive wood in the garden." I had never cooked rabbit like this and I didn't know how they would turn out. These rabbits were a revelation—very large, well fattened, and as fresh as can be.

It was lunch for nine people. I had made some fish soup from tiny Mediterranean fish—none of which was bigger than a minnow—plus a hunk of conger eel for richness. Wild thyme and rosemary were picked from the surrounding countryside on the return journey. Dessert was to be some summer fruits. Raspberries, red currants, black currants, white currants, strawberries, and cherries, in a light sugar syrup and served with unpasteurized crème fraîche.

The rabbits were a sensation. Having first been marinated with a splash of local rosé, olive oil, garlic, and some of those heady herbs, they sizzled and spluttered and really just cooked themselves to perfection on the fire. I also threw on some wedges of eggplant, which blackened magnificently and accentuated their own smokiness.

On that occasion, Gay and I agreed that it was one of the best meals we had ever eaten. She kindly mentioned that, if I were to admit it, it was one of the best meals I had ever cooked. One tries not to have arguments with good friends on holiday.

BRAISED RABBIT WITH WHITE WINE, SHALLOTS, ROSEMARY, AND CREAM

This is the sort of recipe that is very easy to make, as it requires simple preparation on the stove with only a few ingredients and little effort. The end result is very satisfying and it is a good, rich dish.

2 small rabbits, each jointed into 6 pieces
salt and pepper
½ cup butter
6 shallots, peeled and chopped
½ 750 ml-bottle of dry white wine
4 rosemary sprigs
1½ cups whipping cream
juice of ½ lemon

Season the rabbit with salt and pepper. Melt the butter in a large, heavy-bottomed, shallow pan until foaming. Put in the rabbit pieces and turn the heat down. Gently fry for about 30 minutes or until pale golden brown, no more, turning from time to time. Lift out the rabbit pieces and put on a plate. Tip out any excess fat, leaving yourself with about 3 tbsp in the pan. Fry the shallots until pale gold and return the rabbit to the pan. Add about a quarter of the wine, and allow to simmer. Baste the rabbit pieces with the wine and shallots until it has become a syrupy sauce. Add a further splash of wine and carry on with this process until the wine has been used up and there is about a wineglass of liquid left in the pan. This should be tawny colored and syrupy. Add the rosemary, turn down to the lowest possible heat, cover, and allow to cook for a further 10 minutes. Remove the lid, add the cream, turn up the heat, and bring to the boil. Let the cream amalgamate with the sauce, making sure that you scrape up any bits in the bottom of the pan. Simmer until the sauce is a pale coffee color and of an unctuous consistency. Add the lemon juice and correct the seasoning. Serve with buttered noodles or boiled potatoes.

This is not a dish to be hurried, rather it is one that should be nurtured as you are pottering about the kitchen doing other chores.

STEWED RABBIT WITH BALSAMIC VINEGAR
AND PARSNIP PURÉE

This is another simple, gently cooked dish. It requires little extra liquid apart from the balsamic vinegar and a small amount of concentrated meat glaze.

2 small rabbits, each jointed into 6 pieces
salt and pepper
1 tbsp sugar
4 tbsp clarified butter (see page 31)
½ cup balsamic vinegar
4 tbsp concentrated Meat Glaze (see page 204)

For the parsnip purée

4 large parsnips, peeled and cut into chunks
2 cups milk
salt and pepper
6 tbsp butter
1 tbsp smooth Dijon mustard

Season the joints of rabbit and sprinkle with the sugar, turning them over with your hands to ensure an even coating. Heat the clarified butter in a large, heavy-bottomed, shallow stew pan. Gently fry the rabbit until the sugar has caramelized and turned the pieces of rabbit a rich, mahogany brown. Do be careful, as the sugar burns easily. Tip off any excess butter and add the balsamic vinegar and meat glaze. Allow to bubble, cover, and simmer extremely gently for 45 minutes–1 hour. Check regularly that the liquid has not boiled dry, and if it does add a little water plus a touch more balsamic.

Meanwhile, simmer the parsnips in the milk, seasoned with salt and pepper, until tender. Drain, reserving the milk, and process to a purée with the butter and mustard, adding a little of the reserved milk when necessary. To achieve a super-smooth texture, it is worth passing the purée through a fine sieve. Keep warm.

Uncover the rabbit and check the sauce; there shouldn't be much, but if there is, reduce it to a sweet sticky syrup that will just about coat the pieces of rabbit. Transfer to a serving dish and offer the purée separately.

RABBIT TERRINE

Rabbit makes a tasty terrine that is neither too gamey nor nondescript, as many terrines can be. I think it is important to take the time and trouble to hand-chop the ingredients for terrines. The resultant texture produces a nice chunky mouthful, and it allows the separate ingredients to speak for themselves.

1 small rabbit with its liver and heart, boned to give about 8 oz meat
4 oz pork fatback
9 oz skinless pork belly
3 oz pork fillet
4 bacon slices
1 onion, peeled and finely chopped
2 garlic cloves, peeled and finely chopped
¼ cup butter
1 egg
1 heaped tsp herbes de Provence
2 tbsp fresh breadcrumbs
½ small wine glass of Cognac
salt and pepper

Preheat the oven to 325°F. Finely dice the rabbit (with its liver and heart), fatback, pork belly, pork fillet, and bacon. When this is all done, put it all together in the middle of your largest chopping board. With a heavy knife, mix and chop all the meats together to form a cohesive mass. Tip into a mixing bowl. Fry the onion and garlic in the butter and add to the rabbit mixture with all the other ingredients. Mix thoroughly. Pack into a terrine of 1¼-pint capacity, press down well, cover with aluminum foil or wax paper, and bake in a bain-marie (water bath) for 1–1½ hours. The cooked terrine will have shrunk away from the edges and be surrounded by clear fat. Press with a light weight if you want a dense and firm terrine, and leave to cool. Serve from the dish with some gherkins.

ROASTED LEG OF RABBIT WITH BACON
AND A MUSTARD SAUCE

The rabbit that you use for this dish should be the French-farmed variety. They are tender, large, and succulent. If you find it impossible to obtain one and make do with a smaller variety, then you may have to serve two legs per person. A wild rabbit will not do. If you have an enterprising butcher, then hopefully you can buy just the rabbit legs. If not, then buy two rabbits and use the remaining parts for another dish.

4 rabbit legs
½ cup unsalted butter, softened
1 garlic clove, peeled and chopped
1 tbsp chopped fresh tarragon

1 tbsp chopped fresh parsley
grated rind of 1 lemon
salt and pepper
20 thin bacon slices

For the mustard sauce

1½ cups whipping cream
2 tbsp smooth Dijon mustard
salt and pepper

Preheat the oven to 425°F. With a small sharp knife, remove the thigh bone from the rabbit leg by forming a little tunnel around the bone rather than coming through from the side. This is only slightly tricky and just takes a little time and trouble. Mix together the butter, garlic, tarragon, parsley, lemon, and seasoning. Divide this among the four cavities and wrap each leg with five slices of bacon, then place on a lightly buttered baking tray. Make sure that the ends of each slice meet on the underside. Roast the legs in the oven for about 10 minutes until crisp and golden brown. Remove from the oven and leave to rest for a further 10 minutes in a warm place (back in the oven with the door ajar, for instance). Meanwhile, make the sauce. Simply heat the cream with 1 tbsp of the mustard and a little salt and pepper. Simmer for 5 minutes or so until slightly thickened. Keep warm. To serve, cut three slices from the bulbous end of each leg and, being careful to collect the herby juices, arrange neatly on four plates. Sit the bony part upright alongside the slices. Add the second spoonful of mustard to the sauce, whisk, reheat, and serve separately in a sauce-boat. A dish of plain boiled potatoes and a green salad would be a fitting accompaniment.

SAFFRON

It is unfortunate that saffron carries a "luxury food" tag, for it is the most beguiling of culinary flavors. It is the world's most expensive spice; it takes 20,000 crocus stigmas to yield 4 oz of saffron. Saffron often comes from Spain and other Mediterranean countries, but the best I have ever come across is Indian.

The pungency and color that result from its addition to a soup or stew, risotto, or ragoût is, to my mind, worth all the expense. You will not need much and a generous pinch is enough—two generous pinches will work wonders.

Because its flavor is unique and so individual, it marries well with a great many preparations, both sweet and savory. It can be used in cakes and biscuits, custards and creams, with vegetables and legumes, eggs and rice, and in endless sauces, dressings, and purées. But with fish, particularly fish soups and stews, is where saffron comes into its own.

I was once enjoying a particularly fine bouillabaise at a restaurant called Michel in Marseille. This was about ten years ago and I had never eaten this fabled dish before. The unfamiliar fish that were to be included were displayed at the entrance to the restaurant. I had never seen such splendid specimens. Glistening skins and scales, and stiff with rigor mortis freshness. There was rascasse, wrasse, red mullet, John Dory, monkfish, sea bass, and a gigantic length of conger eel. All these were included whole or in chunks for my mammoth lunch to come. They were stewed in what I can only describe as a distillation of all things fishy. And this particular fish broth was the burnished terra cotta line of a Provençal roof tile. There would have been many tomatoes added, some white wine, and of course saffron. The strong and fiery paste called rouille added extra pungency and the dish arrived with some boiled potatoes on the side. These had also been cooked in the soup and were yellow; saffron stains soaked up by the soft potato.

When I had finished eating the fish, I found myself—as one does—crushing the potatoes into the soup dregs. An interesting thought occurred to me. Mashed potatoes, creamed with saffron, using olive oil instead of butter and adding a little garlic (to account for the remnants of rouille left in the plate) could be a dish in its own right.

Well, all I can say is that it works brilliantly and I urge you to make it. It is one dish that I can truly call my own.

SAFFRON MASHED POTATOES

If you are going to serve these potatoes with fish, then it is nice to cook them in fish stock. If you are not, then don't bother.

2 lb russet potatoes, peeled and cut into chunks
salt
a generous tsp saffron threads
1 large garlic clove, peeled and finely chopped
¾ cup plus 2 tbsp whole milk
¾ cup plus 2 tbsp virgin olive oil
Tabasco sauce, to taste

Boil the potatoes in fish stock or water with some salt. Heat together the saffron, garlic, and milk, cover, and infuse while the potatoes are boiling. Add the olive oil to the milk infusion and gently reheat. Drain and mash the potatoes—I think the best texture achieved is through a *mouli-légumes*. Put the potatoes in the bowl of an electric mixer, switch on, and add the saffron mixture in a steady stream. Add Tabasco to taste and adjust the seasoning. Allow the purée to sit in a warm place for about 30 minutes so that the saffron flavor is fully developed.

ROUILLE

Apart from being essential to fish soup, this is a wonderful pungent sauce in its own right and could be used as a dip for all sorts of things—deep-fried calamari, goujons of sole, or grilled chicken, for instance. It is also delicious smeared on a baked potato.

2 hard-boiled egg yolks
2 egg yolks
½ tsp saffron threads
3 anchovy fillets
1 garlic clove, peeled and crushed
1 tsp tomato purée
1 tsp mustard
pepper and a little salt
1 tsp lemon juice
8 drops of Tabasco, or more to taste
1 cup plus 2 tbsp olive oil

Blend the first 10 ingredients in a blender until smooth. Add the oil in a thin stream, until the rouille is thoroughly homogenized.

SAFFRON CREAM DRESSING

This is a delicious lotion for shellfish of all sorts, white crab meat particularly, but lobster, shrimp, scallops, etc., are good, too.

1 tsp saffron threads infused in 2 tbsp boiling water
juice of ½ lemon
salt
pinch of cayenne
1 tsp smooth Dijon mustard
¾ cup heavy cream

Mix together the saffron, lemon juice, salt, pepper, and Dijon mustard. (Do not use a whisk, as all the saffron threads get tangled up in it.) Leave to infuse for 5 minutes. Stir in the cream. Use straight away, as if kept for too long it becomes too thick.

SAFFRON SOUP WITH MUSSELS

½ cup butter
2 large onions, peeled and very finely chopped
2 garlic cloves, peeled and finely chopped
2 tbsp Pernod
½ 750 ml-bottle dry white wine
1 bay leaf
1 thyme sprig
1 cup light chicken stock
2 ¼ lb mussels, de-bearded, thoroughly scrubbed and washed
2 waxy, all-purpose potatoes, peeled and diced
1 tsp saffron threads
salt and pepper
½ cup heavy cream
2 tarragon sprigs, leaves only, finely chopped
lemon juice, to taste
croûtons, to serve

Melt the butter and in it cook very gently the onions and garlic until pale golden. Add the Pernod, allow to froth, then pour in the white wine. Add the herbs. Bring to the boil and simmer gently for 15 minutes, uncovered. Add the chicken stock and reheat.

Put the mussels in a large pot and strain the soup over them. Leave the onion in the sieve, because it's going back into the soup. Bring the mussels to the boil until they are *just* open. Drain them and keep the liquor. Strain this through a very fine sieve or cheesecloth back into the original soup pan; this is to catch any grains of sand or bits of shell. Return the onion to the broth, discarding the bay leaf and thyme, and add the potatoes and saffron, salt, and pepper. Bring back to the boil and simmer until the potato is tender. Keep warm.

Shell the mussels, watching out for any reluctant beards, and discard any that aren't open. Put them into the soup. Reheat with the cream and tarragon, and lemon juice to taste. Finally, adjust the seasoning and serve with croûtons.

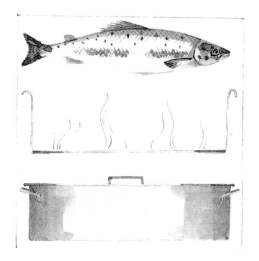

SALMON

In my view there is no substitute for seasonal wild salmon caught from our rivers in the British Isles. Many, I know, disagree with me and would wish to put me to the test and see if I could tell the difference between a fish from the Tay and a bright red, too-evenly textured specimen from a computer-controlled farming station. Let's face it, flavor and texture are paramount. The very appearance of a fine wild salmon is a joy to behold. Its life has been full of adventure. Swimming up and down river and stream, out to sea and back, leaping up gushing waterfalls and spawning in the most natural way.

When you see the real thing alongside its lowly pretender on a fishmonger's slab, all is revealed. Shining, glossy skin with large scales, a resolute firmness of flesh, prominent well-formed fins and tail, and a brightness of eye.

Its neighbor, however, sports stunted growth in the fin and tail departments, and has softer flesh. After all, man cannot "farm" characteristics.

It is very easy to cook salmon. Its fatty makeup allows a few degrees of heat either way that will not spoil the texture or taste of the fish. That is not to say that you can put it on a low heat and go out to the pub.

Like many fish (or for that matter meat or poultry), its taste and texture are far superior when cooked on the bone. This applies to a whole fish, a piece cut from it, or even a steak. That is not to say that salmon cannot be enjoyed as a fillet; indeed, for some recipes it is essential.

I love whole salmon poached in a good court-bouillon (vegetables, a splash of wine, herbs), simply lifted off the bone, skinned, and served with hollandaise sauce, new potatoes, and a cucumber salad dressed with a little wine vinegar. It is the perfect summer lunch.

When I was a child this was a special Saturday night supper, always cooked by my father. The smells emanating from the kitchen said summer had arrived. Apple mint in the new potatoes; the aroma of cucumber mixed with vinegar, parsley being minced (he used a funny multi-chopper that always left a deep green ring on the chopping board) and fresh peas simmering. Also the slightly nutty smell of butter seeping out of the foil-wrapped salmon cooking in the oven (we didn't have a fish kettle and if you don't have one either this is another successful way to cook salmon).

Thinking of other ways of cooking salmon, a fond memory of a delicious supper cooked by a friend several years ago comes to mind. This was a small fish weighing around 5 lb. It had been gutted, its head removed, and the scales scraped off. Its skin had been rubbed with salt. The friend in question had a very well-equipped kitchen that included a huge heavy cast-iron frying pan into which she melted much farmhouse butter. The pan amply accommodated the whole fish and it was vigorously fried until the skin attained the texture of sandpaper.

All that was served with this fabulous fish were peas and pink fir apple potatoes gathered from her garden that very evening. Butter from the frying of the fish, and some cut lemons were the only accompaniments.

It just goes to show that simple preparations, good ingredients, and a confidence in what you feel to be just right is the key to good food.

FANFARE

George Perry-Smith

I would like here to sing the praises of George Perry-Smith, one of the great pioneers who changed the eating habits of an apathetic British public. Alongside Kenneth Bell, Francis Coulson, Ray Parkes, William Heptinstall, and others, George Perry-Smith breathed new life into the hearts of a post-war restaurant-going public.

He made his name at The Hole in the Wall in Bath, which he opened in the late 1950s. And Elizabeth David was his biggest influence.

An early menu from the 1960s that I have would not be out of place today. Moreover, it reads like a testament of sensibility, good taste, and fine tradition—much in fact that is missing in a fiercely competitive restaurant scene today. Only the prices seem mythical.

With much respect and a great deal of admiration, I hereby salute you, George, with my version of your most famous creation.

SALMON IN PASTRY WITH CURRANTS AND GINGER

I think this derives from an old English recipe where sweet ingredients were often used with meat and fish. It may sound odd to use preserved ginger together with further sweetness from the currants, but it works like a dream.

12 oz brioche paste or puff pastry
3–4 globes of preserved (stem) ginger
2 tbsp currants
½ cup butter, softened
salt and pepper
a pinch of ground mace
1½ lb filleted salmon, skinned and boned, cut from a central piece
1 egg yolk

Divide the brioche paste or puff pastry into four 3-oz pieces. Roll out very thinly to approximately 5-inch squares and chill on a lightly floured pan in the fridge. Cut the stem ginger into slivers, and pour a little boiling water on the currants and leave to swell up for 5–10 minutes. Drain the currants and stir into the butter together with the ginger, salt and pepper, and the mace. Divide the salmon into four equal pieces and spread each one with the seasoned butter. Chill. Mix the egg yolk with a little water and with a pastry brush paint one side of each piece of pastry. Place each piece of salmon in the middle of the eggy side, butter-side down, and form a parcel with the join on top. Now turn the parcel over so that the butter-side of the fish is uppermost. Chill once more for about 30 minutes. Meanwhile preheat the oven to 400°F. Brush the parcels of salmon with more egg yolk, mark a crisscross pattern, if desired, with a small knife, and place on a buttered baking sheet. Cook for 20–30 minutes or until golden brown.

George Perry-Smith used to serve a sauce Messine with this—an herb and cream sauce sharpened with lemon juice. I prefer a hollandaise sauce lightened with whipped cream. But as the dish itself is very rich, it is equally nice just served with a wedge of lemon. A big bunch of watercress and some new potatoes are all the accompaniments necessary.

POACHED SALMON WITH BEURRE BLANC

One might say that this recipe is old-hat but the combination of salmon with this classic French sauce is truly remarkable. There have been many recipes for beurre blanc in many books and too many comments about its trickiness. It is in fact very easy.

I first tasted beurre blanc in the Loire valley when I was about twelve. It was served with local salmon and I shall never forget its buttercup yellow color, sweet yet sour taste, and its divine richness. The very finest chopped shallots had been left in the sauce. These days they are often sieved out, which is a shame because then it just becomes another little butter sauce. To add cream is heresy, and so is using onions in place of shallots. Also, some people suggest using white wine and vinegar or just white wine. I find that white wine is unnecessary. Just vinegar with a little water is the right thing to do.

For the court-bouillon

2 pints water
2 carrots, peeled and sliced
1 large onion, peeled and sliced
1 celery stick, sliced
2 cloves
a few peppercorns
2 bay leaves
1 tbsp salt
2 tbsp white wine vinegar
2-lb piece of wild salmon on the bone

For the beurre blanc

6 tbsp white wine vinegar
¼ cup water
4 shallots, peeled and very finely chopped
salt and white pepper
1 cup cold, unsalted butter, cut into cubes
a squeeze of lemon juice

Put all the ingredients for the court-bouillon in a large pan, preferably stainless steel or enamel. Bring to the boil and simmer for 20 minutes. Slip in the salmon, bring back to the boil, switch off the heat, cover, and leave for 20–30 minutes. The fish should easily be cooked through after this time, but a few minutes longer left in this liquid is not going to spoil the fish.

To make the beurre blanc, take a small stainless steel or enamel pan and in it put the vinegar, water, and chopped shallots. Add a pinch of salt and a grinding of pepper. Over a high heat, reduce until all the liquid has evaporated. Over the lowest thread of heat, whisk in the butter piece by piece until all has been incorporated. The result should be of a consistency similar to thin cream. Taste for seasoning and add lemon juice to taste. Keep warm.

Carefully lift the salmon out of the court-bouillon. Remove the skin and lift the flesh off the bones onto a warmed dish. Serve with boiled potatoes, a fresh green vegetable such as string beans, and hand the sauce separately.

GRILLED SALMON, SAUCE VERTE, AND FENNEL SALAD

To cook salmon in this way, with the skin intact, produces a marvelous crust with the flesh of the fish being just cooked. The accompanying sauce is aromatic and mayonnaise-like in consistency and the fennel salad provides a nice crunchy contrast. You will need a stove-top cast-iron ribbed grill for this dish.

1½-lb piece of boned fillet of salmon, scaled but not skinned, cut into 4 pieces
a little olive oil
1 tbsp Maldon sea salt
pepper

For the salad

2 fennel bulbs, well trimmed and very thinly sliced
salt and pepper
juice of 1 lemon
3 tbsp olive oil

For the sauce

a bunch of flat-leaf parsley, leaves only
a bunch of watercress, leaves only
4 tarragon sprigs, leaves only
4 mint sprigs, leaves only
10 basil leaves
2 anchovy fillets
1 quantity aïoli made with half the amount of garlic (see page 29)

Put the fennel in a bowl, season with salt and pepper, add lemon juice, and mix thoroughly. Spoon over the olive oil and leave to marinate.

Preheat the grill. Bring a large pan of water to the boil, throw in the parsley and watercress leaves, give a quick stir, and drain. Rinse briefly with cold water and squeeze dry in a tea towel. Chop the tarragon, mint, and basil leaves with the anchovies until extremely fine. Do the same to the parsley and watercress, and stir all of them into the aïoli. Check the seasoning and sharpen with a little extra lemon juice if necessary.

Brush the skin side of the salmon with olive oil and sprinkle evenly with the Maldon salt. Grind pepper over the flesh side. Place on the grill, skin side down, and cook for about 3–5 minutes or until the skin is well crisped and almost blackened. Turn over and cook on the flesh side for about the same amount of time. Transfer to a hot plate and rest in a lukewarm oven for 5 minutes. Arrange on individual plates together with the fennel salad and a spoonful of the sauce verte. Serve with lemon wedges if you wish.

POACHED SALMON, HOLLANDAISE SAUCE, AND PICKLED CUCUMBER

Although this is another traditional, and one might think uninspired, recipe, it is one of the nicest ways to eat salmon. Hollandaise and salmon were made for each other and the cucumber salad is just delicious.

For the cooking of the salmon, follow the recipe for Poached Salmon with Beurre Blanc (see page 181).

1½ lb salmon, on the bone
1 quantity court-bouillon (see page 181)

For the hollandaise

¾ cup unsalted butter
2 egg yolks
salt and pepper
juice of ½ lemon

For the pickled cucumber

1 cucumber, peeled and thinly sliced
3 tbsp white wine vinegar
½ tbsp chopped fresh dill
salt and pepper
½ tbsp sugar

Place all the ingredients for the pickled cucumber in a bowl and mix thoroughly. Leave to marinate.

Melt the butter, leave to rest for a few moments, and skim off the froth that will collect on top. Whisk the 2 egg yolks with a splash of cold water over a very low heat until thick. Continue whisking while adding the melted butter. Incorporate all of it but leave the milky residue behind. Season and add the lemon juice.

Fillet and skin the cooked salmon and serve with some new potatoes. Serve the pickled cucumber and the hollandaise separately.

CEVICHE OF SALMON

For this recipe I use a basic salsa, as ceviche itself derives from Mexico and is, when all's said and done, raw fish "cooked" (i.e., marinated) in lime juice. The other basic ingredient in ceviche is usually just onion but together with the tomato, cilantro, and chilli, this dish comes into its own. The chopped and seasoned avocado is an addition of my own and closely resembles that other Mexican favorite, guacamole.

1 lb fillet of salmon, skinned and boned
4 ripe tomatoes, peeled, seeded, and finely chopped
green chillies, seeded and chopped, to taste (I would use between 4 and 6 small hot chillies, which will produce quite a fiery ceviche)
juice of 2 limes
1 small red onion, peeled and finely chopped
1 bunch of cilantro, leaves only
salt

For the guacamole

2 small ripe avocados
1 garlic clove, peeled and finely chopped
juice of 1 lime
2 tbsp olive oil
salt and pepper

Cut the salmon into chunky slivers and mix together with the tomatoes, chillies, lime juice, and onion. Chop the cilantro leaves coarsely and add to the mixture, and season. Leave to marinate for about 1 hour but no longer; any longer than this and the fish will be too "cooked."

Meanwhile, peel the avocados, coarsely chop, and put in a bowl. Mix with the garlic, lime juice, olive oil, and seasoning.

The nicest way to serve this dish is to put a bowl of ceviche and a bowl of the avocado on the table, and let people help themselves. Serve with crusty bread or, to be really authentic, corn chips. Also a bowl of sour cream is an added indulgence.

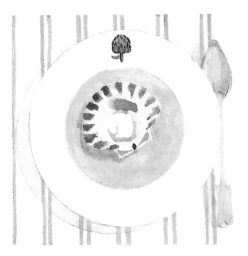

SCALLOPS

These remarkably versatile discs of pure muscle could have been created for the table. They are a portion control officer's dream and lend themselves to the neatest of presentation in perfect little circles. Sliced ever so thinly and dribbled or dressed with a sauce, they are also a boon to the profit-conscious. It is a pity to muck them about with too many other flavors or, similarly, with too many other textures. I was once served one raw scallop cut so paper-thin that you could see the pattern of the plate on which it lay. It had been smeared with a sticky sour-sweet dressing that reminded me of burned ketchup. This meager portion had then been topped up with a hive of deep-fried strips of leek that resembled unraveled Shredded Wheat. Naturally, any flavor, or texture for that matter, had been completely obliterated by a cowboy cook. I happen to like sashimi (Japanese raw fish) but prepared by someone Japanese who has the sensitivity to know when to leave well enough alone.

But this sweet and succulent mollusc comes into its own when it is shown the heat of a hot frying pan. Generally, I find that many cooks are not brave enough when frying or grilling scallops—or for that matter any fish or meat that requires a crust to bring out its savory qualities. The oil or butter must be hot enough to create a seal, otherwise water and juices flow forth and boil the chosen morsel into submission.

My favorite way of cooking scallops is to leave them whole and give them a thorough frying in very hot olive oil until one side forms the sort of jammy crust that you might find on an excellent roast potato. I then flip them over and cook for a few seconds longer. Then straight out of the pan onto the plate. Much garlic and chopped parsley are then thrown into the pan with a little more oil, sizzled briefly, and poured over the scallops. (The smell, by the way, is just fabulous.) Some bread, a piece of lemon, and a glass of cold Sancerre would be fitting accompaniments to a dish that I dare say is almost without peers.

Versatility is the scallop's middle name, however, and some of the following recipes are also delicious. But you can't beat the simple ones, can you?

SCALLOPS SAUTÉ PROVENÇAL

The recipe for this is so simple that it almost doesn't need recording. However, it's good to have it written down so that it doesn't get forgotten. The word "Provençal," in everybody's language, usually means tomatoes, garlic, and olive oil; in this recipe it is just that.

The definitive version of this particular dish I first ate at Chez L'Ami Louis.

2 large or 4 small very ripe tomatoes
¼ cup olive oil
salt and pepper
20 medium scallops, cleaned, roes intact
¼ cup butter
4 large garlic cloves, peeled and coarsely chopped
1 small bunch of flat-leaf parsley, leaves only, coarsely chopped
lemon wedges, to serve

If the tomatoes are large, slice them in half horizontally. Season and either broil or bake with a little of the olive oil until on the point of collapse and a little blistered. I always think that if you are going to cook a tomato, then cook it right through—there's nothing worse than a hot, raw tomato. Meanwhile, heat a heavy-bottomed frying pan with a little more of the olive oil until almost smoking. Season the scallops and fry until really crusty and browned. The secret is to give them longer than you think before turning them over. When cooked—which should only take a matter of minutes—remove from the pan and keep warm with the tomatoes, which should be cooked by now. Add the butter to the pan and heat until foaming. Throw in the garlic, sizzle well, and add the parsley. Spoon over the scallops and tomatoes and serve with the lemon wedges.

SCALLOPS BERCY

Sauce Bercy is one of those classic French sauces that is just perfection. It is as simple as can be—a few shallots, a little white wine, and some parsley. But it is extremely versatile and with slight variations can accompany both fish and meat. The making of it has similarities to beurre blanc but its taste is quite different. It is delicious spooned over grilled and sliced fillet steak, calves' liver, kidneys, and suchlike, and here one would introduce a touch of meat glaze to the sauce (see page 204).

4 shallots, peeled and finely chopped
1 cup dry white wine
1 thyme sprig

6 tbsp strong fish or chicken stock
6 tbsp cold unsalted butter, cut into chunks
salt and pepper
20 scallops, trimmed, roes intact
1 tbsp olive oil
1 tbsp very finely chopped flat-leaf parsley
a squeeze of lemon juice

Preheat a cast-iron ribbed or flat-topped griddle. In a stainless steel or enamel pan, combine the shallots, wine, and thyme. Bring to the boil and reduce by three-quarters. Remove the thyme, add the stock, and further reduce by a quarter. On a very low heat, whisk in the butter, piece by piece. Check for seasoning and keep warm. Season the scallops, brush with the olive oil, and grill them until they are nicely charred on each side. Finish the sauce by adding the parsley and lemon juice, and spoon it over the scallops. Serve with boiled potatoes.

.

SCALLOP AND ARTICHOKE SOUP

The first time I saw this recipe was in *The Four Seasons Cookery Book* by Margaret Costa. I have seen other versions since, so here's another one. The marriage of scallop and Jerusalem artichoke is astonishingly good.

¼ cup butter
1 large onion, peeled and finely chopped
1 cup either fish or light chicken stock
1 bay leaf
1 thyme sprig
1½ cups milk
8 oz Jerusalem artichokes, peeled and coarsely chopped
salt and pepper
8 scallops, cleaned, roes intact, cut into large chunks
½ cup heavy cream
2 tbsp chopped flat-leaf parsley
croûtons to serve

Melt the butter and fry the onion until thoroughly soft without coloring. Add the stock, bay leaf, and thyme, cover, and simmer gently for 10 minutes or so. Add the milk and the artichokes, bring to the boil, season well, and simmer once more until the artichokes are completely collapsed. You may find that the liquid has a messy separated look about it, but once it has been blended until smooth (and it must be mixed in the blender), it will all come back together. Before processing the soup, strain off a large ladle of the liquid and in a small pan gently poach the scallops for a few seconds until just firm. Lift out with a slotted spoon, put on a warm plate, and cover. Return the liquor to the soup, remove the thyme and bay leaf, and blend until smooth. Pass through a fine sieve, reheat with the cream and parsley, and, finally, stir in the scallops to warm through. Serve with croûtons.

SMOKED HADDOCK

I look upon smoked haddock as being essentially British. There is something about its distinctive smoky, fishy odor when being cooked that is familiar and comforting. It's fireside stuff, soft and buttery. Sunday evening food.

Smoked foods have always been favorites with the British, and we smoke foods superbly well. Scotland is best known for all things smoked. Salmon is the most famous (though sadly most of it is from farmed fish these days and I actually prefer Irish smoked salmon). But I love smoked haddock, particularly those done in Arbroath, and known colloquially as "smokies." They are undyed, the palest golden yellow and, unlike those big slabs of artificially colored fish—often cod in fact—these are whole, small haddock that have been split with the bone left in and gently smoked to produce the most delicate of flavors. They are not something that you will necessarily find on your local fishmonger's slab, but if you do, I urge you to try them.

When cooking dishes using smoked haddock, try to find fillets that have been smoked in the traditional way. Smokies are really not suitable because they have so many little bones. They are best eaten as they are, either grilled with butter or poached in milk, and certainly with no more embellishment than a simple poached egg.

SMOKED HADDOCK BAKED WITH POTATOES AND CREAM

I have adapted this from a dish I cooked several years ago using flakes of salt cod. This is every bit as good and the smoky flavor of the haddock lends a particularly savory note. This is the sort of dish you want to come home to after having been to see a really good movie.

2 lb smoked haddock, skinned and all bones removed (use tweezers)
2 cups heavy cream
½ cup milk
1 lb potatoes, peeled and thinly sliced
1 small bunch of flat-leaf parsley, leaves only, finely chopped
4 firm yet ripe tomatoes, peeled and thickly sliced
3 garlic cloves, peeled and finely chopped
salt and pepper
freshly grated nutmeg

Preheat the oven to 425°F. Gently poach the smoked haddock in the cream and milk. Do not overcook; undercook if anything. Drain and flake the fish and reserve the liquid. Butter a deep-sided, oval ovenproof dish. Cover the bottom with one layer of sliced potatoes, and sprinkle with parsley. Add about a third of the smoked haddock, a little more parsley, and top with some slices of tomato. Stir the garlic into the haddock-flavored cream/milk mixture, season, and ladle some of this into the dish to come up to the level of the tomato. Repeat this process until all the ingredients have been used. (In some recipes, when these instructions for layering and using all the ingredients are given, it doesn't work. This can depend on the size of potato used, the size of your dish, how big or small the tomatoes are, and so on. So I suggest that you leave a little bit of leeway and put it down to trial and error the first time, but remember to write down any adjustments for the next time.)

The final top layer should be potatoes. Over these, grate the nutmeg. Put into the oven and bake for 20 minutes. Turn down the heat to 375°F and bake for a further 40 minutes until the top is golden brown and the potatoes are cooked through (check with a thin skewer). The finished result should be rich and creamy—if you've ever made a gratin dauphinois, then you should get the picture.

OMELETTE ARNOLD BENNETT

I was invited to dinner at the Savoy Grill by some friends who had pre-planned our meal. I was very excited, as it was my first visit and, for me, the choice of dishes could not have been more perfect. It started with this famous omelette, was followed by roast saddle of lamb from the trolley, served with the best deep-fried zucchini I've ever eaten, and we finished up with raspberries and cream. This recipe comes from *The Savoy Food and Drink Book*.

10 oz smoked Finnan haddock fillets
1 cup milk
12 eggs
salt and pepper
3 tbsp unsalted butter
1 cup béchamel sauce (see page 6)
6 tbsp hollandaise sauce (see page 183)
¼ cup heavy cream, whipped
1 heaped tbsp freshly grated Parmesan cheese

Poach the haddock in the milk for about 3 minutes. Remove from the pan and flake the fish. Whisk the eggs, then add salt and pepper and half the haddock.

Heat an omelette pan, add a quarter of the butter, and swirl around the pan. Add a quarter of the egg mixture and cook very quickly, stirring constantly, until the mixture is lightly set. Slide the omelette out on to a plate.

Mix the béchamel and hollandaise sauces together quickly. Add the remaining flaked haddock and fold in the whipped cream carefully. Cover the omelette completely with a quarter of the sauce. Sprinkle with a quarter of the Parmesan and glaze under a hot broiler.

Repeat with the remaining mixture to make three more omelettes.

Personal note: If this were my recipe, I would use the milk that the haddock is poached in to make the béchamel.

CURRIED SMOKED HADDOCK SOUP

There is a Scottish smoked haddock soup called Cullen skink and there is kedgeree and there is mulligatawny. This is a combination of all three.

6 tbsp butter
2 large leeks, white parts only, sliced and washed
2 garlic cloves, peeled and crushed
1 heaped tbsp curry powder
salt and pepper
2 cups light chicken stock
1 potato, peeled and chopped
1 cup milk

1 lb smoked haddock, skin and bones removed
1 tbsp basmati rice, cooked in a little chicken stock
1 small bunch of cilantro, leaves only, finely chopped
a squeeze of lemon juice
a pinch of saffron threads
½ cup heavy cream
croûtons, to serve

Melt the butter and in it stew the leeks until soft. Add the garlic and the curry powder and stew gently for 5–10 minutes with a little salt. Add the chicken stock and the potato and simmer for 15 minutes. Adjust the seasoning, blend until smooth in a blender, and strain through a sieve. Poach the smoked haddock in the milk, break up with a fork, and add both the milk and the fish to the soup. Stir in the rice, the cilantro, the lemon, the saffron, and the cream. Reheat gently and serve with croûtons.

SPINACH

I have come to the conclusion that there is only one way to eat spinach that respects its pure iron-packed goodness. That is to sauté it briefly in nut-brown butter. It takes seconds using a good-sized frying pan or, even better, a wok-like receptacle. Season it with salt and pepper, and a grating of nutmeg if you like. The taste, as a result of this preparation, is sweet and nutty, and the glossy green leaves, shiny with butter, are what spinach is all about.

However, spinach *is* a versatile vegetable and lends itself to numerous treatments and presentations that can be extremely successful. Richard Shepherd, from Langan's Brasserie in London, is justly famous for having created a spinach soufflé with anchovy sauce. I always order it when I get a chance to eat there. Not wishing to be a plagiarist, but wanting to do something similar, I reworked the theme and turned the soufflé into a mousse. However, the success of the anchovy sauce with the spinach is an unbeatable combination that can't be bettered, and believe me, I've tried.

Other ideas with spinach take in roulades, soups, salads, stuffings, and tarts. And one of my all-time favorites is Eggs Florentine. Cold spinach and lemon soup is delicious; the lemon being added at the moment of serving, as the acidity causes the lovely spinach-green to become an unappetizing sludge-gray sooner than you can say "Popeye."

In the late 1970s there was a fashion for raw spinach salads. I have rarely eaten a good one. In those days it was to be found on the menu of any restaurant with trendy aspirations. It was quite normal to find tough and badly washed leaves mixed with rock-hard pieces of bacon, stale croûtons, a rancid dressing—or no dressing at all—black and blue chunks of discolored avocado, and, if you were really lucky, lumps of old Danish Blue.

This is one of those dishes that is so easy to make and has been abused right, left, and center. All it takes is a few tender young leaves, which the French call pousse d'épinards, broken-up chunks of best Roquefort, finely chopped shallots, perhaps, or spring onions, a scrap of garlic if you like, a splash of good vinegar, and a slug of olive oil. Strips of crisp bacon are delicious, too, as are crisp chunks of fried potato, and, of course, croûtons. It is also nice sometimes if the leaves become slightly wilted. The best way to achieve this is with bacon. Toss it onto the leaves while still hot and sizzling, rinse out the pan with a splash of vinegar, and pour that over the salad too.

SPINACH MOUSSE WITH ANCHOVY HOLLANDAISE

For the mousse

2 eggs
4 oz cooked spinach, thoroughly squeezed dry
1 cup heavy cream
salt, pepper, and nutmeg

For the hollandaise

3 egg yolks
1 tbsp water
1 cup clarified butter (see page 31), melted
2-oz can of anchovy fillets, squeezed free from oil
lemon juice, to taste
a pinch of cayenne

Preheat the oven to 350°F. In the blender, purée the eggs and spinach until completely smooth. Stir in the cream and season with salt, pepper, and nutmeg. Pour into buttered dariole molds or ramekins, cover each one with aluminum foil, and bake in a bain-marie (water bath) in the oven for 20–30 minutes, or until set. Meanwhile, make the sauce. Whisk together the egg yolks with the water over a gentle heat until pale and creamy. Off the heat, add the clarified butter in a thin stream, whisking constantly until glossy and thick. The easiest way to purée the anchovies completely into the sauce is to put the sauce and the anchovies into a blender. Purée together, add the lemon juice to taste, the cayenne, and any extra salt if necessary.

Turn the mousses out of their molds onto individual plates and spoon the sauce over.

SPINACH DUMPLINGS

I call these "dumplings" because I think it's a nice name, but they really are a sort of gnocchi. These are delicate dumplings, not your sturdy suet numbers, and can be a mite tricky when they are being poached. The recipe does not call for any flour in the mixture itself, just for rolling. The beauty of these dumplings is their lightness and lovely soft texture.

1½ lb raw spinach
4 oz ricotta
3 egg yolks
5 oz Parmesan, freshly grated
salt, pepper, and nutmeg

flour
½ cup butter
20 sage leaves
1 lemon, cut into 4 wedges

Blanch the spinach briefly in fiercely boiling water, drain, and refresh in ice-cold water. Squeeze in a kitchen towel until as dry as possible. In a food processor, purée together the spinach, ricotta, egg yolks, 3 oz Parmesan, and seasoning. Spread out in a shallow tray, cover with plastic wrap, and allow to firm up in the fridge for a minimum of 3 hours.

Using two teaspoons, form the mixture into little balls and roll immediately in the flour. In a large pan, bring at least 3½ pints lightly salted water to the boil, and at a gentle simmer poach the dumplings, five or six at a time, and remove with a slotted spoon after about 5 minutes when slightly swollen. Transfer to a hot serving dish, cover, and keep warm. Melt the butter until nut brown, throw in the sage leaves, turn until evenly coated and slightly crisp, and spoon over the dumplings together with the butter. Sprinkle with the remaining Parmesan and serve with lemon wedges.

COLD SPINACH WITH CRÈME FRAÎCHE, GARLIC, AND BLACK PEPPER

This is a good cold vegetable dish to have on a hot summer's day for lunch in the garden, to go with poached salmon or cold rare beef.

4 tbsp olive oil
2 small garlic cloves, peeled and finely chopped
4 lb raw spinach, trimmed and thoroughly washed
grated rind of 1 large lemon
3 tbsp crème fraîche
juice of ½ lemon
coarsely ground black pepper
Maldon sea salt

Heat the olive oil, add the garlic, stir briefly, and put in the spinach. Stir-fry together, being careful not to allow the garlic to brown. Tip onto a large plate and spread out to cool. When cold, pick up the spinach with your fingers and arrange in loose mounds on four individual plates. Sprinkle with the lemon rind. Add the lemon juice to the crème fraîche, and stir to thin slightly. Spoon the cream over the spinach, grind over plenty of black pepper, and add a pinch of Maldon sea salt.

SQUAB

There are two types of squab worth eating: wood squab and the corn-fed farmed variety.

Wood squab live wild in forests and are regarded as all-year game. It's not brilliant, but it should not be dismissed out of hand, because there are some nice preparations that suit this tough little critter. One of the best is to braise it slowly with some punchy wine, root vegetables, and, perhaps, juniper and cloves. Even then, it needs red currant jelly and a good slug of port or Madeira to sweeten the pot.

Another way is to part-roast it, remove the breasts, and cook them in a sauce made from the carcass and legs. I am not convinced that wood squab is worth this effort but on the other hand it is very cheap. This preparation is actually called salmis and is a classic French treatment, best suited to older game birds past their prime. Wild duck, old grouse, cock pheasant, and partridge are most often cooked in this way. And it can be a fine dish.

The corn-fed farmed variety of squab is another matter altogether. In France, it is called pigeonneau and highly regarded, with a price to match. It is extremely tender, due in part to a cosseted breeding program, which produces a fine layer of fat and a rich flavor. It does not have a gamy flavor and, in fact, bears no relation to its wild cousin. If one were to make a flavor comparison, then a well-fatted young red-legged partridge comes to mind. The following recipes use farmed squab.

ROAST SQUAB WITH BRAISED LETTUCE, PEAS, AND BACON

4 corn-fed squab
salt and pepper
4 garlic cloves, peeled and crushed
8 bacon slices
1 glass of dry white wine
¼ cup butter
24 pearl onions, peeled
8 Bibb lettuce hearts
8 oz shelled fresh or frozen peas
1 tsp thyme leaves
2 tbsp rich, jellied chicken stock
1 bunch of watercress, to garnish

Preheat the oven to 450°F. Season the squab inside and out with salt and pepper. Put a clove of garlic inside each cavity and wrap each bird in two slices of bacon. Roast in the oven for 5 minutes, then turn the oven temperature to 400°F and roast for a further 10 minutes. Remove the squab from the roasting pan, take off the bacon (and reserve), and keep the birds warm while they rest.

Pour the white wine into the roasting pan, and use a whisk to scrape up any crusty bits. Place the pan over a brisk heat and boil to reduce by three-quarters. Add the butter and the onions and cook gently, stirring occasionally, while the wine reduces further and the onions turn golden. Add the lettuce hearts, the peas, the thyme, and the stock. Cut the bacon into slivers and add this, too. Cover the pan with foil and cook in the oven (400°F) for about 20 minutes. Remove and turn the oven back up to 450°F. Take off the foil, put the squab on top of the vegetables, and return to the oven for 5 minutes to reheat and crisp their skins. Transfer to an oval serving dish, and garnish with the watercress. A bowl of perfect buttery new potatoes would be the ideal accompaniment.

GRILLED SQUAB WITH SHALLOTS, SHERRY VINEGAR, AND WALNUT OIL

I was inspired to cook squab in this way by reading a simple recipe for grilled chicken in Pierre Koffmann's *Memories of Gascony*. Ideally, the squab would be best cooked over charcoal as the chicken is in M. Koffmann's book.

While eating at his London restaurant, La Tante Claire in Chelsea, several years ago, I noticed how he "seasoned" certain things with a sprinkling of finely chopped raw shallots. They impart the most wonderful savory flavor to a salad, for instance, and I once had a lovely fillet of grilled red mullet that had been given this treatment.

In this recipe, by covering the squab after grilling, the shallots do cook slightly but they still retain their raw aromatic pungency. You will need "spatchcocked" squab for this recipe. These are boned and flattened-out birds that are a little tricky to prepare, so ask your butcher to do it for you.

4 corn-fed "spatchcocked" squab

salt and pepper

5 tbsp walnut oil

4 shallots, peeled and finely chopped (onions will *not* do)

2 tbsp sherry vinegar

1 tbsp chopped flat-leaf parsley

Heat a charcoal or cast-iron ribbed grill until very hot. Salt the squab on their skin and pepper the fleshy undersides. Brush with a little of the walnut oil. First grill on the skin side, turning once through 45 degrees to achieve an attractive crisscross effect—this should take a couple of minutes. Flip over and grill the flesh side for a minute or so without turning. Divide the squab between two plates, skin-side up. Sprinkle evenly with the chopped shallots and spoon over the vinegar and the remaining walnut oil. Grind a little more pepper over the surface. Cover each plate with another plate and put into a warm oven (300°F) for 15–20 minutes. This allows the meat to cook a touch more—it should be pink—and rest at the same time. What also happens is that the vinegar/walnut oil/shallot mixture effectively forms its own "vinaigrette" as it mingles with natural juices from the squab. Remove from the oven, arrange on a serving dish, and sprinkle with the parsley.

Very good with mashed potatoes, or a legume such as lentils. A green salad made with a cream dressing (1 tbsp vinegar mixed with 6 tbsp heavy cream, a scrap of garlic and seasoning) would also be most agreeable.

STEAK

I first cooked steak with my father on Saturday evenings at home. It was a great treat. Steak nights had my father—an inveterately neat cook—with all his ingredients laid out in precise display, almost like a cookery demonstration (or like his dental practice). I am grateful that he passed his sense of order on to me.

There would be the steak, chopped mushrooms, butter, garlic, Worcestershire sauce, brandy, parsley, cream, salt, and pepper. The steaks were fried in the butter, doused in a little Worcestershire sauce, mushrooms added and fried with the garlic, and then the brandy was added. Flames shot up and, of course, this was the exciting bit. (I recall that pyrotechnics never occurred in any other dish.) Finally, cream was poured in and the cooking was over. Steak Diane? I'm not too sure. But it was delicious.

However, it was not until I went to work at the Normandie (see Endive, p. 87) that I really came to understand steak. It was the best thing that Yves Champeau cooked. I think he really understood, and what's more, enjoyed cooking steak more than anything else. After roasting a chicken, I find myself admitting to the same inclination. There used to be a simple steak sauté on the menu at the Normandie. It was a piece of fillet, seasoned and fried in foaming butter. Nothing else. Just that. Gently, carefully fried, coated in buttery, meaty juices. Heaven. Also, there were rump steaks, single and double, grilled and served for one or two people, and côtes de bœuf. All served with béarnaise and pommes frites. There was also entrecôte marchand de vin—literally, wine merchant's steak but, in fact, steak in a red wine sauce.

Then there was the steak au poivre. A real masterpiece of a dish. Simple, of course, but remarkable for its unchanging format.

When it comes to choosing the right steak for the right dish, it is, to a certain extent, a matter for you. But there are a few things to remember: fillet steak is tops for tenderness but forgoes flavor; sirloin or entrecôte is the most common steak that you will come across. I find it boring, to be quite honest, and it falls between the good flavor of my favorite, rump steak, and the texture of a buttery fillet.

Grilling produces a terrific crust on beef that contrasts well with a rosy-red and juicy inside. For this reason, I have never understood the wish for a well-done steak. I understand that the sight of underdone and bloody meat can be off-putting, but I would rather have a stew any day if I wanted to eat well-cooked meat. The most important thing about grilling steak is to make sure that the grill is very hot, and your chosen steak must be well-oiled and seasoned. The combination of these two things produces the desired savory crust. Similarly, when frying, the oil should be almost smoking before you start to cook.

There is one other cut of meat I must mention. The French call it onglet and we British have a little more trouble in giving it one name. Sometimes it is called feather steak, sometimes skirt, and in France they classify it under offal. It is to be found inside the rib cage of the animal close to the vital organs. In fact, often when I have bought it, there is a stray piece of liver attached to one end of the cut. It has a real meaty flavor and, if you like that sort of thing, this is the steak of all steaks. The classic way of cooking it in France is onglet aux échalotes. It is grilled or sautéed and smothered in fried shallots. Many people may find it unacceptably tough. I would disagree, but then I like to use my teeth and I like to use my tastebuds.

STEAK AU POIVRE

This recipe remains unchanged since I first saw it cooked by Yves Champeau at the Normandie some twenty-odd years ago. This isn't your steak au poivre with five different peppercorns, or cream, or mustard, or anything else. It's the steak, the pepper, butter, and brandy and, if you wish, a little meat juice. Though, in fact, there isn't really a sauce to speak of, it's just buttery-brandy juices. The best steak to use for this is a fat little rump steak that you can only come by if you've boned out your own rump of beef. In Britain, rump steaks are sliced straight across the whole thing and what you end up with is a thin and ineptly cut piece of meat. This is where French butchery comes into its own, as their preparation of only the best parts of the rump will produce a good, thick steak. More often than not, I end up using a fillet steak (nowhere near as much flavor as rump), as it ideally lends itself to this recipe.

2 tbsp white peppercorns
2 tbsp black peppercorns
four 6-oz fillet steaks
salt
3 tbsp olive oil
6 tbsp unsalted butter
2 good slugs of Cognac
2 tbsp meat juices/glaze (see page 204) (optional)

Crush the peppercorns coarsely in a pestle and mortar or in a coffee grinder. Tip the pepper into a sieve and shake well until all remnants of powder have been dispersed. (This is very important because the excess powder will cause the steaks to be far too hot.) Press the peppercorns into both sides of each steak with your fingers, pressing well with the heel of your hand. Only now season with salt, because salting first will not allow the pepper to stick to the meat.

Heat the olive oil in a frying pan until hot. Put in the steaks and fry on one side thoroughly, but not on full heat, until a good thick crust has formed. Add 4 tbsp of the butter and allow to color to nut brown. Turn the steaks over, and finish cooking to suit your taste. Try to resist turning too often—the aim is to produce a good crusty coating on each surface. Baste with the buttery juices as you go. Remove the steaks to hot plates, add the Cognac to the pan, and whisk together with the butter. It matters not whether the brandy ignites, but the alcohol must be boiled off. Add the meat glaze, if using, scrape and stir together any gooey bits from the bottom of the pan, and whisk in the final bit of butter. Give a final boil and pour over the steaks. Serve with fries and a green salad.

MEAT GLAZE

Every now and again, when you need to boost a sauce or a gravy, then a spoonful or two of meat glaze can work wonders. Make it on a day when you really feel like cooking, because it is not something that you can rush or be slap-dash about. This is not just a stock made from bits and pieces, it is a carefully thought-out combination of ingredients that, after long, slow cooking and final reduction, will result in a tasty and intensely flavored savory syrup. It is not something that is usually used in its own right—the recipe for Lacy's Oeufs en Cocotte (see page 85), which only uses a very small amount, is an exception—rather, it is used to embellish, enrich, and add depth of flavor.

2 tbsp oil

2 lb veal bones (preferably knuckle), chopped into small pieces by your butcher

1 lb cheap, fatless beef, such as chuck or shin, chopped into lumps

6 large flat, black mushrooms

3 carrots, peeled and chopped

2 onions, peeled and chopped

3 celery stalks, chopped

4 garlic cloves, peeled and crushed

1 tbsp tomato purée

1 wineglass of red wine

1 wineglass of white wine

2 thyme sprigs

1 bay leaf

½ chicken or beef stock (bouillon) cube

8 cups cold water

Preheat the oven to 425°F. Drizzle the oil over the bones in a heavy-duty roasting pan, and with your hands move them around so that they are evenly coated. Roast in the oven until golden brown, turning them from time to time to prevent them scorching. This is important, as burned bits will turn a stock bitter. This should take between 30 and 40 minutes.

Remove the roasting pan from the oven to a burner and, over a moderate heat, put in the beef. Turn around with the bones until similarly browned, add the vegetables, garlic, and tomato purée, and stir them around with the meat and bones until they are lightly colored. Add the wines, and with a wooden spoon, scrape up any crusty bits from the bottom of the pan. Allow to bubble until well reduced. Tip into a large pot—rinse out any left-behind bits with a little water. Put in the herbs and stock cube, and add the cold water. Stir together and bring to the boil very gently, then turn down to a mere simmer. A great froth of scum will settle on the top, which has to be removed with a ladle, for as long as it is generated. The idea is to remove as many impurities as possible, which will include fatty particles that also conveniently settle on the surface. The stock should cook, uncovered, for about 4 hours on the gentlest heat possible; little blips on the surface are all that should be happening.

With a large ladle, carefully lift the bones and liquid into a colander sitting over a clean pan. Allow to drain for a good 20 minutes until every drop has passed through. Throw away all the solids, and allow the liquid to settle completely so that any fat comes to the surface. Remove this fat with several sheets of paper towels by placing directly on the surface of the stock and lifting off immediately. This can be very successful, but if you want to do the best job possible, then allow the stock to cool, place in the fridge overnight so that any fat will completely solidify. This can be lifted off in a solid disc.

All the defatting finished, place the clean stock on the heat and once again bring slowly to the boil. Yet more scum is about to be thrown off. So watch like a hawk for a thin blanket of creamy scum to form on the surface, and then whip it off in one go with a large spoon or ladle—this is actually very satisfying. Turn down to a simmer and look out from time to time for more scum to appear. (I often ask myself where does it all come from.) Gently reduce until the stock has turned the color of a horse chestnut, and is of a light and syrupy consistency. This meat glaze will be about one-tenth of the original volume. Pour into a small porcelain or stainless steel pot, cover when cool, and it will keep in the fridge for a couple of weeks. Or, you can pour it into ice-cube trays and store in the freezer.

SWEETBREADS

This delectable morsel has a kinder name than its partners in the offal family. Kidney, liver, and brain are just that and have connotations that are all too familiar. "Gland"—for that is what a sweetbread is—would not be appropriate on a menu. Gland en croûte, gland glazed with this or that, or creamed glands with wild mushrooms would not be runaway best-sellers. So, someone, heaven knows when, came up with the name sweetbreads and everyone was happy. The French name, incidentally, is ris, either de veau (veal) or d'agneau (lamb), and the Italians call it animelle.

If you are as partial to offal as I am, then sweetbreads are the most luxurious of "variety meats" (the American nomenclature). They are generally the one that is the most acceptable to offal-worriers, due no doubt to their unknown origins. "I'm not too sure *what* they are, but I do like them," is one ostrich-like remark that comes to mind.

There are two distinct varieties of sweetbread. In the catering trade they are called throatbreads or heartbreads. The latter are more luscious, more tender, and much more expensive. Throatbreads have a more pronounced flavor, perhaps, but can toughen up easily if overcooked. It is interesting to hear what the *Larousse Gastronomique* (the technical food bible) has to say about sweetbreads: "Chemical analysis of this substance shows that it contains three times more albumen and four to five times more gelatin than beef and only half as much fiber." I thought you should know this.

Both types of sweetbread need careful and controlled cooking. Gentle braising over root vegetables with a little white wine and seasoning is how I usually go about it. This gives a modicum of flavor to what is essentially a delicate meat. They should still retain a little bit of wobble when cooked, or, rather, part-cooked, as this is only the preliminary stage of preparation. Between this initial cooking and beyond, the sweetbreads should be cooled and pressed slightly for an hour or so between two plates. Although not compulsory, this allows the sweetbread to firm up and facilitates the removal of a thin membrane. This must be peeled off, along with small lumps of fat and gristle. If this is not done, then when it comes to eating, it can be like trying to put a knife through a rubber band.

The finest sweetbreads come from the calf. When at their freshest they are pinky white and smell sweet and milky. Lamb's sweetbreads are identical in look but about one-fifth the size. They are also about one-fifth the price. Best veal heartbreads are very expensive, even at wholesale. So don't be shocked when you see a dish of veal sweetbreads on a menu for an astonishing sum. Or, contrarywise, be suspicious if you are offered them cheap. Either it's going to be a child's portion or they are lamb's sweetbreads masquerading as veal.

RIS DE VEAU AUX MORILLES

This is one of the richest dishes it is possible to eat. The sweetbreads themselves are rich enough, but together with a wine-laden cream sauce and the highly flavored mushrooms, it is truly *cuisine riche*.

25–30 dried morels
6 tbsp butter
2 carrots, peeled and chopped
1 celery stalk, chopped
1 large leek, cleaned and sliced
2 tomatoes, chopped
salt and pepper
½ 750 ml-bottle of dry white wine
1½ lb calves' sweetbreads, preferably
"heartbreads" or noix—ask your specialist butcher

For the sauce

¼ cup butter
2 large shallots, peeled and finely chopped
1 small wineglass of dry Madeira
1½ cups whipping cream
juice of ½ lemon

Begin by soaking the morels in 2 cups warm water for 30 minutes. Fry the carrot, celery, leek, and tomatoes in the butter in a wide, shallow pan until pale golden. Season and add the white wine. In a single layer, put in the sweetbreads and over a gentle heat braise them, turning from time to time. Cover and cook for about 10 minutes. Keep a look out as sweetbreads cook very quickly and you don't want to end up with tough little nuggets. The gentlest heat possible is my advice. When cooked, lift them out, putting any remnants of vegetable that stick to them back into the pan. Transfer to a plate, put another weighted plate on top, so that the sweetbreads are pressed flat, and leave to cool. The reason for this is that when they are firm and cold they are easier to peel. Meanwhile, strain the vegetables, retaining the cooking liquor. Strain the morels, squeezing them with your hands to extract the last bit of the soaking water, and add it to the cooking liquor. Pour through the finest sieve you have (or through cheesecloth) into a clean pan. Boil gently to reduce by three-quarters, skimming off any froth that collects.

Meanwhile, peel off the thin membrane that surrounds each sweetbread—it comes off quite easily—with a small knife. Also remove any obvious bits of gristle or little lumps of fat. Cut into reasonably small slices and reserve.

To make the sauce, rinse out the pan that you initially fried the vegetables in, and in it melt the ¼ cup butter. Fry the shallots until pale gold, add the morels, lightly season with salt and pepper, and gently sauté for 5 minutes without browning. Pour in the Madeira, allow to bubble, and reduce until almost disappeared. Add the reduced morel/vegetable liquor. Stir together and cook until the mixture takes on a syrupy look. Add the cream. Slip in the pieces of sweetbread and gently bring the whole lot to a simmer. Cook very gently, stirring carefully from time to time, until the consistency of the sauce is unctuous but not too thick; rather like custard in fact. Add the lemon juice, and serve piping hot with plain boiled potatoes and a plainly cooked green vegetable.

BREADCRUMBED VEAL SWEETBREADS WITH TARTAR SAUCE

Everybody loves things baked in breadcrumbs. Think of deep-fried fish, scampi, and chicken Kiev—surely some of the most popular (though often disgusting) dishes everywhere. It is a shame that this method of cooking can be so abused, though it is often the simplest things that are the hardest to get right.

Other sauces that go well with this are béarnaise (see page 85), aïoli (see page 29), salsa (see page 43) with crème fraîche, or other mayonnaise-based sauces like tartar.

1½ lb veal sweetbreads, cooked and prepared as for Ris de Veau aux Morilles
(see page 208)
salt and pepper
4 tbsp all-purpose flour
2 eggs, beaten
breadcrumbs made from 1 small, day-old white loaf
¾ cup clarified butter (see page 31)
watercress and lemon wedges, to garnish

For the sauce

2 egg yolks
1 tsp Dijon mustard
salt
a few dashes of Tabasco sauce
2 tsp (or more) white wine vinegar
1 cup peanut oil

4 tarragon sprigs, leaves only, finely chopped
1 heaped tbsp chopped parsley
1½ tbsp chopped capers
1½ tbsp chopped gherkins

Preheat the oven to 425°F. Beat together the egg yolks, mustard, salt, and Tabasco until thick. Add a touch of vinegar and start adding the oil little by little until very thick. Thin with a little more vinegar and continue to do this until all the oil is used up and the mayonnaise is thick and glossy. Stir in the tarragon, parsley, capers, and gherkins. Pour into a bowl for serving later.

Cut the sweetbreads into pieces measuring about 2 × 1 inch. Season with salt and pepper and dip in the flour, then the beaten egg, and finally in the breadcrumbs, making sure that all surfaces are evenly coated. (A good tip here: always keep one hand for doing the dry bit and one for doing the wet bit, otherwise you end up with breadcrumbed fingers instead of breadcrumbed food.)

Put the butter in a cast-iron oven dish—a large oval Le Creuset would be ideal. Whatever you choose, make sure that it is going to be large enough to accommodate all the sweetbreads without crowding. On the stovetop, heat the butter until hot; there should be enough of it so that the sweetbreads fry in a good ¼-inch depth. Put in the sweetbreads, allow to sizzle, and put straight into the oven. (I call this "oven-frying.") Bake for 5–7 minutes or until a good golden crust has formed on the underside. Flip over and cook for a further 5 minutes. Baste a few times during this process. Drain on paper towels and serve immediately, piping hot and simply garnished with some watercress and lemon wedges. Needless to say, French fries are good with this.

BLANQUETTE OF LAMB'S SWEETBREADS

It is advisable to buy lamb's sweetbreads in spring when the lamb itself is young and tender. The sweetbreads, too, are in a similar state and are meltingly soft and succulent. Do make sure that they are spankingly fresh, as otherwise they can go off, after being cooked, quicker than anything I know, particularly in warm weather.

This is very similar to the classic blanquette de veau in which an egg and cream liaison is used to thicken the sauce.

1½ lb fresh lamb's sweetbreads (never use frozen)
1 cup dry white wine
1 cup chicken stock
salt and pepper
12 small, young carrots

12 large spring onions, bulb end only, trimmed
12 very small new potatoes, scraped
12 button mushrooms
2 tbsp butter
2 tsp flour
2 strips lemon rind, totally pithless
2 tbsp fresh peas
¾ cup heavy cream
2 egg yolks
juice of ½ lemon
2 tarragon sprigs, leaves only

Place the sweetbreads in a saucepan, cover with cold water, and bring to the boil. Just as it is about to boil, drain the sweetbreads and discard the water. Allow to cool only enough to be able to handle the sweetbreads. Peel off the thin membrane and set aside. In a stainless steel or enamel pan, reduce the dry white wine by half. Add the chicken stock, season, and bring back to the boil, and in this liquid poach all the vegetables, except for the peas, until tender. Add the sweetbreads and heat through for 3–4 minutes. Melt the butter in a saucepan and add the flour. Make a roux. Strain all the liquid from the sweetbreads and vegetables. Keep both warm. Stir the liquid into the roux. Whisk to make completely smooth, bring to a simmer, add the lemon rind and cook very gently for 10–15 minutes. Pick out the lemon rind and return the sauce to the sweetbreads. Reheat, together with the peas. Whisk together the cream and egg yolks and, over a very gentle heat, add to the pan and incorporate the liaison gently but thoroughly until completely blended into the sauce. Do not bring back to the boil, otherwise the sauce will separate, but sufficient heat is needed to make the egg yolk thicken the sauce. Stir in the lemon juice—do not worry, this will not curdle the sauce—and the tarragon, and give the blanquette a few more stirs. Serve with some fresh noodles.

TOMATOES

We shouldn't really eat tomatoes as much as we do in Britain. It's silly. It's as worrying as consuming strawberries and asparagus at Christmas. What's wrong with cabbage and rutabaga, apples and pears? I don't think that home-grown tomatoes, even in summer, are that good. Tomatoes need really hot sunshine to grow properly, to ripen and have the correct flavor. Yet it's quite extraordinary that when we are out shopping, suddenly as if from nowhere appears that bag of tasteless tomatoes in the supermarket, force-ripened and hard as rock. There is also a mad desire on the part of the British to insist on wanting something called "salad tomatoes." By this is meant easy-to-slice, underripe to the point of being half-green, and tasting of nothing.

Tomato salad is one of the most glorious of eating pleasures. Naturally red, sweet tomatoes, salt, pepper, and a slick of olive oil. Nothing else. And when it comes to using tomatoes in sauces and stews, the canned Italian ones will do a much better job than most of the fresh varieties that are available to us. We have French and Italian plum tomatoes imported during the summer, but even then they are mostly ripened up after picking. Ripe from the field is a long way from being ripe from the box. I just wish sometimes that we could be more aware of what is good *when* it is good, rather than eating things or buying ingredients purely out of habit and ignorance. In many parts of America, tomatoes are glorious in the summertime.

CREAMED TOMATOES ON TOAST

This was inspired by reading Edouard de Pomiane's *Cooking in Ten Minutes*. It is a smashing little book, full of humor and acute perception about cooking simple things without fuss. If you ever come across a copy, buy it.

1½ cups heavy cream

2 garlic cloves, peeled and crushed

6 ripe plum tomatoes, cut in half lengthways and cored

salt and pepper

12 basil or mint leaves, torn into pieces

4 slices of French country bread, grilled or toasted and brushed with a little olive oil

Preheat the oven to 375°F. Simmer the cream with the garlic and reduce by one-third. Put the tomatoes, cut-side uppermost, in an ovenproof dish and season them. Strain the cream into a bowl and stir in the basil or mint. Lightly season and pour over the tomatoes. Bake in the oven for 20–25 minutes or until the cream has reduced and is thick, and the tops of the tomatoes are slightly blistered. Meanwhile, have ready the bread on four individual plates and spoon three halves of tomato onto each slice. Spoon the residual cream over the top.

TOMATO AND PESTO TARTS

Use the pastry recipe from Anchovy and Onion Tarts (see page 8) but instead of forming an irregular square shape, make circles that measure 6 inches in diameter.

4 large ripe tomatoes, peeled and cored

4 puff pastry circles

salt and pepper

2 heaped tbsp pesto (see page 78)

2 tbsp freshly grated Parmesan cheese, plus a little extra

4 lemon wedges

Preheat the oven to 425°F. Thinly slice the tomatoes. If they are exceptionally juicy, lay them on a paper towel for a few minutes to soak up the excess juice. Grease a flat baking sheet and lay out the pastry circles. Lightly prick the pastry with a fork but not quite to the edge. Cover the pastry with overlapping slices of tomato, leaving a ½-inch rim—one pastry circle should accommodate one tomato. Lightly season with salt and pepper and spoon the pesto over the tops of the tomatoes, spreading it to cover. Sprinkle the Parmesan so that it covers both the tomatoes and the edge of the pastry. Bake in the oven for about 15 minutes or until puffed up and golden and, most importantly, until the underneath of the pastry is cooked through and not soggy. Dust with the extra Parmesan and serve piping hot with wedges of lemon.

PAPPA AL POMODORO

"Pap n. Soft or semi-liquid food for infants or invalids" is the *Oxford Dictionary* definition. You need not be very young or very old or very ill to eat Pappa al Pomodoro, but the description of the consistency is spot-on. I spooned myself this ambrosial stuff for the first time while on holiday in Italy. It was high summer and we ate it outside in a charming restaurant just outside Florence. It is served warm rather than hot and the tomatoes must be full of flavor, very ripe and soft. This recipe comes from Lindsey Bareham's *A Celebration of Soup*.

3½ cups light chicken stock
3 garlic cloves, peeled and crushed
4–5 tbsp olive oil
1½ lb very ripe tomatoes, peeled and cut into chunks
7 oz country bread, crusts removed and broken into chunks
salt and pepper
10 basil leaves (at least), torn

Bring the stock to the boil. Fry the garlic in the olive oil, add the tomatoes and the bread, and stir until the bread flops and merges in with the tomatoes. Slowly stir in the hot stock, a little at a time, until the mixture starts to resemble thin porridge. Season to taste with plenty of pepper, add the basil, and simmer gently, stirring every now and then, for 10–15 minutes. Serve warm with an extra slick of olive oil in each bowl.

TRIPE

It is a sad thing that, having been brought up in Lancashire, England, I was never given tripe as a boy. It is, after all, a great northern staple. However, "lamb's fry" (lamb's testicles), a more unusual offal, was a frequent treat cooked by my father for weekend breakfasts. I hadn't a clue what they were for ages, but found them absolutely delicious.

I used to love all those tasty bits, and looked forward to them. In the north of England, where eating offal is part of the fabric of life, I formed none of the usual prejudices that seem to go with offal. The fact that it was always available helped. Liver was there, kidneys, and on rare occasions, sweetbreads. And my mother had fond memories of beef and cow heel pie, although she never made it for me.

In Bury, where I grew up, there were the best black puddings (a family favorite; eaten boiled with buttered baps [soft white rolls] and English mustard) to be found on the market stall, and chitterlings, udders, and cow heel. The one and only offal that I've had to discover for myself is tripe. Clearly not Mum and Dad's cup of tea.

I remember a shop called the UCP in the middle of Bury that had sheets of precooked tripe sitting in the window. To eat there or take away. It was a sort of café-cum-dining-room, extremely basic, and what I remember most was the smell of fries and vinegar. That's what I wanted to eat, but I was fascinated by that tripe in the window. It looked so unlike food at all that I was curious to try it.

My grandmother used to buy it, and I remember her saying often, "I'm just off to the UCP for some tripe, love" (like something out of a play by Alan Bennett). She liked it in the traditional manner, just doused in malt vinegar and eaten cold. Nothing else. And, I suppose, if I had been given it like that then, I would not have found it, how shall we say, delectable.

But northern folk like it like this; they also like it cooked with onions. Not in the Lyonnais fashion with lots of heavily stewed golden onions and rich meat juices, but with a bland, milky sauce thickened with flour and tasteless, slippery onions. This method I do *not* care for.

Also, unlike the French, we bleach our tripe too much when washing out its impurities, and much of its flavor goes too. On the Continent, all tripe sold is naturally brown. And, happily for the French housewife, most of it has been pre-prepared. She would throw up her hands in horror if she came across our pale equivalent. Hers has been carefully cooked with vegetables and calves' feet, giving it a richness and body that sets to a jelly and also provides a delicious and gelatinous sauce. In any good charcuterie there is always a bowl of it ready to be served by the slice.

In Italy you will also find extremely good tripe dishes. I once could not resist, even after a copious lunch, sampling three different varieties of tripe in a bun, with salsa verde, from the tripe van in the Piazza del Duomo in Florence.

Rome also has its own style of cooking tripe, braised with garlic, white wine, and herbs. And then there is Trippa alla Parmigiana, when it is fried and served with fresh Parmesan.

Not long ago, I bought some good chorizo sausage and was inspired to cook Callos alla Madrilena—tripe Madrid-style, where the tripe is cooked with a pig's foot, the said chorizo, chopped ham, paprika, chillies, garlic, herbs, and spices. Even from the sound of it, you can tell it is one hell of a bowl of tripe.

Finally, it has to be said that my two favorite tripe dishes are French. They are Tripes à la Lyonnaise and, best of all, Le Tablier de Sapeur. This I first ate in a Left Bank Parisian restaurant called Meissonier, where it is their speciality. The name means "fireman's apron" and the dish consists of a square sheet of tripe, breadcrumbed, fried, and served with a sharp mustardy-type sauce such as a ravigote (see page 19), tartar, or béarnaise.

The French find such evocative names to describe their dishes, don't they?

TRIPES À LA LYONNAISE

Whether this is the definitive version or not, I am not sure. All I know is that it is lip-smackingly good and simple to prepare.

½ cup butter
2 lb onions, peeled and thinly sliced
1 tbsp tomato purée
1½ lb cleaned ox tripe, preferably the honeycomb variety
salt and pepper
2 tbsp red wine vinegar
6 tbsp concentrated meat glaze (see page 204)
3 tbsp finely chopped flat-leaf parsley

Heat the butter until pale nut brown and add the onions. Stew gently until gooey and golden brown—this can take up to 1 hour. Add the tomato purée and continue to cook until the tomato purée has lost its bright red color and has turned rusty. Put the tripe in a pan, cover with water, bring to a boil, drain, and cut it into thin strips. Add to the onions and season. Stew for 30 minutes, covered, on a very low heat. Turn up the heat and fry vigorously so that parts of the onion and tripe become burnished. Add the vinegar and allow it to burn off most of its harshness. Stir in the meat glaze, and let the whole stew bubble for a few moments before adding the parsley. Serve immediately, piping hot, with plain boiled potatoes.

CALLOS A LA MADRILENA (TRIPE MADRID-STYLE)

This recipe is adapted from the excellent *The Foods and Wines of Spain* by Penelope Casas. It is a heart-warming dish that should be cooked for a long time, and eaten on cold, wintry days.

1 lb ox tripe
½ cup dry white wine
2 ripe tomatoes, peeled and chopped
1 pig's foot, split in half
2 parsley sprigs
10 peppercorns, lightly crushed
2 cloves
a few gratings of nutmeg
2 bay leaves
2 thyme sprigs
salt

1 onion, peeled and coarsely chopped
8 garlic cloves, peeled
2 tbsp olive oil
1 onion, finely chopped
4 oz chorizo sausage, peeled and sliced
3 oz diced, cured ham (prosciutto-style)
1 tbsp paprika
1 tbsp flour
2 dried red chillies, seeded and crumbled
1 small bunch of flat-leaf parsley, leaves only

Place the tripe in a pot and cover with water. Bring to the boil and drain. Cut the tripe into small squares and put it in a pan with 3½ cups water, the wine, tomatoes, pig's foot, parsley, peppercorns, cloves, nutmeg, bay leaves, thyme, salt, the coarsely chopped onion, and the garlic. Cover and cook over a very low heat, or in a low oven (275°F, but make sure it comes up to the boil before it goes in the oven), for 2 hours.

In a frying pan, heat the oil and fry the finely chopped onion until it is lightly colored. Add the chorizo and ham and cook for 5 minutes. Stir in the paprika, fry for a few moments, and then add the flour. Cook over a low heat for a few minutes, and then add a large ladle of the cooking liquid. Stir until the mixture thickens. Return the tripe to the pan, together with the chilli, and cook for another hour.

Carefully lift out the pig's foot and remove the bones. Break up the meat and return to the tripe. Coarsely chop the parsley, stir it into the tripe, and serve immediately in a suitably rustic, terra cotta bowl.

Penelope Casas suggests serving this with a green salad and plenty of good crusty bread. That would be *in situ*; here, I would suggest plenty of boiled potatoes, either served separately, or stirred into the stew.

DEEP-FRIED TRIPE WITH GREEN PASTE

This is a pleasing alternative to a tripe stew; the cooked pieces of tripe take on a melting quality surrounded by a crisp breadcrumbed coating.

2 cups beef stock (canned beef stock would be fine)
1 carrot, peeled and sliced
2 celery stalks, chopped
1 onion, peeled and sliced
3 cloves
2 garlic cloves, peeled and crushed
1 bay leaf
2 thyme sprigs

6 peppercorns
3 tbsp oriental fish sauce (nam pla)
2 tbsp soy sauce
3 dried chillies, crumbled
1 tbsp red wine vinegar
1½ lb ox tripe, preferably honeycomb variety, blanched in
boiling water for a few seconds, and drained
salt
all-purpose flour
2 eggs, beaten
fresh breadcrumbs made from half a standard white loaf, crusts removed
peanut oil for deep-frying
Green Paste (see page 43)

Put the first 13 ingredients together in a large pan, preferably stainless steel or
enameled, and bring to the boil. Put in the tripe, and poach at a gentle simmer for
about 1 hour. Remove, drain, and cut into ½-inch strips. Season with salt and
dip each strip first in flour, then in egg, and finally in the breadcrumbs. It is good to
do them one at a time to avoid one strip glueing itself to another. Also, it is an idea
to have a platter ready to receive them, which has been strewn with breadcrumbs so
that they do not stick to the surface.

Heat the frying oil to a temperature of 360°F and cook the tripe in batches for 2-3
minutes or until golden brown and crisp. Drain on paper towels and serve the Green
Paste in a separate bowl for dipping.

VEAL

There is no doubt that the Italians cook the finest veal dishes anywhere in the world. It is their number one meat and I have found great pleasure—probably only in the last seven or eight years—in learning how to roast veal properly. Not only veal, in fact, but pork and lamb too. This type of cooking is called "wet roasting" in Italy. It involves seasoning the roast, then scaling and coloring it in butter or oil. White wine is added, perhaps with a scrap of garlic and some chopped-up tomato, suitable herbs, and maybe a squeeze of lemon juice. All this serves to moisten and flavor the meat as it roasts. Some of this "wet roasting" actually takes place completely on the burner and never goes into the oven. The meat is frequently turned as the juices gently reduce and attach themselves to the roast. The final result should be no more than a few tablespoons with which to anoint the slices of meat as opposed to drowning them. If we are talking gravy, this is the best. And it makes itself.

It is a pity that the ubiquitous escalope or scaloppina has had such a rough time in the past. Its life has been just one long trudge through soggy breadcrumbs, cheese, and ham slices and finally blanketed with thick, white sauces. I think it could be called the trattoria story. This slice of veal is for simple preparations. A little lemon juice, a few sage leaves and some butter, a dash of Marsala perhaps. Chopped artichokes, some roasted peppers or grilled slices of fennel might be suitable accompaniments. And my favorite of all is the one where a thin slice of prosciutto is pressed into the meat along with a sage leaf. I know this dish—Saltimbocca alla Romana—is famous the world over, but have you ever had a good one?

Shin of veal is a magnificent cut. The great thing about it is that it is tender enough to roast as well as being braised gently or cut into thick slices for osso buco. Cooked in its whole piece it is called stinco, the English translation being shank or shin, I presume.

ROAST SHIN OF VEAL

This is my favorite cut of veal by far. Do not be put off by thoughts of tough meat or difficulty when it comes to carving. A shin of veal can look unwieldy when you see the whole thing, but ask your butcher to saw right through the bone at the thin end of the shin, about an inch above the meat. This releases the tendons and allows the meat, while it is roasting, to shrink down the bone and "collect" at one end.

1 prepared shin of veal (see above)
4 garlic cloves, peeled and sliced
2 rosemary sprigs
salt and pepper
a little flour
6 tbsp olive oil
6 tbsp butter
½–¾ 750 ml-bottle of dry white wine

Preheat the oven to 375°F. Make deep incisions in the meat with a small knife and push the slices of garlic and little bits of rosemary into these. Season all over with salt and pepper and rub with the flour. This helps form a crust on the meat and helps with the gravy too. Melt the olive oil and butter in a heavy-bottomed roasting pan, on the burner. When foaming, put in the shin and brown very well on all surfaces. Put in the oven for 20–30 minutes, basting occasionally. Take out, tip off most of the fat, and add some of the white wine. Turn the temperature down to 325°F and roast for a further 1½ hours, topping up with splashes of white wine now and again when needed. This is one of those "wet roasting" dishes (see page 221) and the wine, combined with the juices that will drip from the meat, constitutes the gravy. Transfer the shin to a serving dish and keep warm. Put the gravy back on the burner and stir and scrape around to make sure that any gooey bits are lifted from the bottom. Taste for seasoning and, if too strong or too salty, then add a little water. The consistency should be one of juice rather than sauce, and the color should be mahogany. When carving, hold the "handle" of the bone and carve downward in chunks rather than thin slices. Flageolet or haricot verts beans in a creamy sauce are very good with this.

SALTIMBOCCA ALLA ROMANA

A trattoria standby, good old saltimbocca can be really delicious. And I have often found that it is one of the safest choices when you feel a little dubious about some of the other dishes on offer. It takes literally minutes to cook and is a truly perfect marriage of flavors.

8 veal escalopes, beaten very thin between waxed paper
pepper
16 sage leaves
8 paper-thin slices of prosciutto
6 tbsp butter
all-purpose flour for coating
salt
1 small glass of dry white wine
a splash of Marsala (optional)
4 lemon wedges

Grind pepper over one side of the veal escalopes. Place one sage leaf on each escalope and cover with a slice of prosciutto so that it fits as neatly as possible to the shape of the escalope. Fold in half, put back in the waxed paper, and lightly beat to sandwich the two together. Melt the butter in a large frying pan until about to turn nut brown. Quickly dip the saltimboccas in the flour and fry briefly on either side until golden brown, about 2 minutes a side. Do this in two batches if necessary to avoid overcrowding. Keep warm in a low oven. While the fat is still hot, throw in the remaining sage leaves and sizzle for a few moments until they are crisp. Lift them out onto paper towels, sprinkle with salt, and put them on top of the veal in the oven. Tip out most of the fat and pour in the wine and Marsala, if using. Allow to bubble and reduce until it forms a light, syrupy gravy. Spoon this over the saltimboccas, and serve immediately with the lemon wedges. Delicious with mashed potato and buttered spinach.

SALTED CALVES' TONGUE WITH MADEIRA SAUCE

Traditionally, tongue with Madeira sauce would refer to salt ox tongue. This is absolutely delicious in its own right. But I thought, as I wanted to give a recipe for calves' tongue, it would be useful, and interesting, to give a good brine recipe (which comes from Jane Grigson's *Charcuterie and French Pork Cookery*) to salt the tongue yourself. Plain, boiled calves' tongue needs a sauce such as ravigote (see page 19) or mustard sauce; certainly something piquant. Madeira sauce would be too rich. The salting process hardens the meat somewhat and gives it a sharper taste, which then marries wonderfully with the Madeira sauce.

The brine recipe is given in its original quantities and I would halve it for two tongues. It seems sensible to give the full quantities because having a brine bath sitting around is very useful for all sorts of things. You could brine your own pieces of pork and beef—particularly belly pork—which is the classic Petit Salé (see page 159) that you see all over France, served with lentils. Brine keeps for ages in a cool place. Saltpeter is a preservative and available from pharmacies. Soak the tongues for three days in the brine, so make it in advance.

2 calves' tongues
2 carrots, peeled and chopped
2 onions, peeled and quartered
3 celery stalks, chopped
3 thyme sprigs
2 bay leaves
1 tsp peppercorns
2 tbsp red wine vinegar

For the brine

10 cups water (Jane Grigson specifies soft or rain water. Use mineral if you feel
strongly about it)
¾ cup sea salt
1½ cups packed brown sugar
¼ cup saltpeter
1 tsp juniper berries
a pinch of grated nutmeg
2 bay leaves
3 thyme sprigs
1 tsp black peppercorns
4 cloves

For the Madeira sauce

2 tbsp butter
2 bacon slices, chopped
1 small onion, peeled and finely chopped
1 small carrot, peeled and finely chopped
1 celery stalk, finely chopped
1 leek, washed and trimmed, finely chopped
2 tsp tomato purée
1 heaped tsp all-purpose flour
¾ cup plus 2 tbsp dry Madeira
3 tbsp Meat Glaze (see page 204)
salt and pepper
¼ cup butter
1 tbsp chopped parsley

To make the brine, boil together the water, sea salt, brown sugar, and saltpeter.
Coarsely grind the herbs and spices and add to the liquid. Cover and leave to cool

completely. Strain into a stainless steel or china dish. It is now ready for use. Soak the tongues in the brine for 3 days, then drain.

Put the tongues, vegetables, herbs, peppercorns, and vinegar in a large pan. Cover with cold water, bring to a boil, and simmer gently, covered, for 2 hours or until very tender when tested with a thin skewer—there should be no resistance. Turn off the heat and keep warm in the liquid. This, by the way, can be done a day in advance.

Meanwhile, to make the sauce, fry the bacon in the 2 tbsp butter until crisp. Add the vegetables, stir until well colored, and add the tomato purée. Carry on cooking over a low heat until the tomato purée has turned a rusty red color. Stir in the flour and cook gently for a few minutes, stirring constantly, so that it is well blended into the vegetables. Heat the Madeira in a small pan, ignite with a match, and boil until the flames have subsided. Add to the vegetables with the meat glaze and stir until smooth. Season with salt and pepper. If you find the sauce is too thick, add a little of the cooking liquor from the tongues. Conversely, if you find that the sauce is too thin, allow it to reduce slightly. Whichever is the case, the sauce should simmer gently for at least 20 minutes to attain a syrupy consistency that is going to coat the slices of pink calves' tongue. Strain the sauce through a very fine sieve, pressing well against the solids with the back of a ladle to extract all the flavor. Reheat gently, removing any scum that forms in the process. Keep warm.

While the tongue is still warm, peel off the skin. Cut the tongue into slices and arrange on a serving dish. Over a gentle heat, whisk the ¼ cup butter into the sauce and spoon over the meat. Sprinkle with the chopped parsley and serve with spinach and boiled potatoes.

INDEX

Aïoli:
Le Grand, 48
Grilled Breast of Chicken with Provençal Vegetables and, 29–30
Anchovy(ies), 4–10
Hollandaise, Spinach Mousse with, 196
Jeremiah Tower's Montpellier Butter, 6
Old-Fashioned Egg Sauce, 6–7
and Onion Tarts, 8–10
Roast Leg of Lamb with Garlic, Rosemary and, 115
and Rosemary Butter, Grilled Veal Kidneys with, 109–10
Rouille, 175
Rowley's Vinaigrette of Red Peppers and, 151
Salade Niçoise, 7–8
Artichoke(s):
Salade Niçoise, 7–8
and Scallop Soup, 188–89
Asparagus, 11–15
Délices d'Argenteuil, 13–14
Grilled, with Parmesan, 14–15
Soup, 13

Bacon, 154–55
Oeufs en Meurette, 82–83
Piperade, 82
Roasted Leg of Rabbit with a Mustard Sauce and, 171–72
Roast Squab with Braised Lettuce, Peas and, 199
Salade Frisée aux Lardons, 83–84
Bareham, Lindsey, 146, 161, 214
Basil:
Chilled Pimiento Soup with, 153
Cream Sauce, Roast Best End of Lamb with Eggplant and, 117–18
Grilled Eggplant with a Dressing of Olive Oil, Garlic and, 75
Grilled Eggplant with Pesto, 78
Potato, and Tomato Soup, 165–66
Tomato and Pesto Tarts, 213–14
Bertolli, Paul, 156
Bilson, Gay, 69, 91, 150, 167
Parsley Salad, 145–46
Blanc, Georges, 30, 127
Brains, Calves', 16–21
Cervelles au Beurre Noir, 18–19
Deep-Fried, with Sauce Gribiche, 20–21
Gratin of, with Sorrel, 18
Salad of, with Sauce Ravigote, 19–20
Sauté of, with Cilantro, Chillies, Ginger, and Garlic, 21
Bread and Butter Pudding, 68–69

Butter:
Jeremiah Tower's Montpellier, 6
Rosemary and Anchovy, Grilled Veal Kidneys with, 109–10
Snail, 96

Cabbage, Roasted Lambs' Kidneys with Mustard Dressing and, 109
Capers, Warm Hake with Thinned Mayonnaise and, 104
Caramel:
Crème Brûlée, 62–63
Crème Renversée à l'Orange, 69–70
Ice Cream, 64–65
Carey, Charles, 75
Casas, Penelope, 217
Cèpe(s), 22–25
and Potato Broth, 25
Tarts, 24
Champeau, Yves, 87, 88, 92, 203
Cheese:
Creamed Goat's, Baked New Garlic with, 94
Endives au Gratin, 89–90
See also Parmesan
Chicken, 26–33
Grilled Breast of, with Provençal Vegetables and Aïoli, 29–30
Poulet Poché à la Crème with Crêpes Parmentier, 30–32
Poulet Sauté au Vinaigre, 32–33
Roast, 28
Chilli(es):
Green Paste, 43
Grilled Red Onion Relish, 135–36
Salsa, 43–44
Sauté of Calves' Brains with Cilantro, Ginger, Garlic and, 21
Vinegared Eggplant with Spring Onion and, 79
Chocolate, 34–40
Bavarois, 35
Milk, Malt Ice Cream, 37
Petit Pot au Chocolat, 39–40
Pithiviers, 38–39
Saint-Émilion au Chocolat, 36–37
Tart, 36
Cilantro, 41–46
and Coconut Soup, 45–46
Dipping Sauce, 45
Green Paste, 43
Marinated and Grilled Lamb Cutlets with Hummus, Olive Oil and, 115–17
Oriental Salad, 44–45

Pimiento Salsa, 149–50
Salsa, 43–44
Sauté of Calves' Brains with Chillies, Ginger, Garlic
   and, 21
Coconut and Cilantro Soup, 45–46
Cod, 47–53
   Brandade de Morue, 52–53
   Deep-Fried, 50–51
   Le Grand Aïoli, 48
   Poached, with Lentils and Salsa Verde, 49–50
   Poached, with Pickled Vegetable Relish, 51–52
Conran, Terence, 167
Cost, Bruce, 79
Costa, Margaret, 66–67, 188
Coulson, Francis, 62
   Strawberry Pots de Crème, 61
Crab, 54–57
   Tart, 57
   Vinaigrette with Herbs, 56
Crackers, Crisp Parmesan, 142
Cream, 58–65
   Braised Rabbit with White Wine, Shallots, Rosemary
     and, 169
   Caramel Ice Cream, 64–65
   Crema Catalana, 71
   Crème Brûlée, 62–63
   Crème Chantilly, 60
   Eggplant Baked with Herbs and, 77–78
   Francis Coulson's Strawberry Pots de Crème, 61
   Fruit Fool, 60–61
   Leeks with Mint and, 122
   Milk Chocolate Malt Ice Cream, 37
   Rice Pudding, 63–64
   Saffron Dressing, 176
   Sauce, Basil, Roast Best End of Lamb with Eggplant
     and, 117–18
   Smoked Haddock Baked with Potatoes and, 191
   Vanilla Ice Cream, 65
Crêpes Parmentier:
   Duck Livers, and Onion Marmalade, 127–28
   Poulet Poché à la Crème with, 30–32
Croûtons, Parmesan, Garlic and Sorrel Soup with,
   96–97
Cucumber, Pickled, Poached Salmon with Hollandaise
   Sauce and, 183–84
Currants, Salmon in Pastry with Ginger and, 180
Curried Smoked Haddock Soup, 192–93
Custard, 66–72
   Bread and Butter Pudding, 68–69
   Crema Catalana, 71
   Crème Brûlée, 62–63
   Crème Renversée à l'Orange, 69–70
   Francis Coulson's Strawberry Pots de Crème, 61
   Lemon Surprise Pudding, 68
   Orange Mousse, 72
   Passion Fruit Bavarois, 71–72
   Sauce, 70

David, Elizabeth, 5, 36, 60, 76, 113, 129, 130, 148, 156,
   179

Dipping Sauce, 45
   Rouille, 175
Dumplings, Spinach, 196–97

Egg(s), 81–86
   Délices d'Argenteuil, 13–14
   Florentine, 84–85
   Lacy's Oeufs en Cocotte, 85–86
   Oeufs en Meurette, 82–83
   Omelette Arnold Bennett, 191–92
   Piperade, 82
   Salade Frisée aux Lardons, 83–84
   Salade Niçoise, 7–8
   Sauce, Old-Fashioned, 6–7
Eggplant, 73–80
   Baked with Herbs and Cream, 77–78
   Creamed, 77
   Grilled, with a Dressing of Olive Oil, Garlic, and
     Basil, 75
   Grilled, with Pesto, 78
   Grilled, with Sesame, 79–80
   Grilled Breast of Chicken with Provençal Vegetables
     and Aïoli, 29–30
   Roast Best End of Lamb with Basil Cream Sauce
     and, 117–18
   Roulade of Peppers and, 150
   Salad, Spiced, 76–77
   Vinegared, with Chilli and Spring Onion, 79
Endive(s), 87–91
   Braised, 89
   Creamed, 90
   au Gratin, 89–90
   Pickled, 91

Fennel, Grilled Salmon, and Sauce Verte Salad, 182–83
Fool, Fruit, 60–61
Frisée, Salade aux Lardons, 83–84
Fritters, Parmesan, 141–42
Fruit Fool, 60–61

Garlic, 92–97
   Baked New, with Creamed Goat's Cheese, 94
   Cold Spinach with Crème Fraîche, Black Pepper and,
     197
   Deep-Fried, 94–95
   Grilled Eggplant with a Dressing of Olive Oil, Basil
     and, 75
   Purée and Sauce, 95–96
   Roast Leg of Lamb with Anchovy, Rosemary and, 115
   Roast Potatoes with Olive Oil, Rosemary and, 163
   Sauté of Calves' Brains with Cilantro, Chillies, Ginger
     and, 21
   Slow-Braised Belly Pork with Soy, Ginger and,
     158–59
   Snail Butter, 96
   and Sorrel Soup with Parmesan Croûtons, 96–97
Ginger:
   Salmon in Pastry with Currants and, 180
   Sauté of Calves' Brains with Cilantro, Chillies, Garlic
     and, 21

Ginger (continued)
 Slow-Braised Belly Pork with Soy, Garlic and, 158–59
Girardet, Frédy, 131
Glaze, Meat, 204–5
Gratin:
 of Brains with Sorrel, 18
 Endive au, 89–90
Green Paste, 43
 Deep-Fried Tripe with, 218–19
Greens, Warm Wilted, Prosciutto with, 156–57
Grigson, Jane, 223
Grouse, 98–101
 Roast, with Bread Sauce and Game Crumbs, 99–100
 Soup, 101
Guérard, Michel, 32, 127

Haddock. See Smoked Haddock
Hake, 102–6
 Basque Chiorro, 105–6
 Fillet of, with Herb Crust, 105
 Warm, with Thinned Mayonnaise and Capers, 104
Ham:
 Boiled, a Sauce to Serve with, 156
 Endives au Gratin, 89–90
 See also Prosciutto
Hummus, Marinated and Grilled Lamb Cutlets with Olive Oil, Cilantro and, 115–17

Ice Cream:
 Caramel, 64–65
 Milk Chocolate Malt, 37
 Vanilla, 65

Kidneys, 107–11
 Grilled Veal, with Rosemary and Anchovy Butter, 109–10
 Roasted Lambs', with Cabbage and Mustard Dressing, 109
 Sauté of Veal, with Shallots, Sage, and Beurre Noisette, 110–11
Koffman, Pierre, 199

Lacy's, 66–67
 Oeufs en Cocotte, 85–86
Lamb, 112–18
 Breast of, Ste-Ménéhould, 114
 Marinated and Grilled Cutlets with Hummus, Olive Oil, and Cilantro, 115–17
 Roast Best End of, with Eggplant and Basil Cream Sauce, 117–18
 Roast Leg of, with Anchovy, Garlic, and Rosemary, 115
 Sweetbreads, Blanquette of, 210–11
Leek(s), 119–23
 with Cream and Mint, 122
 Parsley Soup, 146–47
 Tart, 121–22
 Vichyssoise, 122–23
 Vinaigrette, 121

Leigh, Rowley, 151
 Vinaigrette of Red Peppers and Anchovy, 151
Lemon Surprise Pudding, 68
Lentils:
 Petit Salé aux Lentilles, 159–60
 Poached Cod with Salsa Verde and, 49–50
Lettuce, Braised, Roast Squab with Peas, Bacon and, 199
Liver(s), 124–28
 Calves', Venetian Style, 125
 Duck, Crêpes Parmentier, and Onion Marmalade, 127–28
 Poultry, Richard Olney's Terrine of, 125–27

Madison, Deborah, 165
Marfell, John, 119
Meat Glaze, 204–5
Mint:
 Leeks with Cream and, 122
 Pimiento Salsa, 149–50
Molyneux, Joyce, 16–17
Mousse:
 Orange, 72
 Spinach, with Anchovy Hollandaise, 196
Mushrooms:
 Blanquette of Lamb's Sweetbreads, 210–11
 Oeufs en Meurette, 82–83
 Ris de Veau aux Morilles, 208–9
 See also Cèpe
Mussels, Saffron Soup with, 176–77
Mustard:
 Dressing, Roasted Lambs' Kidneys with Cabbage and, 109
 Sauce, Roasted Leg of Rabbit with Bacon and, 171–72

Olive Oil, 129–32
 Grilled Eggplant with a Dressing of Garlic, Basil and, 75
 Marinated and Grilled Lamb Cutlets with Hummus, Cilantro and, 115–17
 Mashed Potatoes, 131
 Roast Potatoes with Rosemary, Garlic and, 163
 Sauce Vierge, 131–32
 Vinaigrette, 132
Olney, Richard, 125–26
 Terrine of Poultry Livers, 125–27
Onion(s), 133–38
 and Anchovy Tarts, 8–10
 Blanquette of Lamb's Sweetbreads, 210–11
 Creamed, with Rosemary, 137
 Grilled Red, Relish, 135–36
 Marmalade, Duck Livers and Crêpes Parmentier with, 127–28
 Piperade, 82
 Roast, 135
 Soup, 137–38
 Spring, Vinegared Eggplant with Chilli and, 79
 Tart, 136–37
Orange:
 Crème Renversée à l'Orange, 69–70
 Mousse, 72

Parmesan, 139–42
  Crackers, Crisp, 142
  Croûtons, Garlic and Sorrel Soup with, 96–97
  Fritters, 141–42
  Grilled Asparagus with, 14–15
Parsley, 143–47
  Potato Purée with, 145
  Salad, Gay Bilson's, 145–46
  Soup, 146–47
Parsnip Purée, Stewed Rabbit with Balsamic Vinegar
  and, 170
Passion Fruit Bavarois, 71–72
Pastry:
  Salmon in, with Currants and Ginger, 180
  See also Tarts
Peas, Roast Squab with Braised Lettuce, Bacon
  and, 199
Pepper(s), 148–53
  Chilled Pimiento Soup with Basil, 153
  Gazpacho, 152–53
  Grilled Breast of Chicken with Provençal Vegetables
    and Aïoli, 29–30
  Piedmontese, 149
  Pimiento Salsa, 149–50
  Piperade, 82
  Red, Rowley's Vinaigrette of Anchovy and, 151
  Red, Tart, 151–52
  Roulade of Eggplant and, 150
Perry-Smith, George, 36, 119, 179
Pesto:
  Grilled Eggplant with, 78
  and Tomato Tarts, 213–14
Pomiane, Edouard de, 213
Pork, 154–55
  Petit Salé aux Lentilles, 159–60
  Slow-Braised Belly, with Soy, Ginger, and Garlic,
    158–59
  Terrine, Old-Fashioned, 157–58
  See also Bacon; Ham
Potato(es), 161–66
  Blanquette of Lamb's Sweetbreads, 210–11
  Cakes, 163–64
  and Cèpe Broth, 25
  French Fries, 164
  Olive Oil Mashed, 131
  Purée with Parsley, 145
  Roast, with Olive Oil, Rosemary, and Garlic, 163
  Saffron Mashed, 175
  Salad, 165
  Salade Niçoise, 7–8
  Smoked Haddock Baked with Cream and, 191
  Tomato, and Basil Soup, 165–66
  Vichyssoise, 122–23
Prosciutto:
  Délices d'Argenteuil, 13–14
  Saltimbocca alla Romana, 222–23
  with Warm Wilted Greens, 156–57
Puck, Wolfgang, 37
Puddings:
  Bread and Butter, 68–69

Lemon Surprise, 68
  Rice, 63–64
  See also Custard
Rabbit, 167–72
  Braised, with White Wine, Shallots, Rosemary, and
    Cream, 169
  Roasted Leg of, with Bacon and a Mustard Sauce,
    171–72
  Stewed, with Balsamic Vinegar and Parsnip Purée, 170
  Terrine, 170–71
Rice Pudding, 63–64
Rosemary:
  and Anchovy Butter, Grilled Veal Kidneys with,
    109–10
  Braised Rabbit with White Wine, Shallots, Cream
    and, 169
  Creamed Onions with, 137
  Roast Leg of Lamb with Anchovy, Garlic
    and, 115
  Roast Potatoes with Olive Oil, Garlic and, 163
Saffron, 173–77
  Cream Dressing, 176
  Mashed Potatoes, 175
  Rouille, 175
  Soup with Mussels, 176–77
Sage, Sauté of Veal Kidneys with Shallots, Beurre
  Noisette and, 110–11
Salads:
  Calves' Brains with Sauce Ravigote, 19–20
  Frisée aux Lardons, 83–84
  Gay Bilson's Parsley, 145–46
  Grilled Salmon, Sauce Verte, and Fennel, 182–83
  Niçoise, 7–8
  Oriental, 44–45
  Potato, 165
  Spiced Eggplant, 76–77
Salmon, 178–84
  Ceviche of, 184
  Grilled, Sauce Verte, and Fennel Salad, 182–83
  in Pastry with Currants and Ginger, 180
  Poached, Hollandaise Sauce, and Pickled Cucumber,
    183–84
  Poached, with Beurre Blanc, 180–82
Salsa, 43–44
  Ceviche of Salmon, 184
  Pimiento, 149–50
  Verde, Poached Cod with Lentils and, 49–50
Sauces:
  Aïoli, 29–30
  Basil Cream, 117–18
  Béarnaise, 85–86
  Béchamel, 89–90
  Bread, 99–100
  Custard, 70
  Dipping, 45
  Garlic, 95–96
  Gribiche, 20–21
  Hollandaise, 183–84, 196

Sauces (continued)
Madeira, 223–25
Mustard, 171–72
Old-Fashioned Egg, 6–7
Ravigote, 19–20
Rouille, 175
Saffron Cream Dressing, 176
to Serve with Boiled Ham, 156
Tartar, 209–10
Verte, 182–83
Vièrge, 131–32
Scallop(s), 185–89
and Artichoke Soup, 188–89
Bercy, 187–88
Sauté Provençal, 187
Sesame, Grilled Eggplant with, 79–80
Shallots:
Braised Rabbit with White Wine, Rosemary, Cream and, 169
Grilled Squab with Sherry Vinegar, Walnut Oil and, 199–200
Sauté of Veal Kidneys with Sage, Beurre Noisette and, 110–11
Shepherd, Richard, 194
Silverton, Nancy, 37
Smoked Haddock, 190–93
Baked with Potatoes and Cream, 191
Omelette Arnold Bennett, 191–92
Soup, Curried, 192–93
Snail Butter, 96
Sorrel:
and Garlic Soup with Parmesan Croûtons, 96–97
Gratin of Brains with, 18
Soups:
Asparagus, 13
Cèpe and Potato Broth, 25
Chilled Pimiento, with Basil, 153
Cilantro and Coconut, 45–46
Curried Smoked Haddock, 192–93
Garlic and Sorrel, with Parmesan Croûtons, 96–97
Gazpacho, 152–53
Grouse, 101
Onion, 137–38
Pappa al Pomodoro, 214
Parsley, 146–47
Potato, Tomato, and Basil, 165–66
Saffron, with Mussels, 176–77
Scallop and Artichoke, 188–89
Spinach, 194–97
Cold, with Crème Fraîche, Garlic, and Black Pepper, 197
Dumplings, 196–97
Eggs Florentine, 84–85
Mousse with Anchovy Hollandaise, 196
Spry, Constance, 105
Squab, 198–200
Grilled, with Shallots, Sherry Vinegar, and Walnut Oil, 199–200

Roast, with Braised Lettuce, Peas, and Bacon, 199
Steak, 201–5
Meat Glaze, 204–5
au Poivre, 203
Stein, Ricky, 54
Strawberry Pots de Crème, Francis Coulson's, 61
Sweetbreads, 206–11
Blanquette of Lamb's, 210–11
Breadcrumbed Veal, with Tartar Sauce, 209–10
Ris de Veau aux Morilles, 208–9
Tarts:
Anchovy and Onion, 8–10
Cèpe, 24
Chocolate, 36
Crab, 57
Leek, 121–22
Onion, 136–37
Red Pepper, 151–52
Tomato and Pesto, 213–14
Taruschio, Franco, 23, 148
Tomato(es), 212–14
Ceviche of Salmon, 184
Crab Tart, 57
Creamed, on Toast, 213
Eggplant Baked with Herbs and Cream, 77–78
Gazpacho, 152–53
Pappa al Pomodoro, 214
and Pesto Tarts, 213–14
Pimiento Salsa, 149–50
Piperade, 82
Potato, and Basil Soup, 165–66
Salade Niçoise, 7–8
Salsa, 43–44
Sauce Vièrge, 131–32
Scallops Sauté Provençal, 187
Spiced Eggplant Salad, 76–77
Tower, Jeremiah, 5
Montpellier Butter, 6
Tripe(s), 215–19
Deep-Fried, with Green Paste, 218–19
à la Lyonnaise, 217
Madrid-Style (Callos a la Madrilena), 217–18

Vanilla Ice Cream, 65
Veal, 220–25
Roast Shin of, 222
Salted Calves' Tongue with Madeira Sauce, 223–25
Saltimbocca alla Romana, 222–23
Veal Sweetbreads:
Breadcrumbed, with Tartar Sauce, 209–10
Ris de Veau aux Morilles, 208–9
Vinaigrette, 132
Crab, with Herbs, 56
Leeks, 121
Rowley's, of Red Peppers and Anchovy, 151

Waters, Alice, 93, 156